LIVING ABROAD IN
France

FIRST EDITION

Terry Link

© Corel/Velocity Stock

AVALON
TRAVEL

CONTENTS

Daily Life

Resources

Preface

I moved to France 14 years ago, having signed the papers to buy a vacant bakery on my 50th birthday. The day of the signing was hot. It was also a holiday, and I had to take the notaire (notary) away from a family gathering because I was returning to California the next day. I signed with as much trepidation as I had experienced 30 years before in asking my girlfriend to marry me, and just as much certainty that this was what I wanted, no matter what the future held.

After seeing so many years of that future unfold, I have only two regrets: I did not make the move sooner, and I did not study more French before doing so.

The old bakery my wife and I bought and turned into a *chambre d'hôtel* (bed-and-breakfast) was neither the culmination of a dream nor the beginning of one. Rather, it was the next logical step in a process that began with my first trip to Europe—an eight-week trip that turned out to be little more than a tour of France. I was crazy about the country!

My wife was, too. As a partner in a cheese and wine shop, she specialized in French cheeses. Soon she left the cheese shop and opened her own *charcuterie* (butcher's shop), making pâtés, sausages, quiches, and salads, as well as selling cheese and wine. This endeavor required more trips to France, and when our eldest son decided to attend university in France, rather than in the United States, we easily agreed to his choice.

Eventually, together with our son and his wife, we bought a small house in a village that served the four of us as a vacation home. Working on remodeling projects in that house, with its meter-thick stone walls, was a new experience for me, and one I thoroughly enjoyed.

By this time, our other children were grown, and my wife and I were ready to move to France permanently if we had some means of support. When the newspaper where I was working offered an "early retirement" buyout to older workers, we had the solution: Use the buyout money to start a bed-and-breakfast.

I enrolled in a French class five mornings a week, and we began making two-week trips looking for a suitable property. We took one of these in January to see what the winter weather was like. (My wife already knew, having spent two weeks one February on a farm learning about foie gras production.)

The building we eventually bought was sound—it had housed the ovens of an abbey, according to a map of the village from 1668. It then continued as a bakery until the late 1980s, when the owner, who had grown up in the house to become a baker like his father, retired. But it had minimal electricity and no hot water. (The communal bathhouse up the street has since been converted to a senior citizens' center.)

Thus began my real education in *bricolage*, the French term for do-it-yourself construction. As a learning process, it was largely enjoyable. But not all the lessons were. When my mother-in-law had a heart attack while visiting us, we received a close look at French medical care. In the end, it turned out well, but we had an anxious few weeks. Meanwhile, my father-in-law and I built a second bathroom so she would not have to climb the stairs, and they spent Christmas with us until she was able to travel.

A plan to supplement our income by renting bicycles to the general public ran afoul of French bureaucracy: We were a *chambre d'hôtel*, not a bicycle shop. We could rent rooms, but not bicycles, without establishing a separate business.

When our first car threw a rod and had to be scrapped, we learned just how isolated a small village can be—with no used car lots and no easy way to shop for another car—and how dependent we were upon the friends we had made.

There were numerous similar incidents, small enough in themselves, but for an immigrant beginning a new life in another country, they loomed large. After deciding to leave your native land, making the move, and getting settled, there comes a point when you begin to wonder if you have done the right thing.

For my wife and myself, our moment of realization came after a rainy winter day of fruitless shopping for furniture. The dollar had dropped from 6.25 francs (when we came to France) to 4.53 francs, it was raining, the heater in the car wasn't working, and we were cold, hungry, and tired. We started to voice our fears aloud.

Then, as we came over a rise and saw our village, we also saw a double rainbow that seemed to end there. Looking at each other, we both grinned and said, "There's our home!"

—Terry Link

Introduction

Welcome to France

After World War I a popular song asked "How are you gonna keep 'em down on the farm after they've seen Paris?" Numerous Americans, from Ernest Hemingway to Gertrude Stein, answered: "You can't."

France is still a magnet for Americans today. The world's number one travel destination draws hundreds of thousands of American tourists each year, some of whom fall so deeply in love with the country they return to stay. Why?

The attraction, just as it has been for generations, is the extraordinary quality of life the ordinary person can enjoy. France is both modern and old-fashioned. French science and technology rival those of any nation, yet the country appreciates fine food, a slow pace, and the good things in life. Indeed, a French phrase describes it best: *joie de vivre* (joy of living).

That joy of living can be experienced throughout the entire country. In Paris, you can sit in front of Notre-Dame Cathedral and watch pigeons bob along, as they have for the past 700 years, while talking on your cell phone. Then you can catch a high-speed train to charming Beaune, where farmhands snip clusters of grapes from the vines the way they did in Roman times.

At the local market, you can buy cheese from the person who made it, and fruit and vegetables from the farmer who grew them. The *charcutier* (butcher) can tell you where his meat comes from. You can sit along the quai in Honfleur and savor a bowl of *moules* (mussels) while gazing at the boats in the harbor. Here, though boats may be powered by diesel motors, little else has changed since Samuel Champlain sailed off to the New World. And while the barges that ply the Canal du Midi between Bordeaux and the Mediterranean transport passengers today, rather than haul freight, their captains still banter with the lockkeepers, just like in the old days.

> *Throughout most of France, you can find a quality of life that is difficult to match anywhere in the world.*

You can drive through the south of France on two-lane roads edged with wildflowers and shaded by sycamore trees generations old. In olive groves and orchards, wild thyme, lavender, and rosemary grow in rocky patches of soil. The scent of pine and heather perfumes the air. You can linger over dinner, just like the French do. When you reserve a table at a restaurant in France, it's yours for the night—the waiter won't ask you to wait in the bar for 30 minutes before seating you, or hustle you along so he can seat another party before the night is over.

This is contemporary France, a land that has preserved what is good and beautiful and true from its past and made it work in the present. Other nations have also preserved their historical charm, and other industrialized nations also boast ultra-modern amenities, but no country combines these two so successfully as France. This is true not only in Paris, but also, remarkably, in the smaller towns and villages. The successful blending of past and present permeates the entire society and every region.

One of the secrets of this successful blending lies in the fact that the French have managed to combine an agricultural base within a modern industrial economy. High-tech agricultural methods mingle with the rural charm of hand-hewn stone walls and tile roofs. Farmers—individual, small producers—are still important to the French economy. When French farmers take their complaints to the streets, the government pays attention to them. After all, France is the food basket of Europe thanks not to corporate agribusiness, but to the family farm.

At the same time, France prizes its modernity. The country boasts a surplus of electric power from nuclear plants and builds rockets to launch its own satellites into orbit. It is Europe's largest producer of automobiles and host to its commercial aircraft industry. In most years, exports surpass imports; when they do not, as in 2004, it becomes a national issue. French medical researchers rival their peers anywhere in the world, and the health of French citizens is taken seriously. Employers provide mandatory health care, and the government offers extensive benefits for the needy and unemployed.

France also educates its people, providing a university education at nominal cost for anyone who graduates from high school and wants to continue in school. Even in present times, an extremely popular annual event is the televised *dictée* (dictation), in which millions of French people sit in front of their televisions and try to write a paragraph of dictation correctly, just as they did in school. The correct version is later published, along with the results.

France is a well-educated, well-run nation, internationally famous for its culture, art, and cuisine; Americans living in France enjoy the benefits of all this as much as French citizens do. And the weather's nice, too. The country enjoys a temperate climate, an added boon to Americans from harsher climes. The southern Atlantic and the Mediterranean coasts rarely dip below freezing and enjoy pleasant daytime temperatures of 50°F nine months out of the year, from February through November. The country's coldest region, north above the Loire River, does not rest long under a blanket of snow. July and August are the only months with stretches of 95-degree highs.

With such a nice climate, it's no surprise France offers abundant recreational opportunities for outdoors enthusiasts. Two massive mountain ranges, the Pyrénées and the Alps, border the country on the south and the east, respectively, providing Olympic-caliber skiing on nearly 80,000 miles of runs, plus hiking, biking, and other activities, all within a few hours from any location in the country. On the two coasts, extensive beaches offer chances to laze away the day, comb for seashells, or go boating—not to mention eat abundant fresh fish and seafood.

From the rolling plains of Champagne to the forests of the Massif Central, France boasts a tremendously varied geography paralleled only by its cultural variety. A distance of 10 miles can bring noticeable changes in the language, in the crops, in the architecture, and certainly in how the local population defines itself.

The Lay of the Land

PARIS AND THE ÎLE-DE-FRANCE

Paris remains the primary attraction for American visitors, if not all immigrants to the country. This is where Gene Kelly was "Singin' in the Rain." African-American musicians like Bud Powell, Charlie Parker, and Ben Webster discovered that the French cared more about their music than the color of their skin. Among those who found postwar Paris a congenial milieu was a young wife who took cooking classes to while away the hours when her businessman husband was at work. Julia Child later collaborated with two of her teachers on the two-volume *Art of French Cooking,* which helped transform American cuisine.

Paris is still a magical city—at least to visit. The region around the city itself, the Île-de-France, shares more and more in the cultural and social wealth of Paris, as a great transit system accommodates an increasing population. Paris can hold only so many people and institutions within its boundaries. Research and academic institutes and business, commercial, and manufacturing centers have all pushed outward, both following the burgeoning population and attracting it. Many of these

© Corel/Velocity Stock

The French countryside still has an old-world sensibility.

suburbs offer small-town charm mixed with big-city excitement in woodsy settings cut by streams and rivers.

Paris and the surrounding departments average 25 inches of rain per year. January is usually the coldest month with an average temperature of 40°F, but it can drop below freezing about 25 days per year. July and August are the warmest months, and the temperature usually passes 77°F.

THE MIDI AND LANGUEDOC

Between the Atlantic Ocean to the west, the Mediterranean Sea to the east, the Massif Central to the north, and the Pyrénées to the south, lies Bordeaux and the Midi region. Bordeaux, with its three centuries of English rule beginning with Eleanor of Aquitaine's marriage to Henry II in the mid-1100s, offers a sophisticated and cosmopolitan city where foreign trade is lifeblood. Surrounding this gem are rustic villages, an Atlantic coast of sandy beaches, and a great flat pine forest-park that attracts thousands of vacationers each summer. Along the coast toward Spain are cities such as Biarritz and St.-Jean-de-Luz, rivals of Cannes and Cap d'Antibes on the Mediterranean.

The Bay of Arcachon, just west of Bordeaux, is not only a source of seafood, but has also become quite a yachting center—its protected harbor offers pleasure-craft shelter from Atlantic storms.

Bordeaux and the surrounding area average 25 inches of rain per year on the coast and 35 inches inland. January is usually the coldest month, with an average temperature of 42°F; July and August are the warmest months, but the temperature rarely passes 86°F along the coast. Fog is frequent in fall and winter in the valleys of the Garonne and Dordogne rivers.

Basque Country

The Basques tend to be concentrated in the foothills of the Pyrénées and along the southern coast. However, much of the country north of the Basque lands and southwest of Bordeaux is a region known in former times as Gascony, a rich agricultural area noted today for its poultry, foie gras, and Armagnac brandy, among other things. Its wines, though not widely known outside the region, are well worth getting acquainted with.

Marciac, one of Gascony's tiny villages lying between Bordeaux and Toulouse, has become known throughout Europe for its annual weeklong

A Look at the Regions

Alsace
Population: 1,775,000; 214 people per square kilometer
Departments: Bas-Rhin (67), Haut-Rhin (68)

Aquitaine
Population: 2,988,000; 72 people per square kilometer
Departments: Dordogne (24), Gironde (33), Landes (40), Lot-et-Garonne (47), Pyrénées-Atlantiques (64)

Auvergne
Population: 1,351,000; 51 people per square kilometer
Departments: Allier (03), Cantal (15), Haute-Loire (43), Puy-de-Dôme (63)

Basse-Normandie
Population: 1,436,000; 82 people per square kilometer
Departments: Calvados (14), Manche (50), Orne (61)

Bretagne
Population: 2,978,000; 109 people per square kilometer
Departments: Côtes-d'Armor (22), Finistère (29), Ille-et-Vilaine (35), Morbihan (56)

Burgogne
Population: 1,612,000; 51 people per square kilometer
Departments: Côte-d'Or (21), Nièvre (58), Saône-et-Loire (71), Yonne (89)

Centre
Population: 2,467,000; 63 people per square kilometer
Departments: Cher (18), Eure-et-Loir (28), Indre (36), Indre-et-Loire (37), Loir-et-Cher (41), Loiret (45)

Champagne-Ardenne
Population: 1,337,000; 52 people per square kilometer
Departments: Ardennes (08), Aube (10), Haute-Marne (52), Marne (51)

Corse
Population: 266,000; 31 people per square kilometer
Departments: Corse-du-Sud (2A), Haute-Corse (2B)

Franche-Comté
Population: 1,131,000; 70 people per square kilometer
Departments: Belfort (Territoire de) (90), Doubs (25), Haute-Saône (70), Jura (39)

Haute-Normandie
Population: 1,787,000; 145 people per square kilometer
Departments: Eure (27), Seine-Maritime (76)

Île-de-France
Population: 11,131,000; 927 people per square kilometer

Departments: Essonne (91), Hauts-de-Seine (92), Paris (75), Seine-et-Marne (77), Seine-Saint-Denis (93), Val-de-Marne (94), Val-d'Oise (95), Yvelines (78)

Languedoc-Roussillon
Population: 2,408,000; 88 people per square kilometer
Departments: Aude (11), Gard (30), Hérault (34), Lozère (48), Pyrénées-Orientales (66)

Limousin
Population: 711,000; 42 people per square kilometer
Departments: Corrèze (19), Creuse (23), Haute-Vienne (87)

Lorraine
Population: 2,319,000; 99 people per square kilometer
Departments: Meurthe-et-Moselle (54), Meuse (55), Moselle (57), Vosges (88)

Midi-Pyrénées
Population: 2,368,000; 58 people per square kilometer
Departments: Ariège (09), Aveyron (12), Haute-Garonne (31), Gers (32), Hautes- Pyrénées (65), Lot (46), Tarn (81), Tarn-et-Garonne (82)

Nord-Pas-de-Calais
Population: 4,013,000; 323 people per square kilometer
Departments: Nord (59), Pas-de-Calais (62)

Pays de la Loire
Population: 3,312,000; 103 people per square kilometer
Departments: Loire-Atlantique (44), Maine-et-Loire (49), Mayenne (53), Sarthe (72), Vendée (85)

Picardie
Population: 1,869,000; 96 people per square kilometer
Departments: Aisne (02), Oise (60), Somme (80)

Poitou-Charentes
Population: 1,668,000; 65 people per square kilometer
Departments: Charente (16), Charente-Maritime (17), Deux-Sèvres (79), Vienne (86)

Provence-Alpes-Côtes d'Azur (PACA)
Population: 4,665,000; 149 people per square kilometer
Departments: Alpes-de-Haute-Provence (04), Alpes-Maritrimes (06), Bouches-du-Rhône (13), Hautes-Alpes (05), Var (83), Vaucluse (84)

Rhône-Alpes
Population: 5,814,000; 133 people per square kilometer
Departments: Ain (01), Ardèche (07), Drôme (26), Haute-Savoie (74), Isère (38), Loire (42), Rhône (69), Savoie (73)

jazz festival, attracting thousands to hear the best in the business, such as Wynton Marsalis and Diana Krall.

The rural northern area drained by the Dordogne river has been much favored by the English and Americans in recent decades; newcomers here will not lack for English-speaking acquaintances. The countryside is wooded and green, the towns small and comfortable with open-air markets and local produce. Ridges channel small streams into larger rivers. Besides the Dordogne river, there is the Lot.

Besides wine and truffles, this is also the land of Lascaux and the other great caverns preserving prehistoric art. Human habitation goes back 400,000 years in this region. There are medieval castles as well as the caves of the troglodytes and the farmhouses of the past two centuries.

Toulouse

Further east lies the great university city of Toulouse, surrounded by rolling plains with fields of grain, sunflowers, and corn reminiscent of the American Midwest. Toulouse has become a high-tech aerospace center and has been for centuries the capital of Occitan—a land where *oc,* not *oui,* means yes. Though long ago subjugated militarily by Paris, the area retains a sense of political independence. The linguistic difference today is relatively minor; far more people speak standard French than anything else.

Along with the tens of thousands of students are thousands of teachers and professors and researchers. The educational level is high, cultural activity geared toward youth—music, film, etc.—is plentiful in the center city, and the suburbs are filled with middle-class families.

South of Toulouse are the sparsely populated Pyrénées; to the north are the edges of the Massif Centrale, the great uplifted plateau of the center of France. The small farms here are losing their economic viability and gradually being reoriented towards tourism and service, although vineyards continue to maintain their importance.

Rainfall in Toulouse and the surrounding departments varies from 25–35 inches per year. January is usually the coldest month, with an average of 37 days below freezing per year (only about 10 percent of these drop below 20°F). July and August are the warmest months, with an average temperature of 86°F.

Languedoc

Along the western shore of the Mediterranean and then further north stretches Languedoc, a semi-arid region once neglected by much of the rest of France, but now proving attractive to northerners due to its climate, beaches, and sparse population. With Provence growing steadily in population and property prices rising just as steadily, Languedoc has become more attractive to retirees and relocators to France, and its coastal cities, such as Perpignan and Narbonne, have expanded. The capital city, Montpellier, famed for centuries for its university and medical school, remains the largest city in the region.

Summers here are hot, and temperatures over 104°F are not uncommon. Winters may be called mild, but they are not warm; snow and ice are not unknown, although seldom below an altitude of 2,000 feet, and daytime temperatures often hover near freezing. Rainfall varies with the distance from the sea and averages 22–40 inches per year.

Beginning in 1999, cheap direct flights from London opened the area to the British, who have come by the tens of thousands in search of sunshine and second homes. The vineyards that carpet so much of the landscape produce a lake of wine, still the region's most important crop. Languedoc remains largely agricultural, dotted with small farming villages. In addition to its hot summers, this area provides easy access to the ski slopes and other winter sport areas of the Pyrénées. Spain is two hours or less from almost anywhere in Languedoc, and Barcelona is reachable in a four-hour drive.

PROVENCE AND THE CÔTE D'AZUR

In the famed South of France is Provence, sandwiched between the Rhône River running east to Italy. Provence shows several faces, depending on your desires; perhaps that's why it has proved so popular for so long. To begin with, there are the climate and the terrain. The former is mild, but not tiresome; and the latter rugged, but not hostile. The most famous face is worn by the glamorous Côte d'Azur and Riviera: expensive villas, celebrities, and starlets in a playground of the rich and the merely well-to-do. The sleepy fishing villages that once hugged the cliffs around the inlets between Nice and Toulon and Toulon and Marseille are long gone, swallowed in a rising tide of tourism.

Then there is the urban face—cities like Marseille and Nice, Aix and Avignon—full of life and jostling crowds, but also eminently livable. The arts have not been neglected in Provence, and they are cultivated in the cities.

Behind the mountains that wall off the Mediterranean remain small towns where traces of the world of Marcel Pagnol's peasants can be found. The villages of the Luberon, such as Roussillon, offer this charming rusticity. Provence is a multifaceted world; to dismiss it because of any single aspect is a mistake.

Rainfall along the coast averages 27 inches per year and rises to an average of 35 inches inland; October and March are the wettest months, while July is the driest. Snow is rare, occurring only 10–14 days annually above 2,500 feet elevation. Along the coast, it rarely freezes and temperatures can occasionally surpass 86°F. In the interior of the region, especially in the higher mountains, temperatures can drop dramatically below freezing while the number of hotter days dwindles.

NORMANDY AND BRITTANY

Normandie (Normandy) and the English Channel lie west of the Île-de-France and Paris, while storms lash the more westerly coast of Bretagne (Brittany). Normandy is especially attractive for those seeking a rural retreat, but one with big city comforts nearby. Not only is Paris close at hand, so are other major French cities, such as Rouen and Lille. The latter provides quick access to London as well, via the tunnel under the English Channel. Normandy remains a favorite weekend getaway English and Parisians alike, with expensive resorts on the coast and bucolic hideaways further inland.

Rainfall in Normandy varies from about 30–50 inches per year, with the heaviest amount falling on the coast in autumn and winter. January is usually the coldest month, with an average of 39°F; but the temperature can drop below freezing an average of 51 days per year. July and August are the warmest months, but the temperature rarely passes 95°F. Local fog is frequent between October and February, with visibility often reduced to 200 yards.

Brittany is several steps further from these central urban areas; while its population is relatively dense for rural France, the region has no large city besides Rennes. With its Celtic language, cuisine, and traditional dress so different from the capital, it offers a greater sense of separation and isolation—not necessarily negative, just different. Take the cuisine: Crêpes and galettes, made with buckwheat flour and consumed with the ever-present apple cider, are an important part of Breton culinary heritage; crêperies are everywhere. And while galettes are available throughout the country, it is usually a Breton running the shop.

The rugged granite coast of Brittany also sets the region apart. Often lashed by storms, it nonetheless offers a beauty unmatched by tamer, more sheltered shores. This granite has served to construct many of the 4,000 chateaux and manor houses that dot the landscape.

Rainfall in Brittany varies from 30–60 inches per year. The Atlantic-exposed west coast actually receives lesser rainfall, while the inland highlands may get twice that amount. More than half of Brittany's annual rainfall comes between October and March; June and July are the driest months. Winters on the coast are often mild, though there is greater variation around Rennes. Nonetheless, temperatures above 95°F and below 15°F are rare. On the coast, freezing seldom occurs, but winds in winter can be significant. Summer temperatures average 68–80°F.

BURGUNDY AND THE RHÔNE VALLEY

Like the Midi, the Rhône Valley and Bourgogne (Burgundy) constitute a great wine-producing region. Pleasant villages and market towns lie along the banks of the Rhône River and farming is the big industry here. Lyon is the largest city in the region, and many consider it the gastronomical center of France. Lyon offers the advantages of a large city, such as its university, and is also something of a crossroads of Europe, with links to Switzerland, Italy, Spain, and Germany, as well as the rest of France. Nearby are several major nature preserves.

To the east, the Alps offers summer and winter recreation areas within easy reach of much of the Rhône Valley. These hillsides have plenty of opportunities for a different kind of life other than that of the valley. Weather in the Rhône Valley generally follows that of Provence; however, the mild temperatures are exacerbated by the mistral winds sweeping down the valley. At higher elevations, it naturally grows much colder.

Burgundy is similar and farming here consists of grapes and fruit, although it is too far north for olives. A lack of larger cities outside of Dijon has made employment here difficult. Ownership of the most famous vineyards is jealously guarded, and land is expensive. But away from these celebrated parcels, Burgundy remains its historic self; and its picturesque little villages lie only a few hours from Paris. The regional park of Morvan, with its heavily forested hills, provides excellent summer recreation, and the slopes of the Jura Mountains to the east provides access to many winter sports.

The valley watershed of three great rivers is here in Burgundy—the Loire, the Seine, and the Rhône. Boating on the hundreds of miles of rivers and canals in Burgundy can be a pastime or a business; live-aboard barges are part of the local scene. All these streams of water, as well as 50,000 acres of lakes, makes Burgundy a great location for anglers.

Burgundy's rainfall varies from about 24–32 inches annually. While the average low temperature remains 40°F, the summers are cool, with temperatures seldom straying above 85°F.

Social Climate

"Vive la difference!"—cultural difference, that is. Indeed, the disparities in lifestyle between the two countries comprise the main attraction to France for many Americans. Few French people spend hours commuting to work, for example, like millions of their American counterparts. And lunch "hour?" What's that? The French linger over meals, and, as a rule, eat healthier, better food than the average American. They don't sit in front of the TV for hours each day, but rather visit friends and spend time with their families. And the French government debates issues for months, not years, and acts decisively at the end of the process.

> To the French, other values are just as important as productivity, an attitude many Americans living in France find balm to their overworked souls.

There is no better example of the French dedication to quality of life than the country's adoption of a 35-hour workweek—heresy to the American business mindset, where productivity is king. But the French ask, "Is that our only goal? What about expanding employment opportunities? What about family life?" To the French, other values are just as important as productivity, an attitude many Americans living in France find to be balm to their overworked souls.

Anyone who moves to France should do so with the same intention he or she would have in moving from Boston to San Diego—to become a fully functioning member of a new community, despite the distance from friends and family. Travelers should pack an ample supply of patience, curiosity, and desire to participate in their adopted culture. The sort of person who should *not* consider moving to France (or to any other foreign country, for that matter) is one likely to keep sighing, "Back home, we do things *this* way."

FRANCE AND FOREIGNERS

Along with welcome differences in lifestyle, Americans living in France enjoy a certain resonance with the French. After all, historical ties have connected the two nations for more than 200 years. We may speak different languages, but Americans and the French share many cultural symbols and philosophical beliefs.

The mutual attraction between the two nations has existed since the beginning of the United States. For starters, the American Revolution provided an impetus for France's own. French Protestants fleeing persecution by an intolerant monarchy sought refuge in America just as, generations later, American free thinkers and artists found welcome refuge from puritanical mores in Paris, long viewed as the cultural center of the Western World. The two nations' concern with the human spirit and intellect—and the freedom to explore ideas—formed the first bonds.

Remember, it was French General Lafayette who offered military aid to George Washington. Founding fathers Benjamin Franklin and Thomas Jefferson so admired the French that they visited the country as American ambassadors. French political scientist Alexis de Tocqueville returned the praise in his famous study of the young United States.

These ties continued into the 20th century. When World War I began, American sympathies lay with France and Great Britain, finally prompting our intervention on their side. "Lafayette, we are here," General John J. Pershing intoned when he and his troops landed in France in 1917, acknowledging a 150-year-old debt.

It was the political connections during that war that led to more personal ones. At last, ordinary Americans got a vivid glimpse of a world already known to the well-to-do elite. A world in which wine was an everyday beverage, and meal preparation approached an art form. A world in which common folks' houses were built to last centuries, not a few years. A world in which writers and artists and intellectuals of every stripe were not only welcomed, but celebrated.

These connections endure today, despite the acrimony introduced into the relationship by the second Bush administration. They are enhanced by air travel that brings Paris as close to New York as the Big Apple is to San Diego, by telecommunications that bridge the distance between family members and friends, and by a global economy that produces similar products everywhere. A McDonald's hamburger tastes no different in Toulouse than it does in Topeka. Rest assured, you won't give up any modern conveniences by moving to France.

LOOKING TO THE FUTURE

Modern conveniences do cost, however, and France pays the price. Just like other industrialized nations, France suffers from urban sprawl, congested highways, crime, and poverty. Don't move to France to escape the 21st century or Western civilization. But do admire the nation for its willingness to tackle these problems in a rational way: to study and debate them, then implement positive solutions.

France is poised at the beginning of its third millennium as a nation with great natural and cultural resources, a checkered political history, and a proven desire to surpass the average. Change is coming here as quickly as anywhere in the world.

With an economy firmly tied to the rest of Europe, with trade barriers falling and costing jobs (but lowering prices), the French voice in international affairs is sometimes only one hoarse whisper among a rising clamor. And with a 19.6 percent value-added tax weighing heavy on every purchase of goods, labor, and service, the French can see that the future will not resemble the past.

Most French people look forward to the future, knowing that change is inevitable, and they are willing to work to turn it to their advantage. It is an enviable attitude, one that can make your move to France a pleasant and profitable experience.

History, Government, and Economy

France has been a wealthy land, favored with a temperate climate, a high proportion of arable land, abundant water, forests, and other natural resources. The Romans, eager to exploit that wealth, brought culture and civilization. The better kings and governments that followed them increased that natural prosperity and expanded their intellectual achievements.

The French Revolution overturned the social order in a violent way; indeed, its very violence brought a reaction that for decades stifled representative government. But the popular basis for the revolution was not be denied: With the establishment of the Third Republic in 1870,

France was set firmly on a path toward political and intellectual freedom and economic justice for its citizens. That path has been neither smooth nor straight, but the country and its leaders have not seriously strayed from it despite two world wars.

Today France and the rest of Europe are trying to manage a transformation thrust on them by the rapid pace of industrial and social change throughout the world. Europe is unifying not only out of necessity, but willfully. The 20th century taught well the dangers of nationalistic divisions. In addition to breaking down political barriers, nations of the European Union are forging a new economic unity; the introduction of a common currency was a significant step away from a protectionist past.

This remains very much a work in progress however. France, the great agricultural center of Europe, often finds itself at odds with its neighbors on common policies in this area. Loss of industrial base, persistently high unemployment rates, and immigration all threaten European unity. Despite all that has happened in the past 60 years to bring Europe together, the outcome remains to be seen.

History

Humans settled in what is today France nearly a half a million years ago. The country has a long history. Human remains 450,000 years old were found near Tautavel, a small winegrowing village not far from the Mediterranean. Among the oldest remains ever found in Europe, they reveal little beyond the physical appearance of a young, sturdy adult.

The 2,500-year recorded history of France is a bloody one, a history of invasion and conquest, battles won and lost, heroism and intrigue and the slow forging of a nation.

Fast forward 420,000-plus years: Artists employing sophisticated techniques and materials covered the walls of caves around France with pictures of animals we still find breathtakingly beautiful. Of this culture, little is known beyond the implements they left behind. But their artwork alone is enough to inspire use of the word "civilization."

The 2,500-year recorded history of France is a bloody one, full of invasion and conquest, battles won and lost, heroism and intrigue and the slow forging of a nation. Two great leaders a millennium apart, Charlemagne and Napoleon, brought most of Europe under the French flag. Before and after their reigns, the borders of France ebbed and flowed with the tide of history.

ROMAN RULE

The concept of France was born long before the nation. The Romans, following the Mediterranean trade routes of the Phoenicians and Greeks, found the land across the sea to the west hospitable. Roman soldiers were rewarded for faithful service with land around Narbonne—the Roman capital, well established by 118 B.C.—60 years before Julius Caesar began his conquest of Gaul.

The Gaul of Caesar's great campaigns included Belgium and much of the Netherlands. Caesar pushed his barbarian enemies across the Rhine, a river Napoleon would later proclaim France's "natural boundary." Roman legions quickly moved north up the Rhône River, established a garrison at Vienne, and soon built the city of Lyon as their capital in Provence.

Whatever its faults, Rome provided the barbarian tribes of Western Europe with discipline, law, and education. Roman rule could be harsh, but it also introduced an unmatched standard of civilization. When imperial Rome moved east to Constantinople, the Pax Romana failed and Europe descended into the Dark Ages.

CHARLEMAGNE AND THE CHURCH

Christianity eventually replaced Roman rule. When Clovis, king of the Franks, converted in 493 to marry the Burgundian princess Clotilda, he not only extended his kingdom, he also gained a powerful ally in the Roman church. When Pepin the Short, father of Charlemagne, was anointed by Pope Stephen II, he established the principle of rule by "divine right"—the belief that the king ruled by God's will, so opposition to him was sacrilege.

Charlemagne—Charles the Great—ruled for nearly half a century, extending the boundaries of his kingdom until it included virtually all of Western Europe, except for parts of Italy, Spain, and the British Isles.

But Charlemagne did more than gain ground. He re-established the rule of law, at least for his lifetime, and granted land to the church for monasteries that fostered learning throughout Europe. His rule contributed to the widespread establishment of feudalism, ending the Dark Ages and initiating the Middle Ages. Charlemagne divided his vast empire into counties, ruled by a count, with a viscount as a deputy. Soon these positions became hereditary; the lands on the frontier of the kingdom were called *marches* and the military rulers became *marquis*.

Just before Charlemagne's death, he crowned his son Louis king. But Louis was no Charlemagne, and gradually compromises were made, dividing the royal authority and fragmenting the empire. As a result, powerful aristocrats, who controlled large areas such as Normandy, Toulouse, and Burgundy, were able to act independently and oppose the king.

Tension between the noblemen and the king in Paris shaped much of French history until the revolution, and tension between the crown and the church also grew during this period. The church was often in need of reform, yet with so many churchmen from noble families and such extensive church holdings, any change meant both political and religious ramifications. Kings and noblemen could defy popes, and the bishops whom they named supported them. So, when Pope Urban II called for a crusade in 1095 to seize Palestine from Muslim rule, it gave church and state a chance to unite for mutual benefit. The crusaders were doing "God's work" looting and seizing territory; younger sons from noble families, who had little hope of inheritance, swelled the ranks. By 1100, Europeans—especially the French—were in control in the Near East.

Consolidating Royal Power

The 13th century saw the consolidation of French royal power within much of the territory of today's France. France even elected cardinal Clement V pope and installed him and several successors at Avignon in 1307, holding the papacy a virtual prisoner for 70 years. The 14th century brought the transition from the Middle Ages to the Renaissance and the Hundred Years' War with England.

The war lasted more than 100 years. The conventional dates are 1337 to 1453, but seeds were sown with the Norman Conquest in 1066. The war started over the right of succession to the throne, then swept down through decades of kings. The Hundred Years' War saw no decisive battle, and the plague often took a greater toll than the war.

After nearly a century of struggle, the war gave France its most enduring heroine, Jeanne d'Arc, who did more than anyone to end the fighting. Joan of Arc stepped onto the stage of history in 1428, prepared to put the dauphin Charles on the French throne and push the English back across the Channel.

Joan achieved her first goal; she broke the siege of Orléans, and Charles was crowned at Reims. After the coronation, Joan continued to fight with the army, but was wounded in 1430 and captured by the Burgundians, who sold her to their English allies. The English put her on trial as a heretic in Rouen, where she was convicted, condemned, and burned at the stake in 1431. She had placed Charles on the throne, but he did nothing to save her.

RENAISSANCE AND REFORMATION

Despite his rocky start, Charles VII surrounded himself with wise counselors and pushed the English out of France by mid-century. But he ruled an impoverished land devastated by war and disease. It was left to his son Louis XI, then Louis XII, and then Francis I to rebuild the land and deliver France into the Renaissance.

The 16th century, however, brought the far from peaceful Protestant Reformation. Religious differences served as a new excuse for a civil war that divided families, stifled dissent, and encouraged atrocities on both sides. Jean Calvin fled Paris for Geneva, where he established a theocracy and accepted French Protestants.

Efforts at peacemaking failed to quell sectarian struggles, often in the form of mob violence or assassinations. When Henry III died in 1589, Henry of Navarre claimed the throne as Henry IV.

Henry had been a Huguenot, but as king he returned to Catholicism, supposedly saying, "Paris is worth a mass." He issued the Edict of Nantes in 1598, offering protection for Protestants, and maintained an uneasy truce between the factions until his assassination by a Catholic in 1610.

The religious battles continued sporadically until mid-century. By 1620, Cardinal Richelieu began his devious and successful efforts to bring a measure of order, if not peace, to European politics. Richelieu established the principle of a balance of power, shifting alliances with nations while keeping France's interests in the fore. These policies were followed by his successors and continued to shape Europe until the revolution.

THE SUN KING SHINES

The last century and a half of the French monarchy was dominated by the reign of Louis XIV, the Sun King. This era became "the glory that was France," so-called because of the intellectual growth that took place in so many fields—philosophy, the arts, architecture, mathematics, and science. Descartes, Pascal, Corneille, Molière, Mansart, Le Nôtre, Lully, Rameau, and scores of others advanced education and the arts throughout France and the world. This intellectual and artistic ferment developed its own momentum for more than two centuries.

At this point, Paris and France became nearly synonymous. Louis concentrated power in the court; nobles from the provinces who desired something from the king were obliged to leave their homes and go to court to secure it, often a months-long process as complicated as it was expensive.

Louis himself was a complex figure. His reign began in 1643, when he was five years old. He grew to epitomize the absolute monarch, conceiving of the 10,000-room château at Versailles as a fitting residence for a king. He worked hard and well for France. A patron of the arts, he also built a professional army handsomely outfitted to fight almost continuous wars with Holland, England, and the Holy Roman Empire.

Early in his reign, Louis arrested his corrupt superintendent of finances and took over the job, closely supervising his able aide Colbert. He fostered economic development, increased trade, and colonial expansion; tax reform brought in more revenue. A staunch Catholic and supporter of the church, he nonetheless had numerous mistresses; and secretly married a commoner when his queen, Marie Thérèse, died in 1683.

During the latter part of his reign, which ended in 1715, the Sun King faded. By revoking the Edict of Nantes and renewing persecution of the Huguenots, he aroused negative sentiment. Continuous wars and European intrigues drained the treasury; in the end, France lost much of its hard-won territory in the New World. Despite Louis' accomplishments and devotion to France, his reign laid the foundation for the 75 years leading up to the revolution.

Louis XIV's great-grandson succeeded him—also at age five. Neither Louis XV nor his grandson, who became Louis XVI, showed much talent for government. As the century wore on, taxes multiplied and food grew scarce. The French lost the Seven Years' War in 1763. Reform was blocked at every turn by one faction or another unwilling to compromise. When revolution finally came in 1789, it seemed inevitable.

"LIBERTÉ, ÉGALITÉ, FRATERNITÉ!"

The French Revolution was bloody awful: chaotic, despotic, and necessary. Centuries of serfdom and slavery were not easily erased.

The revolution proceeded from the formation of the National Assembly in 1789 to Napoleon's seizure of power in 1799. The storming of the Bastille was followed by an uprising in the countryside, and the cry of *"Liberté, égalité, fraternité!"* echoed throughout France. Over the next two years, the National Assembly hammered out a constitution that included the king. But when Louis XVI tried unsuccessfully to flee the country that year, the European monarchies threatened France and diplomatic relations grew strained.

The Republic was proclaimed and the king was tried, convicted of conspiracy, and executed in 1793. This was the year of the Terror—when anyone accused of treason was assumed guilty and executed. In Paris, 20,000 people were guillotined, and twice that number in the provinces. Eventually, the tables turned, and the radicals themselves were executed.

NAPOLEON'S RISE AND FALL

The conservative Directory that next held power failed to find answers to economic problems, and protests continued. When a young artillery officer used a cannon to break up one of these riots, the Directory gave him control of the army in Italy in 1796. Napoleon Bonaparte did well, even conquering Egypt. But, alarmed by his independence,

© Corel/Velocity Stock

Arc de Triomphe

the Directory ordered him to return to Paris. Napoleon complied, but only to overthrow the Directory at gunpoint. The lower house of the National Assembly then declared him First Consul of the republic.

Napoleon quickly ended the revolution and set about reconstructing France in his own image. He talked of republicanism, the rights of man, and freedom, but he ruled as ruthlessly as any other despot. Then he set about to do the same for the rest of Europe, declaring himself emperor in 1804.

On the continent, Napoleon appeared unstoppable. But the British owned the seas, and Bonaparte finally overreached himself, invading Moscow for no gain and losing half a million men. When his enemy's army entered Paris in 1814, Napoleon abdicated and accepted exile to Elba, a small Mediterranean island. The brother of Louis XVI was crowned Louis XVII, and the monarchy was restored.

But only temporarily, for Napoleon returned from exile went on the march again. This time, the British stopped him at Waterloo and took him to St. Helena, a small English island in the Atlantic, where he remained until his death.

FROM MONARCHY TO EMPIRE TO REPUBLIC—AND BACK

During the century between Napoleon and World War I, France seemed rudderless, caught in any current that came along. Louis XVII gave the country limited prosperity during 10 years of cautious rule. He was followed by Charles X, who quickly abdicated in the face of a popular uprising in 1830 in favor of Louis Philipe, the duke of Orléans.

Louis Philipe barely managed to balance the various factions until 1848, when a popular uprising forced him to abdicate and established the Second Republic. It was decided France should have a president; the electorate chose Louis Napoleon Bonaparte, nephew of the emperor.

Louis Napoleon bided his time until 1851, when the National Assembly tried to take away the vote from three million people. He arrested the leaders and shut the assembly indefinitely. He then submitted his action to a vote, and won. A year later, he declared himself Emperor Napoleon III.

DIPLOMATIC DEFEATS

The Second Empire started out rigidly conservative and steadily liberalized. Industrialization sped up, financial institutions were established, and economic expansion was supported. Tariffs were reduced, trade en-

Normandy's Other War Memorial

One June day long before 1944, the coast of Normandy saw another battle where Americans fought and died. This was a sea battle in 1864, when the USS *Kearsarge* sank the Confederate raider CSS *Alabama*, seven miles from the port of Cherbourg.

Today, a memorial in Cherbourg's Museum of Nautical History recalls that battle. It is the only Civil War historical site outside of the U.S., and the sunken remains of the three-mast ship are jointly administered by the U.S. and France.

The *Alabama*, built for the Confederacy by the British in 1862, terrified American sailors for nearly two years, sinking more than 60 Union merchant ships and taking 2,000 prisoners.

Captain John Winslow tracked the *Alabama*, commanded by a former shipmate, Raphael Semmes, around the Atlantic to Cherbourg, and waited for the raider to leave port the morning of June 19. For more than an hour, the two ships traded cannon fire before the *Alabama* began to sink.

Semmes and about 40 of his 155-man crew were rescued and escaped aboard a British yacht. The *Kearsarge* took all but the 29 lost in battle prisoner, then continued in naval service for 30 more years before sinking on a reef off the coast of Central America.

couraged, unions and strikes legalized, and political opponents granted amnesty. The political process opened up.

Napoleon III fared less well in foreign policy. He tried to install Prince Maximilian von Habsburg as emperor of Mexico without success. He gained Nice and Savoy for France, but failed to unify Italy.

The disastrous Franco-Prussian war in 1870 cost him the throne. Napoleon III did not want the war, but Otto von Bismarck did. The Prussian prime minister manipulated public opinion so that the war cry sounded as loudly in Paris as it did in Berlin. Napoleon led French troops in battle and was captured. When word reached Paris, the radicals gained control of the assembly, declared a republic, and formed a provisional government.

The new government negotiated peace at a heavy price, giving up Alsace, Lorraine, and five billion francs in indemnities. This set the tone the next 50 years of public life. The various factions that fought so bitterly over the past century—radicals, monarchists, socialists, conservatives, communists, Catholics and anti-clerics, bourgeoisie, peasants, and the nobility—didn't let up.

Scandal was rampant, including one of the worst in French history. The Dreyfus affair nearly split France apart. In 1896, the only Jew on

Jour-J, *le Débarquement,* and the Aftermath

Normandy was unquestionably the scene of the fiercest fighting American troops encountered in France during World War II. The day the Allied troops arrived, June 6, 1944, is known as Jour-J to the French (the equivalent of D-Day in America), and the invasion itself as *le Débarquement.*

The first three beaches chosen for the invasion—Sword, Juno, and Gold—ran from the mouth of the Orne River west, where British forces landed, to Bayeux. From Bayeux west to St-Mère-Église were Omaha and Utah, where the Americans came ashore. The beaches here are narrow strips of sand backed by steep cliffs, like so much of the coast along the English Channel.

More than two months of vicious combat, including tanks, heavy artillery shelling, and aerial bombardments, devastated many cities and towns. However, the reconstruction effort after the war was extraordinary. While scars remain, many parts of this pastoral countryside appear untouched after two generations of healing.

After spending the first week securing their beachhead, the Americans attacked westward across the Cotentin Peninsula to the whaling port of Barneville. The invaders then turned north to take the great port of Cherbourg, critical to maintaining supply lines to the advancing armies, on June 26.

Bayeux was the first city liberated in France, on June 7. Caen fell to British attack on July 9. St. Lô, nearly 40 kilometers (25 miles) southwest of Bayeux, was liberated on July 25. This was a difficult part of the bat-

---

the general staff, Capt. Alfred Dreyfus, was arrested for selling military secrets to the Germans. Anti-Semitism was so rabid among the aristocratic Catholics in France's officer corps that he was convicted on forged evidence and sent to Devil's Island. It took a decade of bitter controversy to exonerate Dreyfus and restore him to his post. But this blot on the face of France is remembered today.

CULTURAL TUMULT

Fortunately, the ugliness of public life during the Third Republic was balanced by great beauty. Manet, Monet, Toulouse-Lautrec, Renoir, Gauguin, Pissaro, Cézanne, Matisse, Degas—a seemingly endless list of artists flourished. So did musicians, such as Georges Bizet, Maurice Ravel, and Claude Debussy; and scientists, such as Louis Pasteur, Marie Curie, and mathematician Henri Poincaré.

In stark contrast, World War I hit with little warning. The 1914 assassination of Austria's Archduke Franz Ferdinand in Sarajevo triggered tle. Troops had to contend with the *bocage* land ("war of the hedges") quartered by dense rows of apple and pear trees, along with roads too narrow for armor and cannon. St. Lô was almost totally destroyed in the war, but rebuilt with charm, and today is a town of 22,000.

Past St. Lô, the countryside opens up, which allowed the tanks to speed ahead, bypassing pockets of German resistance, and to encircle them. Countances, today a pleasant town of 10,000 noted for its jazz festival every May, fell on July 28. Granville and Avranches, opposite Mont St.-Michel, followed on July 31. On August 1, Gen. George Patton took command of the newly formed Third Army and swept into Brittany, taking Rennes on August 4. He then turned east to Orléans and Chartres.

Meanwhile, British forces slowly moved south from Caen. With American success to the west and British and Canadian pressure coming from the north, the Germans decided to counterattack. On August 6, German tanks moved west, intending to cut off Patton's Third Army at Avranches. The American First Army met them at Mortain, today a village of 2,500 at the mouth of a narrow valley and the western tip of the Parc Régional de Normandie. A week of heavy fighting followed, but the Germans were unable to break through. On August 12, they began a retreat eastward. They were too late. French forces that had taken Le Mans on August 9 sped north and captured Alençon on August 12. A day later, they were outside Argentan, cutting off the road to Paris.

Canadian forces entered Falaise on August 17 and pushed forward, connecting with the Americans on August 19. The Germans were caught between the two forces, and on August 21, 1944, the Battle of Normandy ended.

a network of alliances that set half of Europe at the throats of the other half. France bore the brunt of the war, since most of the fighting took place within its borders. Trench warfare produced terrible losses.

France suffered 1.3 million dead and 3 million wounded. An entire generation of young men was crippled or lost. In villages all over France stand memorials bearing the names of the dead.

WAR AND DEPRESSION

The loss of life was matched by economic devastation. Inflation had skyrocketed 400 percent and the national debt had multiplied by five. The French were determined to make the Germans pay reparations, which unwittingly contributed to the rise of fascism.

By the mid-1920s, the economy began to revive and enjoyed full prosperity by 1928—just in time for the Great Depression. The Depression affected France as it did other nations: massive unemployment, falling production, rising deficit, and no real solution in sight.

Economic gloom paralleled Hitler's rise to power and the rearming of Germany. When war struck again in 1939, a thoroughly demoralized France reacted.

While the U.S. remained neutral, Germany launched the blitzkrieg in spring 1940. France surrendered in less than three months. The Third Republic crumbled. Germany occupied Paris, the north of France, and the Atlantic coast; France was reduced to the thinly populated Massif Central, Midi, and Provence. The country's new capital at Vichy was chosen because the resort area had enough hotel rooms to house the new government.

THE VICHY GOVERNMENT

Marshal Philippe Pétain headed the new regime. Little more than a puppet of the Germans, the authoritarian, anti-Semitic, and clerical Vichy government gave the French right wing what it had long demanded. Dissidents and Jews were rounded up and sent east as slave labor or to concentration camps. By 1944, Germany held full control.

But Vichy did not represent the whole country. The other France was headed by General Charles de Gaulle, an abrasive, autocratic, talented soldier who escaped to England and did not surrender. The Vichy government called him a traitor and sentenced him to death. De Gaulle offered the Allies a French component for their propaganda and a conduit to French Resistance groups, who reluctantly agreed to accept the general as their symbolic leader.

The Allies' successful invasion of Normandy on June 6, 1944, was quickly followed by the liberation of Paris in late August. May 8, 1945, is officially recognized as Liberation Day in France, a national holiday.

De Gaulle established a provisional government—giving women the vote for the first time—and brought some order out of the chaos left behind by Nazi occupation. A new constitution was drawn up, based on the old one, and the Fourth Republic was born.

COLONIAL CRISES AND THE COLD WAR

The Fourth Republic never equaled the postwar stresses of anticolonialism and the Cold War. Coalition governments of the Fourth Republic lasted an average of six months; any constructive attempt to resolve a problem seemed to anger one faction or another, which then withdrew and toppled the government. Numerous crises beleaguered the government, the greatest centering on French colonies in Indo-China, North Africa, and the Near East.

Indo-China was the first to break free from colonial rule, in 1954, but not without a bitter war. Tunisia and Morocco followed. Algeria was another story.

An Algerian nationalist group had been waging a guerilla war against the French for years. To counter them, France installed a heavy military presence augmented by troops pulled out of Indo-China. Tough, embittered, and right wing, they were determined to hold Algeria by any means—torture was commonplace. When the government in Paris talked about withdrawal in 1958, the military began planning a coup d'état.

De Gaulle refused to go along with them. Instead, the National Assembly gave him six months of power to rule by decree. He rewrote the constitution, thus giving France a strong presidency. De Gaulle was elected to the post, and his party gained a plurality in parliament. Disgruntled army officers organized their coup, but could not persuade their troops to follow. Instead, the officers formed a terrorist group, the OAS (Secret Army Organization), even attempting an assassination of de Gaulle. They failed. De Gaulle crushed the OAS and recognized Algerian independence in 1962.

The postwar years were not all bad for France. Marshall Plan aid helped revive industrial production, and France took the first steps toward forming the European Union. In 1951, France, West Germany, Italy, Belgium, Holland, and Luxembourg formed the European Coal and Steel Community. In 1957, these nations signed the Treaty of Rome to establish the Common Market. De Gaulle's government also introduced economic reforms, resulting in a 5 percent annual increase in the Gross National Product between 1958 and 1967.

De Gaulle's exit from public life was unusual. In summer 1968, his party won a majority in parliament. Industrial wages increased, and university reforms were soon instituted. De Gaulle then decided to introduce some governmental reforms in a national referendum. When the referendum lost, de Gaulle walked away without explanation, went home, and continued writing his memoirs—almost as if the 1958 call to return to public life had been little more than an interlude in a busy afternoon.

MITTERAND AND THE EUROPEAN UNION

After de Gaulle, the right wing retained the presidency for more than a decade, until François Mitterand's Socialists swept into power in 1981.

Mitterand served two presidential terms, and the right gained control of the National Assembly more than once, but *cohabitation*—when the president and the prime minister are on opposite sides of the political fence—has worked.

In recent decades, the governments of France have persevered in their commitment to a European Union. Valerie Giscard d'Estaing, as finance minister and later president, was instrumental in establishing a framework for the common currency. Giscard d'Estaing presided over the drafting of the EU constitution under discussion by member states in 2005. Mitterand shepherded the acceptance of the Treaty of Maastricht, which opened the borders of EU nations.

President Jacques Chirac, who followed Mitterand, began his term with a legislative majority—but after raising taxes, resuming nuclear tests, and failing to lower unemployment, Chirac was forced into *cohabitation* with the government of Socialist Prime Minister Lionel Jospin.

In spring 2002, France went to the polls. The electoral system anticipates a run-off between the top two vote-getters. For the presidency, it was universally expected that Chirac would face Jospin in the second round. But Jospin, despite achieving such legislative successes as the 35-hour workweek and universal health care, never really unified his party, and many people either cast protest votes or sat out the first round.

To the dismay of the left and delight of the right, Jospin came in third, behind Jean-Marie Le Pen, leader of the extreme right Front National party. Faced with that choice, the electorate gave Chirac a resounding victory and five more years in office. A few weeks later, voters ended *cohabitation* by giving Chirac's party, Union pour un Mouvement Populaire (UMP), a large majority in the National Assembly.

Government

"How can anyone govern a nation that has 246 different kinds of cheese?" asked Charles de Gaulle—who underestimated the number of French cheeses, but not the difficulty of running France.

In fact, de Gaulle finally gave up trying, but his efforts were not in vain. The constitution he helped write in 1958 continues to serve the nation well after more than 40 years, delivering the stability France has historically lacked in modern times.

The French constitution established a parliamentary form of govern-

© Corel/Fotosearch

Assemblée Nationale

ment with parallels to both the British and the American systems, but different from both. Representatives are elected to the Assemblée Nationale (National Assembly), and a prime minister is chosen from among the majority to run the government. But in the French system, there is also an elected president who names the prime minister. Executive power is wielded by a series of ministries whose heads are appointed by the prime minister. Most of the decisions affecting life in France are made at the ministerial level: budget, taxation, health care, and Social Security.

This system has proved an effective antidote to the parliamentary jockeying that paralyzed the Fourth Republic. Since election to the presidency requires a majority vote, the president enters office with a true mandate from the electorate. His appointment of a prime minister depends on the legislature's majority vote. When the president's party controls parliament, this appointment is relatively straightforward; the president installs his own person, and they work in tandem. When another party controls the parliament, the president bows to the will of the majority party and names its leader prime minister, and this appointee then chooses his own ministers to govern.

The president, elected for a five-year term, is charged with guaranteeing proper functioning of public authorities and the continuity of the state—a large, ill-defined task. He serves as head of the armed forces, can dissolve the legislature, and convenes and presides at meetings of the Council of Ministers. He can also call for a national referendum on acts passed by the legislature and require the legislature to reconsider its acts.

The prime minister is responsible for running the government. Although the president actually appoints cabinet ministers, he does so following the suggestions of the prime minister. The sort of cooperation that the constitution forces on these high elected officials is evident in the area of defense. The president commands the armed forces, but the minister of defense heads the agency that manages them, and he or she serves at the pleasure of the prime minister.

At the risk of oversimplifying, the president is responsible for the overall welfare of the country—but the instrument of action is the government, headed by the prime minister. The prime minister and his cabinet are responsible day-to-day operations, while the president serves as Head of State and represents France on the international stage. The president is seen as guardian of the various organs of government and maintains the separation of power between executive and legislative. Nonetheless, it is the prime minister's government that conducts national policy. Given the ambiguous nature of this relationship, much depends on the personalities of the individual president and prime minister and their relative political strength at any given time.

The two houses of the legislature are the Assemblée Nationale (National Assembly) and the Sénat (Senate). Representation in both houses is by department according to population. The 577 deputies of the National Assembly are directly elected for five-year terms, unless the president of France dissolves the assembly and calls for new elections. Because of France's multiplicity of political parties, two votes are held a week apart. If a candidate wins an absolute majority in the first vote, he or she wins the seat. If no candidate gains a majority in the first round of voting, as is often the case, the top vote-getters have a runoff and whoever gets the most votes is declared winner. The French enjoy a high degree of representation: one representative in the national legislature for every 67,000 citizens (compared to one rep for every 510,000 Americans in the U.S.).

The assembly elects its own president for the life of the assembly's term. No deputy may belong to more than one of the six standing committees: Cultural, Family and Social Affairs; Foreign Affairs;

Defense; Finance; Constitution and Administration; and Production and Trade.

The nation's 346 senators serve six-year terms, and half of them are elected every three years. Unlike the deputies of the assembly, they are not directly elected. Instead, an electoral college made up of all the elected officials, including municipal counselors in each department, chooses the senators. This is further complicated by the fact that, in the departments entitled to five or more senators, election is on a proportional basis; whereas in the smaller departments, it is based on majority rule. The senate cannot be dissolved, unlike the assembly. It is the president of the senate who succeeds to the national presidency if that post is vacated.

If your favorite sport is politics, you'll enjoy an unending spectacle.

There are elections almost every year in France owing to differing term lengths—six years for senators, five for the president, six for mayors and city councilors, and five for deputies to the National Assembly, regional councils, and European parliament. Besides election of officials, the French also hold national referendums from time to time on such questions as the vote on the proposed European Union. If your favorite sport is politics, you'll enjoy an unending spectacle in France.

Economy

As the recession of the 1990s waned, France faced the new millennium with stability and confidence. Unemployment declined in 2000, the economy continued to grow without excessive inflation, and consumer confidence remained robust. Unfortunately, this did not last. By November 2004, the number of unemployed was back where it had been five years earlier, and consumers were glum. The expansion of the EU to 25 nations in May 2004 cost France and Germany dearly, as multinational corporations quickly moved some production facilities east to take advantage of cheaper labor and taxes in ex-Soviet bloc countries.

The introduction of the euro in 2002, widely hailed as an initial success, also began posing a drawback in the face of a plunging dollar. The U.S. could run up annual deficits of $500–600 billion and talk about spending another $2 trillion to privatize Social Security, but the narrow fiscal constraints that bound euro nations would not permit such profligacy. As American goods—and more importantly, the Chinese goods also tied to that dropping dollar—undercut European products, doubts surfaced. But at the beginning of 2005, there were no predictions of, or calls for, radical change.

The greatest challenge for France in the coming years may well be the economic unification of the new EU nations. There are precedents: Ireland and Portugal are notable examples of below-par economies boosted by joint EU efforts. Membership for Turkey is more than economic, however, with its overwhelmingly Islamic population. Economic questions are coupled with the European Union's increasing control of much national policy. French duck hunters, for instance, have defied EU regulations of their sport, and a national referendum was called for 2005 on the EU constitution. Nonetheless, the nation's elected leaders on both the right and the left have been at the forefront of efforts to unite the continent, and there is no sign of this ending, no matter how they maneuver to advance France's interests.

People and Culture

French culture is world-renowned. Famous for its cuisine, architecture, and celebration of intellectual freedom, the country remains one of the most important cultural centers on the globe. The French themselves are as individual and diverse as people anywhere, but some generalizations are possible. For starters, French diplomacy is no myth. The society encourages good manners, and you'll find that most French people are polite, as well as reserved by American standards. They are proud of their beautiful country and respond warmly to those who appreciate it.

Class

More than two centuries ago, the French Revolution wiped out the feudal distinctions of l'Ancien Régime historically made between nobility and commoners. Nonetheless, France vacillated from empire to monarchy to empire, flirting only briefly with a democratic government until the Third Republic was established in 1870. You need only note the number of public figures today whose names contain *de* or *d'*—denoting noble lineage—for proof that class still matters in France.

A noble title remains a trump card in the game of high society; even today, there is a movement to restore the monarchy. Ironically, many of the titles their French carriers wear so proudly originated in some other land. Titled nobility from other European countries ended up in France following the dissolution of monarchies in their own lands. The Rothschild banking family, for instance, whose French branch continues in business today, were made barons by the king of Austria. Add to this situation people who, though not of aristocratic birth, used *de* in their names to indicate their origin. Still others simply fake it—laying claim to a title as a form of self-aggrandizement.

EDUCATION

Power and privilege aside, France has always derived its strength from its people, rather than its nobility. The French place a high value on *solidarité,* a populist concept of obligation to one another for the good of all. There is even a *ministère de l'emploi et de la solidarité* (minister of employment and solidarity), one of the most powerful people in the government. This ministry implemented the 35-hour workweek and extended full health-care benefits to welfare recipients.

> *The French place a high value on* solidarité, *a populist concept of obligation to one another for the good of all.*

Along with *solidarité,* the French place a high premium on education. In 2000, the government spent €105.4 billion and the amount has increased annually since then, reaching €111 billion in 2003, the last year for which figures are available. The robust national educational system, which includes an inexpensive university education for qualifying students, produces articulate and competent citizens. Some 25 percent of France's 62 million people are in school. Two million of them are at the university level, where admission depends upon passing *le bac,* shorthand for *le baccalauréat,* the degree granted after passing a national examination at the end of secondary school. *Le bac* is equivalent to a junior college diploma in the United States.

A highly educated population means a skilled workforce. It also explains the disproportionately high number of achievements the French have made in various fields of research, as well as the plentiful supply of professionals. For example, one small agricultural village in Languedoc, population 1,500, counts four doctors, three nurses, a dentist, two pharmacists, and a physical therapist among its citizenry.

Ethnicity

As a group, the French of North African decent have become a target for the Far Right in France. The Front National political party, led by the antisemitic Jean-Marie Le Pen, has captured up to 15 percent of the vote in some elections by campaigning against "immigrants" in general. The party is particularly strong along the Côte d'Azur. Le Pen himself was Jacques Chirac's opponent in the runoff for the presidency in 2002.

With slogans such as "French first," the Front National has tried to cloak its racism as patriotism. But the so-called immigrants are French citizens, some of them second- and third-generation. Some of their grandparents fought or worked for the French in Algeria until that country won its independence in 1962.

The truth is, France is a nation of immigrants, and has been throughout recorded history. Mediterranean ports such as Nice and Marseille began as Greek trading posts. Romans, Germanic tribes, and Scandinavians all emigrated to France. Often they came as invaders, but, over generations, they have become French.

Nor have the Pyrénées been an ethnic barrier in the south. The Basques live on both sides of the border, as do the Catalans. Today, the European Union views the Barcelona-Toulouse axis as an economic unit, just as it was centuries before. In 1886, one million foreigners lived among France's total population of 40 million. By 1930, this figure had swelled to three million, many of them workers recruited from North Africa.

After World War II, France continued to recruit foreign labor from North Africa, Portugal, and Eastern Europe. By 2004, among the nation's total population of 62 million, more than four million foreigners lived in France, one-third of them naturalized citizens, one-third of them other Europeans—Portuguese, Spanish, Italians, and others. Americans accounted for a minuscule fraction. In 1998, France issued just 20,252 long-stay visas to North and South Americans combined, about half of them for students or stays under six months.

Nevertheless, the French perceive themselves as a homogenous country—if you're not French, you're foreign. The American notion that everyone (except Native American Indians) came from somewhere else, and that the chief distinction is the number of generations your family has been on the continent, is to the French, well, foreign. *Integration* (assimilation) is a very important concept in France.

Those who are "outsiders" in some way, not fully assimilated, can meet prejudice. In some cases, it may be nothing more than a rude clerk, but in others, prejudice can take the form of school segregation, refusal of housing—exactly the sort of discrimination people of color have faced in the United States. But not only skin color can set you apart; it can also be your accent or your inability to speak the language.

Even some university graduates with advanced degrees fail to be hired when their ethnic heritage becomes known. Parents find their children segregated when moving from nursery school to primary school or from primary to middle school, whether in Paris or in the provinces. When many of the *sans-papiers* (people without proper visas) were given a chance to regularize their situations in 1997, it was learned that many of them were legally entitled to be in France, but had been denied processing by xenophobic bureaucrats.

Not surprisingly, racial and ethnic tension sometimes erupts on the streets: from racist graffiti to terrorist attacks on the Paris métro. In 2003 and 2004, much of this tension had a three-way focus, as neo-Nazis attacked both Jews and those of African heritage, and the Israeli-Palestinian conflict spilled over into France.

But there is cause for hope. In the same 1999 survey that revealed French xenophobia, 81 percent of the respondents said they objected to the practice of refusing to hire a qualified foreigner, and solid majorities said the same about discrimination in housing or public facilities. The government, both right and left, seems determined to combat the problem. When five provincial council presidents sought to keep their seats by currying favor with the Front National, they were expelled from their parties.

France deals with its social problems the way any democracy must: through discussion and debate, education, and legislation. Despite a history of political instability, the country has made continued social and economic progress. There is nothing to suggest this will not continue in the future.

Customs and Etiquette

Although France and the United States had long enjoyed friendly relations until the U.S. attacked Iraq, contemporary French do not appreciate what they view as American arrogance. For example, the U.S. government's efforts to flood Europe with bananas grown in Central America, genetically modified grains, and hormone-laden meat while maintaining its own barriers to European products has not escaped notice by the general population. Farmers trashing a McDonald's under construction were greeted sympathetically and grabbed national headlines.

At the same time, the popularity of so many things American—Coca-Cola, Hollywood films, logo-bearing sportswear, and, yes, even "Mac-Do's"—mitigates against ill will. After all, the United States is a very popular vacation destination for the French. A joke that made the rounds a few years ago illustrates the view of America as a land of vast abundance: A Frenchman vacationing in Texas goes out to eat one evening. At the restaurant, he asks for a beer and is served a two-quart pitcher. Then he orders a steak and is brought a 32-ounce T-bone. After finishing the meal, he asks directions to the restroom and is told it's out the back door and straight ahead. As he exits the door, the power fails and all the lights go out. The poor fellow stumbles in the dark and falls into the swimming pool. He cries out in a panic, "Don't flush! Don't flush!"

Jokes aside, most French people feel genuine admiration for the United States. Beginning with the Declaration of Independence and continuing through the most recent technological achievements, the French appreciate American accomplishments. And the helping hand the United States has extended militarily and economically to France has not been forgotten.

The anti-French attitude displayed in America during George W. Bush's first administration largely puzzled the French. The unilateral moves of the administration, beginning with its rejection of the Kyoto treaty and continuing through its occupation of Iraq, were attributed to a president who had not been popularly elected. But with Bush's reelection, a certain amount of reassessment is taking place. Widely reported stories of the rejection of the theory of evolution, refusal to accept global warming as a fact, and fiscal irresponsibility on an international level have not only the French, but many other Europeans, reconsidering their attitudes toward America.

The Day of Rest

Like to shop on Sunday? Unless it's window-shopping, you won't do it in France. Most commercial activity takes place between Monday morning and Saturday evening. Many businesses close on Saturday afternoon and reopen on Monday after lunch. Other offices may be open Monday through Friday and closed on the weekend. Each commune (administrative district) can allow up to five Sunday openings per year, but there is no overall formula. There is very little chance you'll be able to spend Sunday shopping for clothes, gardening materials, hardware, or auto parts. Shopping malls and supermarkets are shuttered.

Food shops are allowed to open on Sunday mornings. Grocery stores, butcher shops, and produce markets may open or not, depending on individual owners' preferences. But bakeries are more traditionally open, and many towns and cities have a farmers market on Sunday. Restaurants often close after the Sunday noon meal and do not reopen until Tuesday noon. Service stations usually close, although many have installed pumps that you can operate with a French credit card, even when the station is closed.

It's a given that almost everyone, unless they are in the hotel-restaurant business or are some kind of emergency personnel, will have Sunday off. Amateur sports teams can get together to play—and all the players' friends can come to the game. Saturday night dances and wedding receptions can last until daybreak, because no one has to go to work.

These historical factors are widely recognized, but life is lived person to person. On the human level, anyone who considers moving to France sooner or later must ask him or herself, "Do I belong here?" The answer to this question may well depend on how you are received in France, and that, of course, depends on how you treat the French.

In my experience, the French are a polite, rather formal people, and they expect the same from others. Remember, French has been the language of diplomacy for centuries, and the desire to smooth over conflict is ingrained in the culture. Even so, familiarity often stops at the front door. Once the ice is broken, however, the French respond with warmth and feeling; an invitation to a family gathering should be considered an honor.

Of course, there are cultural differences. Many Americans, particularly women, are likely to find the macho bias of French society, even when politely cloaked, disagreeable at times. On the flip side, Americans used to efficiency in the marketplace may be perceived as brusque by French merchants accustomed to chatting while ringing

In short, Sunday remains a genuine day of rest for most of France, a time to relax and enjoy family time. After the traditional big noon meal, people go for walks or rides in the country, visit friends, take naps, or watch the local soccer or rugby team play.

This takes some getting used to for many Americans in France. After all, most Americans take for granted that their 24-hour supermarkets, drugstores, gas stations, fast-food joints, and building supply stores will remain open 16–18 hours a day, seven days a week. And no matter how welcome the idea of one day sans shopping might be, you never know when you might need to run to the store for a quart of milk, a bag of charcoal, or more nails to finish a do-it-yourself project.

Yet most of us readily adapt to—in fact, yearn for—a more measured pace of life in which work is just one component, necessary but no more important than family life, recreation, or cultural experiences. The French way of life tends to be harmonious; that is, the different aspects blend and fit together, as does French society as a whole. Those who seek a less frenetic way of life, who don't care about shopping for groceries (or anything else) at midnight, and who enjoy being in sync with those around them, will find France a delight.

You could call it an orchestrated way of life, with Custom and Tradition waving a small baton to keep everyone together. The strikes and demonstrations that often as not disrupt that harmony result from some of the musicians telling the conductor he missed a beat or has been neglecting them. They create a certain amount of dissonance as a means of getting everyone's attention, but only to restore the harmony.

up a sale. Yes, it takes longer, but isn't making a human connection worth it?

Here's a litmus test of sorts: What would you do if you ordered a cup of coffee *with* dessert in a restaurant, only to have it served after you've cleaned your plate? This is the norm in France. If you're likely to be exasperated by this custom and make a fuss, France might not be the place for you. If you take this and other differences in stride, and even delight in them, rest assured—you'll have no difficulty making friends in France.

Gender Roles

When it comes to gender equality in France, you could say that the slogan *"Liberté, égalité, fraternité!"* (liberty, equality, brotherhood) has been taken literally. Indeed, the French language itself lacks a feminine equivalent of *fraternité*.

In short, despite great strides in economics and politics, French women

'Til Death Do Us Part?

Divorce did not come easily to France. It took a revolution—and then it was abolished for most of the 19th century. When it finally became permissible again, divorce was granted only for "good cause" (such as a serious transgression by one party or another). In 1975, the law recognized divorce by mutual consent, but even so, more than one-third of divorces continued to be contested with all the venom two people could manage.

Beginning in 2005, the law changed in an effort to facilitate more amiable ruptures. In a society where masculine peccadilloes are taken for granted and the legal standing of concubines is firmly entrenched, the new law speeds and softens the divorce process, allowing both parties to choose the same lawyer.

But it is with marriage, not divorce, that Gallic gallantry comes to the creative fore. A 1959 law, passed at the behest of President Charles de Gaulle, permits marriage between two people, one of whom cannot attend the ceremony because he or she is dead.

Passage of the law came after hundreds of people were killed when a dam burst in Provence. One of the victims was Andre Capra, and when De Gaulle visited the scene of the disaster, Capra's fiancée Irene Jodard implored the general to do something.

De Gaulle's solution permits the marriage to be retroactive to the day before the spouse's death, so that the widow might legally bear her husband's name. In place of the groom's recitation of vows, the mayor or his representative reads the decree authorizing the ceremony.

About 20 such marriages are performed annually. First comes a plea to the president, who orders an investigation of the circumstances by local officials. Parental consent must also be given. But no law can provide a honeymoon for the couple.

still face discrimination. They did not get the vote until after World War II, two generations after their American sisters won suffrage with the 19th Amendment to the U.S. Constitution. But, as if to prove that the vote alone was insufficient, Simone de Beauvoir's *The Second Sex* became a seminal work in the literature of the U.S. women's movement.

Historically, there has been no shortage of strong women in France. The most potent was Jeanne d'Arc (Joan of Arc), whose courage and leadership changed the course of French history. Yet male descendants have prevailed for centuries. Titles passed to sons or to brothers, not to widows. Even today, unless special provision is made in a will, it is the children, especially the sons, who inherit, not the widow. It is possible for a woman to be put out of the house she shared with her husband in the event of his death.

In 2002, women lagged behind men financially in all statistical surveys of employment and income. Women's salaries were 20 percent less, and significantly fewer women have risen through the ranks, even with equivalent education. Even in occupations that are traditionally considered feminine, women are overwhelmingly workers, not managers. The French use the same term as Americans to describe the situation: *plafond de verre* (glass ceiling).

In politics, women fare better. Once given the vote, women won political office. By the 1980s, France had appointed a woman prime minister, Edith Cresson. The head of what would become President Jacques Chirac's party, *Rassemblement pour la Republique* (RPR), was a woman, Michèle Alliot-Marie. One of the most powerful ministers in the government at the same time was Martine Aubry, *ministère de l'emploi et de la solidarité*. When Chirac subsequently reformed his party as the Union pour un Mouvement Populaire (UMP) and regained control of the government from the Socialists, Alliot-Marie became minister of defense.

France has embarked on a path of legislated equality. A new law requires political parties to field candidates comprising equal numbers of men and women. In the mayoral elections of March 2001, 20 percent of the candidates were women. Another recent law requires employers to negotiate on equal employment for women, just as they must negotiate wages and working hours. These changes are not being universally applied, but they are having an effect. In 2005, 73 of the 576 members of the National Assembly, the French equivalent of the House of Representatives, were women.

Just as in the United States, unequal treatment can continue at home. A woman may work at a job as many hours as her male counterpart, and still bear the majority of the responsibility for housework and childcare. The *école maternelle* (daycare) may look after young children while a mother is at work during the day, but laundry, cooking, and cleaning, as well as childcare, are still seen as "women's work" in many households.

GAY AND LESBIAN CULTURE

Paris occupies much the same place in the world of French gays and lesbians as San Francisco does in the U.S.: A large, sophisticated urban landscape offers opportunities for culture, community, employment, and entertainment.

The mayor, Bernard Delanoë, was elected as an openly gay man; the city hosts an annual gay pride parade as outrageous as any in the U.S. One of the regional councilors of the Île-de-France was made knight of the Legion of Honor for his efforts in the fight against AIDS (SIDA is the French term). A 2001 survey estimated there are 3.5 million gays and lesbians in France. In late 2004, Pink TV, a gay- and lesbian-oriented cable channel, made its debut, and it's now available everywhere in France because of the distribution of television via ADSL and telephone lines.

A large, sophisticated urban landscape offers opportunities for culture, community, employment and entertainment

Homophobia certainly exists. In December 2004, a law was passed that put homophobic insults and defamation on the same footing with antisemitism and racism—offenders are subject to prison sentences. In short, the open French attitude toward human sexuality has produced a fairly tolerant society.

In 1999, a law was passed creating the equivalent of domestic partners, called PACS (Pacte Civil de Solidarité). These have been quite successful; more than 130,000 were established in the first four years. A couple, regardless of gender, goes to court and establishes their relationship in a legal contract that gives them all the rights a marriage would: family allocations, inheritance, division of property (50/50 unless spelled out otherwise), and so on. If one partner dies, the other is entitled to two days' bereavement leave from his or her job; children may bear the family name of either parent or both under current law.

Gay marriage so far has met the same fate as in California. A mayor in a small town near Bordeaux performed one ceremony, and it was annulled in court following a national controversy. (In France, it is a mayor, not a judge, who performs marriages.)

Gays and lesbians live in cities and villages far from Paris and I know of several individuals and couples who lead their lives undisturbed in small villages and larger cities.

Religion

France's immigrant groups also account for religious differences among the French, but make no mistake: France is a Catholic country. Nearly 80 percent of the French are at least nominally Catholic.

Surveys of the entire population find approximately 15 percent of French women and 10 percent of the men practice any religion regularly, though nearly one-fourth of the women and a third of the men say they have no religion.

Roman Catholicism became a potent force in France with the conversion of Clovis, king of the Franks, in 493. Charlemagne undertook the protection of the pope in Rome. It was not until 1905 that church and state were definitively separated in France. Even today, some Catholic feast days, such as Ascension Thursday and All Saints' Day, are recognized as national holidays. Other religious holidays that always fall on a Sunday, such as Easter and Pentecost, are followed by recognized Monday holidays.

Only about a million Protestants live in France; over the centuries, Catholic authorities succeeded in driving out most Christian dissenters via persecution and wars. Indeed, Islam is the second-largest religion in France. However, only half of practitioners are French citizens. Surveys have found about 35 percent declare themselves "believers and practitioners" of the faith. There are 1,500 mosques in France, and more than two-thirds have fewer than 150 members; only a score have more than 1,000 adherents.

© Corel/Velocity Stock

Cathédrale Notre-Dame de Chartres

Islam is the country's fastest-growing religion and French Muslims, largely of North African descent, but also black African and Turkish, number about five million. Some French Muslims continue cultural practices that have long been banned in the West, such as female circumcision and arranged marriage, and this perceived gender discrimination also plays a part in France's race and ethnicity problems.

While female circumcision is relatively rare, arranged marriage is not. The women, who were born in France and have lived there all their lives, may be forced as teenagers to decide between fleeing their homes or marrying men they've never met. Older brothers or other family members often help enforce the parents' wishes, leaving the women nowhere to turn unless they are willing to denounce their family to authorities. It is a difficult decision.

This conflict between the Islamic fundamentalists, moderates, and unbelievers was central to France's controversial decision to ban pupils wearing veils or head scarves in school. The veil had become a symbolic means of control: Those who did not choose to wear it could be threatened and intimidated. But the veil is only part of the fundamentalist program; there are also objections to coeducational classes. The big increase in Islamic fundamentalism in the past decade has brought these controversial issues into the limelight.

France is also home to some 750,000 Jews, 400,000 Buddhists, and 200,000 members of the Orthodox Church. In 2004, racist and anti-Semitic incidents ranging from assaults to gravestone graffiti more than doubled, with Jews bearing the brunt of these attacks. Africans were also victims, and the extreme right was blamed for the majority of the incidents.

No matter a couple's religion, however, the only valid marriage is a civil one performed by the mayor or his deputy. A church wedding may follow, but a bride and groom are not legally wed until they have a civil ceremony.

The Arts

France prides itself on its artistic achievements. Although they never equaled the Italian masters, French artists established themselves in the Middle Ages and the Renaissance. Until the 19th century, French painting, sculpture, and music, while often high-caliber, tended to be formal in structure and content. But that all changed with the Impressionists, who influence eventually extended worldwide.

Initially rejected by the French establishment, the Impressionists were especially interested in the play of light and color on the landscape. To capture what they perceived, they threw out the formal rules that had guided French art through the first half of the century. Moreover, they refused to consider the traditional subject matter of mythology and history. Instead, they painted shimmering, vibrant landscapes and subjects engaged in ordinary activities. Major Impressionists were Claude Monet, Pierre-Auguste Renoir, and Camille Pissaro. Others who joined the movement or painted in the same spirit include Paul Cézanne, Edouard Manet, and Edgar Degas.

The name of the movement itself came from a painting of Monet's called *Impression: Sunrise,* which a journalist ridiculed. The artists themselves decided that the term in fact perfectly described what they hoped to do in their work—capture the impression of the moment.

Impressionism as an aesthetic found its way into sculpture in the work of Auguste Rodin and the music of Claude Debussy, Hector Berlioz, Camille Saint-Saëns, and Maurice Ravel, among others. Later painters who were not part of the original movement, but continued it as post-Impressionists, were Henri Toulouse-Lautrec, Henri Matisse, Georges Seurat, and Paul Gauguin.

Pablo Picasso, arguably the most influential artist of the 20th century, was not French by birth, but he lived and worked most of his life in France. Beginning around 1907, he and Georges Braque created the next wave in art, cubism. This angular style of painting that fragmented its subject matter was pursued by others, such as Marcel Duchamps and Fernand Léger. With the advent of cubism, "modern art" was launched—and today, anything goes.

CUISINE

Given people's attachment to the land, the major economic role agriculture has played throughout the nation's history, and French people's penchant for intellectual analysis, the French mastery of cuisine is no surprise. It is a mastery that can border on obsession. The French preoccupation with the quality of food, its style of preparation, and fine distinctions related to smell and taste and service and consumption are well known.

The film *La Grande Bouffe* (*bouffe* is a rough equivalent of "pig out"),

France is world famous for great cuisine.

about a group of men who gather in a hideaway to eat themselves to death, could only be French. There are classes for young children to educate their palates, and university-level "centers of taste" exist on campuses. The Michelin brothers had barely begun producing tires when they launched their famed restaurant guide, *Le Guide Rouge,* which celebrated its centennial in 2000. To the French, *le bon goût* (good taste) is just as important as *le bon mot* (a clever remark).

LITERATURE

One of the joys of mastering French is that it enables you to read French literature. For the most part, this body of work is written in modern French. The few notable exceptions include the poetry of troubadours and François Villon and the epic poem "Song of Roland," celebrating one of Charlemagne's knights. Rabelais, whose name became synonymous with ribald humor, contributed *Gargantua and Pantagruel* in the 16th century. The other giant of that century was Michel de Montaigne, whose thoughtful essays could have been written yesterday.

The 17th century was dominated by three playwrights: the neoclassical tragedians Pierre Corneille and Jean Baptiste Racine, and the comic genius Jean Baptiste Molière. Molière's plays are still produced

French Character

The French national character was tellingly revealed when, in the 18th century, the country was introduced to the humble potato. Despite its potential for feeding a growing population, this tuber from the New World found little popular acceptance.

This resistance dismayed one Antoine Augustin Parmentier, a pharmacist and agronomist. He felt the potato would be a valuable addition to the nation's diet, especially in the event of failures of other crops such as wheat. After making many presentations to the court, Parmentier finally received permission in 1786 from Louis XVI to plant about 50 acres of potatoes in Neuilly—in a vacant field generally regarded as infertile. The potatoes flourished, but still, Parmentier could not persuade people to eat them.

Finally, he hit upon a solution: Hire local police to guard the field—but only in the daytime. His hope was that people would sneak into the field at night, dig up some of the new delicacy, and plant it on their own land. The experiment proved a great success. Parmentier then advised other large landowners to plant a nice big field of potatoes—and forbid anyone from entering. Within a generation, the potato became a staple of the French diet.

The contrast between Parmentier's decidedly French experiment and that of Frederick II of Prussia could not be more striking: Frederick sent his troops in to force the peasants to plant potatoes. Is it any wonder that the one nation gave us the Statue of Liberty and the other, fascism?

today: *The Miser, The Imaginary Invalid,* and *Tartuffe* are three of his better-known works.

The moralistic "fables" of Jean de la Fontaine from this period are still read today, usually as children's literature. For adults, Madame de Lafayette created the first psychological novel, *La Princess de Clèves.*

Philosophers dominated the 18th century. Two major players were Jean-Jacques Rousseau, whose articulation of romanticism in his *Confessions* and *Social Contract* launched the debates of the next century, and Denis Diderot, the philosopher whose prodigious *l'Encyclopédie* attempted to sum up human knowledge. Voltaire, a playwright and writer but primarily a moral philosopher, spelled out his own cynical view of the human condition in the ironical *Candide,* which remains a staple today. A critic of religious and authoritarian hypocrisy, Voltaire protested against injustice and vanity throughout most of his life.

Another novelist of that century, Pierre Choderlos de Laclos, has also endured. His *Les Liaisons Dangereuses* continues to be read and was made into a well-received movie, *Dangerous Liaisons,* starring John Malkovich. It was during this era that the Marquis de Sade detailed his erotic philosophy in several novels, including *The Philosopher in the Bedroom.*

Following the Revolution and Napoleon, French literature exploded on the world scene with novelists such as Honoré de Balzac, whose *Comédie Humaine* collected his numerous novels and stories describing French life in the first half of the 19th century. Stendhal's *The Red and the Black,* Gustave Flaubert's *Madame Bovary,* Victor Hugo's *Les Misérables,* and Émile Zola's *Germinal* still reach wide audiences both in France and abroad.

Poets Charles Baudelaire, Stéphane Mallarmé, and Arthur Rimbaud likewise influenced their peers in world literary circles. Frédéric Mistral, the 19th-century poet of Provence, wrote in Occitan and did much to popularize that language, still spoken widely in southern France. His efforts earned him the Nobel Prize for literature in 1904.

Another early Nobel Prize winner was Anatole France, a novelist and critic of the 19th and early 20th centuries. He became the Voltaire of his day, combining irony and a moral sense to lambast social hypocrisy. He joined Zola's campaign to win justice in the Dreyfus case (see the "Diplomatic Defeats" section of the *History, Government, and Economy* chapter for details) and was outspokenly anti-clerical in his opposition to dogmatism of any sort. Traditional forms were continued by poets such as Paul Valéry, Paul Claudel, and Guillaume Apollinaire.

Marcel Proust, who died not long after the end of World War I, set a new course for the novel with his monumental *Remembrance of Things Past.* Proust was among those influenced by the prolific philosopher Henri Bergson, who celebrated intuition above formal intellectualism.

Louis-Ferdinand Celine, a doctor as well as a novelist, gained many admirers with his staccato style of writing until his support for German fascism during the war cost him support. Other prose writers who came to prominence in the first half of the century include André Malraux, André Gide, and François Mauriac; the latter two won Nobel Prizes in literature. Both Gide, awarded the prize in 1947, and Mauriac, who won it in 1952, were raised in strict Catholic families; their works often touch on the concepts of sin and sensuality.

Surrealism, with its focus on the subconscious, encompassed both art and literature in the 1920s and '30s; André Breton was one of the founders of the movement. Later in the century, particularly following the devastation of World War II, the philosophy of existentialism came to the forefront.

Some of existentialism's best-known French proponents were creative writers, as well as philosophers. The Algerian-born Albert Camus was a journalist in the Resistance; his philosophical works and novels, such as *The Stranger, The Plague,* and *The Fall* won him the Nobel Prize in literature in 1957. Jean-Paul Sartre, who personified the intellectual French Marxist, wrote plays, novels, and philosophical texts. A student of philosophy in Berlin before the war, Sartre not only popularized existentialism among the young but became its chief architect in novels such as *Nausea* and philosophical works such as *Being and Nothingness.* A critic and anticolonialist, Sartre refused the Nobel Prize in 1964.

Traditional lyric poetry flowed from the pen of Alexis Leger, writing under the name Saint-John Perse, for the first three-quarters of the 20th century. Leger, who pursued a dual career as poet and diplomat, was a bitter enemy of Nazism and spent World War II in the United States. Afterwards, he continued his diplomatic career and his writing, winning the Nobel Prize for literature in 1960.

In the theater, important 20th-century playwrights include the poet Paul Caudel and four Jeans—Anouihl, Cocteau, Genet, and Giradoux. Fernando Arrabal, Eugène Ionesco, and a transplanted Irishman, Samuel Beckett, created lasting experimental dramas with the Theater of the Absurd movement. Best known in the United States for his plays *Waiting for Godot* and *Krapp's Last Tape,* Beckett won the Nobel Prize for literature in 1969. The playwright lived most of his life in Paris and sometimes wrote in French, sometimes in English, doing his own translations. The man who said he preferred "France in war to Ireland in peace" was awarded the Croix de Guerre with a gold star for his work in the French Resistance. More recently, novelists such as Alain Robbe-Grillet, Nathalie Sarrute, Michel Tournier and Patrick Modiano, Annie Leclerc, Marguerite Duras, and Hélène Cixous have enjoyed critical acclaim.

The last Frenchman to win the Nobel Prize for literature was Claude Simon, in 1985. Simon, who grew up in French Catalonia, fought with the Republicans in the Spanish Civil War. Perhaps his most important novel, *Les Georgiques,* deals with that experience. Simon became well known in the 1950s as a proponent of the *nouveau roman* ("new novel"), a narrative technique that ignored many conventions of structure, plot, and character development. Because of his complex style, Simon is considered difficult and remains little known, even in France. Other "new novelists" included Beckett, Robbe-Grillet, and Sarrute, although they were never a cohesive group or true literary school.

Prime Living Locations

Overview

The following chapters discuss the characteristics and appeal of the different regions in France. By no means are these the only desirable regions, but they are places where a number of expatriates have decided to live. In fact, they cover about half of France and include the regions where more than two-thirds of the French population lives.

PARIS AND THE ÎLE-DE-FRANCE

First, of course, is Paris, the cosmopolitan capital and the metropolis surrounding it. In many ways, this is both the head and heart of France—its intellectual, cultural, social, economic and political center. There is no other great city like it and few that equal it. For those seeking the cultural France—art, nightlife, high fashion, great food—Paris is the place to be. All of its *arrondissements,* the administrative areas into which large French cities are divided, offer potential homes—although as in any city, some areas are much more expensive than others.

In Paris and the surrounding suburbs, a number of international bilingual schools for pupils below the university level offer parents numerous educational opportunities for younger children.

Prospective Parisian residents should be aware that along with the cultural richness and intellectual stimulation of the region come the drawbacks of a densely packed urban area. In recent years, transit strikes have repeatedly left hundreds of thousands stranded. Controls on both speed and the number of vehicles on the road can be inconvenient. Traffic is terrible, and the resulting air pollution can be a problem. Experts estimate that this pollution is responsible for more than 4,800 deaths annually in the country. Asthmatics should certainly take this into account.

For those seeking the cultural France— art, nightlife, high fashion, great food—Paris is the place to be.

Living in a major metropolitan area anywhere in the world isn't for everyone. Business people may be attracted to towns and regions offering either greater employment opportunities or financial incentives to those who wish to engage in commerce in France. Retirees might find a mountain village, a coastal cottage, or a little farm more appealing. You can live in a small village of 1,000 people and still enjoy good public transportation, find doctors and nurses who actually make house calls, greet merchants who call you by name, and dine on fresh produce and seafood—all without losing access to big-city benefits. But Paris and the Île-de-France do host the greatest number of Americans, mixed among the 12 million French and scores of other nationalities.

THE MIDI AND LANGUEDOC

Bordeaux and the Midi region is a rich, rebellious land that produces enough wine to fill its famous canal connecting the two seas. The western Pyrénées and into the lowlands are Basque Country, where French gives way to a more ancient language—one so different from any other that legend among devout Catholics of region claims that it took the devil seven years to learn his first Basque word. The rural northern area drained by the Dordogne River has been much favored by the English and Americans in recent decades, while the great university city of Toulouse, surrounded by rolling plains with fields of grain, sunflowers, and corn reminiscent of the American Midwest, has become a high-tech aerospace center. Sparsely populated

Languedoc, along the Mediterranean, remains largely agricultural, dotted with small farming villages. Besides the hot summers, this area provides easy access to the ski slopes and other winter sport areas of the Pyrénées.

PROVENCE AND THE CÔTE D'AZUR

In the famed South of France, sandwiched between the Rhône River running east to Italy, is Provence: A land divided between the chic, densely populated coastline from Marseille to Nice and the dry, mountainous interior. This was not the cradle of Mediterranean civilization, but certainly the site of its adolescence. The Côte d'Azur is chic and expensive, while the interior is less costly; but both areas have an international population, having been a vacation favorite with Europeans and British for nearly two centuries. Aix-en-Provence, not far from Marseille and Avignon, is a great center for American and other foreign university students, while the Luberon Mountains provide picturesque villages full of stone houses. You'll probably find more Americans in Provence than anywhere else in France outside of Paris. Les Alpes Maritime (the Maritime Alps), though not as high as their northern cousins, provide winter skiing and summer boating on rivers such as the Durance.

You'll probably find more Americans in Provence than anywhere else in France outside of Paris.

NORMANDY AND BRITTANY

West of the Île-de-France and Paris are Normandie (Normandy) and the English Channel, both more sheltered from the Atlantic storms that can lash the more westerly coast of Bretagne (Brittany). The Seine and numerous smaller rivers wind through this rolling countryside, which is heavily farmed but has pleasant wooded areas as well. Modern transportation—fast and frequent trains and good roads—have brought Paris within reach, much in the way that Long Island connects to New York or Napa to San Francisco. The Eurostar train through the Chunnel has only served to emphasize the proximity of the region to the U.K. It remains a favorite weekend getaway for the English, as well as for Parisians, with expensive resorts on the coast and bucolic hideaways further inland. Its central geographic location within the European Union has made Normandy a great distribution hub as well.

BURGUNDY AND THE RHÔNE VALLEY

The Rhône Valley and Bourgogne (Burgundy) constitute, like the Midi, a great wine-producing region. The southern part of this area below Lyon was historically part of Rome's Provence and remains allied in architecture and lifestyle today. Away from the Rhône river, as well as along its banks, are pleasant villages and market towns. Farming—not only grapes, but also fruit and olives—is the big industry here outside of the only large city in the region, Lyon. The Alps, to the east, and their summer and winter recreation areas are within easy reach of much of the Rhône Valley. In Burgundy, it is much the same—grapes and fruit. Picturesque little villages are only a few hours from Paris, and excellent summer recreation can be found in the regional park of Morvan. The slopes of the Jura Mountains to the east make a day of skiing or other snow sports possible.

Planning Your Fact-Finding Trip

Lots of people fall in love with France the first time they visit. But no one should decide to move there without taking a realistic look at what everyday life in France will be like. The best way to do that is to visit the country and stay where you think you might like to live for as long as you can. At the very least, explore life beyond Paris and the tourist spots. Follow the tips in this chapter to discover for yourself the terrain, climate, and general conditions that appeal to you—don't depend solely on the opinions of others.

Preparing to Leave

It's time to take an inventory of all the factors—practical, cultural, financial, emotional, geographical—that make you feel at home. For example, climate, terrain, and vegetation all have profound effects on people, whether they realize it or not—especially when the familiar supports of culture and acquaintances are abruptly removed. Someone who has spent his or her life on the Midwestern plains, for example, might find the Alps or the Pyrénées a trial; someone from the Rockies might be dismayed by the flatness of the Gers. Many people find the Mediterranean coast too dry and rocky for their tastes; others find the lush greenery of the Dordogne damp and uninviting. Are you more comfortable in certain landscapes than others?

Life is lived in the details, and you should look closely at your own to see if your preferences can be met in France—or if you can comfortably, willingly adapt.

Similarly, are you an aggressive urbanite, or are you a quiet type who likes it when the sidewalks roll up at dusk? Just as in the United States, daily life in a city in France is far different than life in a small village or the countryside. If you've always lived in a city, many conveniences you take for granted will be unavailable in a small town. And if you've only dreamed of living on a farm, don't expect the reality to match your dream—although it may still be the life you want.

Consider your lifestyle. Will you be working, studying, or retired? What about your spouse or partner? Think about how you actually like to spend your free time. Is golf a passion, for instance? Although the sport is gaining popularity, many towns in France have no golf courses nearby. Is a day without soap operas, or any American television, a grim one for you? Your favorite programming may not be aired in France. What about fast food? Yes, there are McDonald's in France, but fast food is not a primary staple in this culinary capital. What about reading? Even if you speak French fluently, you may be reluctant to give up recreational reading in English, and you can't pop around the corner to pick up a copy of the *New Yorker* or the latest John Grisham paperback in a French village. Are you used to endless selection in supermarkets, year-round? Produce is much more seasonal in France. Apples are available all the time, but not apricots; cherries appear in late spring and vanish by mid-summer.

Life is lived in the details, and you should look closely at your own to see if your preferences can be met in France—or if you can comfortably, willingly adapt.

FIRST STEPS

Even before you plan your initial fact-finding trip, do some homework and legwork. Try these few simple ideas to help you decide where to go and what to expect. That way, you'll be sure to get the most out of the time you spend exploring the country—and you'll have some more information to consider while you decide if France is the right place for you.

Talk to Folks

Talk to as many different people as you can who have been in the country. Find out what they liked and disliked about France. Try to meet French people in the United States. Consider hosting a French student, for example, or hire a French au pair. In general, try to establish contacts, so that when you do visit France, you will be able to meet people and discuss your ideas and plans with them. Hearing their viewpoints will be invaluable.

Study Maps

To familiarize yourself with the regions and geography of France, buy good maps and study them. Michelin's are perhaps the best known and they're widely available, but Blay and IGN are also good. A map of the whole country in book format on the scale of 1:200,000 or 1:250,000, with an index, is an excellent place to begin. Such a map will show every commune and even isolated farmhouses; the index will save lots of time, no matter where in France you go. Once in the country, you can use it for touring.

Also get a large map of the entire country. It will give you a better sense of proportion and just how far one place is from another—not in kilometers or miles, but in relation to places you may already know.

Read

Read up on France. You might start with guidebooks, but remember, most are written by and for foreign tourists, not residents. Among the best are the Michelin Green Guides. Available in English or French, they are packed with maps and good information—historical, geological, and archaeological, as well as practical information about places of interest, transportation, and the like. From there, move on to travel literature by authors who have lived in France, such as Peter Mayle; fiction set in France, histories of France, and so on.

Go on the Web and surf French sites. Most cities have websites, Google posts daily synopses of stories in the French media with links to the sources, and Yahoo provides the same sort of portal as it does in the U.S. Many sites, especially touristic ones, have English pages. But just because you don't find something you are looking for on the Web, don't think it doesn't exist.

Once you arrive in France, you'll find more specialized books. However, do not expect them to be in English. Don't overlook magazines as a source of information on a region or topic. Many fine regional guides in France are published as slick magazines, with superb photography, and are sold at newsstands rather than bookstores.

Study French

Before you visit, consider spending some time studying the language. If you move there, you will need to be able to speak at least rudimentary French—after all, you'll be surrounded by French-speakers. Knowing some French before you get there will give you a definite advantage. And if you find that French is just not a language you want to speak, then France might not be the country you want to live in.

Even without actually enrolling in a class, you can find computer-aided lessons in French via CDs from various firms, and online practice is available through such programs as the University of Texas.

When you visit France, consider spending some time there studying French. Language classes are conducted throughout the country; finding one that suits your needs in the region that interests you is likely. The instructors may prove helpful and knowledgeable beyond language lessons in the classroom. Part of class may very well be spent discussing the customs of the country and answering students' questions about French life.

WHAT TO BRING

Here are a few essential items you should take on your fact-finding mission:

- Bring a small calculator—one of those solar-powered, credit-card-sized ones. You will be converting dollars to euros and square feet to square meters or vice versa, and adding up various costs wherever you go. It's a handy tool.
- Also pack a good French-English dictionary, or plan to buy one on arrival. A small paperback version may be nice to carry in the car when

Don't Leave Home Without

The application process for obtaining a visa will require you to collect certain records, such as birth certificates and marriage licenses. Beyond that, in preparing to move to France, don't forget to gather other important documents—some personal, some professional. And don't forget to make copies of them and leave them in a trusted location in the United States. Just as aggravating as finding yourself in France without some necessary document is returning to the States only to discover you left your papers in France.

Be sure to cover all your bases. Write down an inventory of all your important papers—and make a copy of that, too. That way, if you or the person usually responsible for the information is incapacitated, someone else can find it.

Here is a checklist of the documents you should gather:

- If you own real estate in the United States, collect deeds or mortgage papers, insurance policies, tax records, and guarantees on appliances (water heaters, air conditioners, etc.). In the event of an emergency or the need for repairs, make a list of the service people and building contractors you trust.
- Records of all bank accounts, copies of state and federal tax records, insurance policies,

and pension funds. It's probably best to leave stocks with a brokerage, since you may wish to sell or trade them at some point.
- A list of the Social Security numbers, credit card numbers, and passport numbers of all family members.
- Medical records (documenting vaccinations, allergies, eyeglass or contact lens prescriptions, etc.) and a list of the names and phone numbers of your doctors, dentists, optometrists, pharmacists, and other health-care providers.
- An inventory of everything left in storage in the States, including the precise locations. If you or anyone else has to find something, an inventory of numbered boxes detailing the contents of each will be an enormous help.
- Employment and educational records, including awards and letters of recommendation.
- Current addresses and phone numbers of your friends, family members, and business associates. A list of your friends' and relatives' birthdays (and their children's, if applicable).
- Notarized powers of attorney for you and your spouse or companion.

sightseeing, but it won't help you write a letter, frame an argument, or provide a context for many of the words you may encounter. Nor will the paper binding stand much use.

- Depending on your language ability, a phrase book for travelers, such as those published by Berlitz, is handy. This type of book condenses a lot of information and vocabulary, packages it in a useable format, and gives a reasonable guide to pronunciation.

- There are two optional items that may prove a big help: A cell phone and a laptop computer. A cell phone is a definite plus. There are now more cell phones in France than fixed phones, and many public coin- and card-operated phones have been removed. When renting temporary accommodations, you may not have a phone, and there may not be a convenient pay phone.

If your U.S. cell phone will work in France, that's probably the easiest solution. Otherwise, consider either renting or buying a phone in France. Coverage is good in the cities; in 2004, France Telecom's Orange system had an edge over other providers in areas with poor reception.

A laptop is less of a necessity, as many of its functions are possible on third generation GSM phones. Your cell phone may give you access to the Internet; you may have a convenient cybercafé downstairs or around the corner, not to mention Wi-Fi or other possible connections. In 2004, broadband and wireless access became widely available in France. A connection to the Internet may be a real advantage over the Yellow Pages for finding all sorts of phone numbers and email addresses, exploring new travel and housing possibilities as they occur, staying up-to-date on French and American news, viewing property, etc. And a laptop will serve you well when you make the move.

Currency

Traveling in France, a couple should expect to spend a minimum of €150 ($202.50) per day. You probably won't spend that amount every day, but it is better to budget too much than too little. A single person should budget €100 ($135) daily, although students will get by for less. Couples should expect to pay at least €60 ($81) per night for a double room with private bath; you'll probably pay more than that in Paris and other large cities, and perhaps a little less in the provinces, depending on your personal tastes. In cities and larger towns, you will be more likely to find inexpensive lunches—€7–9 ($9.45–12.15). Dinners will run €15–30 ($20.25–40.50), especially with wine. For those on a budget, plan to enjoy your big meal at noon, when better restaurants may offer luncheon specials—the same food as their evening meals, but at a lower price.

Your American ATM debit card will serve you well in France; just make sure to ask your bank to raise your daily withdrawal limit, so that you can make just a handful of bigger withdrawals, rather than lots of small ones—because most U.S. banks charge fees for using ATMs that are not their own. Your Visa or MasterCard charge card will also work everywhere in France, except at 24-hour service stations. French credit cards have a chip embedded in them that American cards do not. The automated fuel pumps cannot read American cards and reject them; if attendants are available, however, they will be able to charge your American account, as will restaurants, hotels and shops.

Do not bother with travelers checks, because French banks charge a fee when a merchant deposits one—therefore, most merchants will not accept them.

As for gratuities in France, tips are always appreciated if you have been rendered a service; 10 percent should be sufficient. In restaurants, if the menu says *"service compris"* (service included), no tip is necessary.

Time Difference

As you're planning your trip, bear in mind the time difference between France and the United States. Without taking into account daylight saving time, when it's 7:00 A.M. in New York and 4 A.M. in Seattle, it's 1:00 P.M. in Paris. In late March, the clocks go forward by one hour; at the end of October, they are put back an hour (spring forward, fall back).

France uses a 24-hour clock, rather than A.M. and P.M. for timekeeping. Informally, people will refer to 9:00 at night or 4:00 in the afternoon, but officially, those hours are 21:00 and 16:00.

WHEN TO GO

For those planning a long-term move, the best time to travel in France is either June or September. Everything will be open and you'll probably have good weather, making your investigations easier. However, outside of Paris, once you have selected an area, you should try to visit it during bad weather. If heat is a problem, then try August; if cold and wet weather is objectionable, try December or January. In other words, try to determine if you will be just as pleased with your choice under less than ideal conditions.

For instance, a small village full of congenial people in summer may seem deserted in winter, when darkness descends about 4:30 P.M., homes are shuttered, the local restaurant is closed until March, and the vacation home occupants are back in their workaday world.

For students or those with a sojourn of a specific duration, you probably do not have a choice; you have to go when and where the situation dictates. Give yourself as much lead time as possible, however, to familiarize yourself with your new surroundings.

Arriving in France

You will need your passport to get into France; in fact, you will need it to get out of the U.S. However, you do not need a visa as long as you do not stay more than three months.

As an American citizen arriving in France, you are going to be treated as if you were any other tourist. You may have your long-stay visa from the consulate, but it won't mean anything until later, when you have presented it to the prefecture and obtained your *carte de séjour* (residence permit). In any event, whether you are coming for three days or 30 years, you'll show your passport and collect your baggage. If you've shipped household goods, they'll arrive elsewhere, not on the plane with you. You need a special license to import firearms; if you are bringing a pet, you should have the required documentation. Duty-free items purchased on the airplane are just that, duty-free; no need to declare them.

Most airports offer a shuttle bus into the nearest city for a nominal fee. However, at Charles de Gaulle airport outside Paris, you can also catch a TGV (fast train) to other cities or an RER (suburban line) train that connects with the Métro. Taxis are expensive, on the order of €30 ($40.50) from the airport into downtown Paris, and limousines even more so. If you do take a cab, be sure to take the one at the head of the line at the taxi stand.

If you are not staying in Paris, but flying on to another city, such as Bordeaux, you will have to go through passport control in Paris and transfer from an international to a domestic terminal. Your luggage, including pets, should be checked through to your destination, and you will take it through customs there. Unlike the U.S. and some other countries, France requires that you go through *la douane* (customs) at the end of your flight, rather than in the city where you first enter the country.

© Corel/Fotosearch

Smaller mountain roads may be your only option to reach some destinations.

TRANSPORTATION

For this kind of research, a car is necessary. Both Renault and Peugeot will sell foreigners a new car and buy it back at the end of their stay, with full insurance and roadside assistance. The plans avoid payment of the TVA added to auto rentals and may be less expensive than ordinary rentals, but require a minimum number of days of ownership. Ordinary rentals are also available either at or near most major airports in the country—agencies include Hertz, Thrift, Alamo, Avis, and other familiar names.

On this score, be aware that distances in France can be deceiving. A journey you anticipate will take an hour becomes 1.5 hours, because the route passes through, rather than around, a medium-sized city. Or you get stuck behind a *convoi exceptionelle* (a truck with an oversized load) and can't pass for kilometers. And, while the *autoroutes* (highways) are fast, they are expensive and do not go everywhere. To reach some destinations, your only options will be smaller, slower roads.

Touring and House-Hunting

No decision-making process about moving to the country is complete before you've actually visited France. Try to stay as long as possible

Housing Size

Following is a breakdown of average-size apartments as used when quoting prices per square meter:

Studio = 25 square meters (269 square feet).
2 rooms = 40 square meters (430 square feet).

3 rooms = 70 square meters (752 square feet).
4 rooms = 90 square meters (968 square feet).
5 rooms = 120 square meters (1290 square feet).

and live as you would at home. If you've never been outside of Paris, definitely plan on touring the country. France has many faces, and finding the countenance that suits you is important. You're an immigrant, not a refugee. You have a choice of where you are going to go, or if you are going to go at all. You may decide that Paris is, after all, where you want to be—but at the same time, you'll know more about your adopted country.

Start looking around. After you've identified the regions you like, rent a house or an apartment for two weeks or a month and try to fit into the daily life around you. Or try several different regions for a week at a time. Do it more than once and at different times of year if you can. You may love Paris in the springtime, as countless others do, but not in the winter. Californians, who have been told they live in a Mediterranean climate, may be surprised to find it can and does rain in Languedoc and Provence any month of the year—and that there really are four seasons, not just a wet one and a dry one. ·

Embarrassing as it may be at first, practice your French. Can people understand you? Do you understand them? These efforts will be informative well beyond language ability itself. They will help you gauge how ordinary people respond to you.

Keep an itemized accounting of your expenditures for food, gas, and anything else you buy. Spend some time going into stores and looking at prices; make a note of them for future reference. Are items you would likely purchase if you lived here readily available, or is there a substitute? If the electric meter where you stay is visible, take a reading to see how much electricity you use in a week or a month.

Whether you are moving temporarily or permanently to France, think about renting a place to live. Even for those who intend to buy eventually, a rental affords the opportunity to get to know a city or village before committing to a purchase, and also gives you time to find the property that you really want, rather than forcing a hurried compromise.

Visit real estate offices, even if you have no intention of buying. Most of them fill their windows with photos and descriptions of property, along with prices. Without even stepping inside the office, you can get an idea of the range of prices for particular types of property and the names of different localities. Before even buying your airline ticket, know that you'll need to budget a minimum of €100,000 ($135,000) to purchase a home or apartment. The initial cost may be less, but renovations and furnishings will almost certainly bring the total actual cost at least to that level.

The rational approach is to prepare yourself carefully, consider all your options and weigh the pros and cons of each choice, avoiding all the possible pitfalls. Then do what most people do when suddenly realizing that they are looking at the home of their dreams: Forget all the good advice and follow your heart.

That amount is a minimum almost anywhere in the country for good basic housing. In Paris, Nice, or dozens of other places, it is a down payment. For a renovated stone *maison* (house) with two hectares (4.94 acres) of land, a view, and a swimming pool, it is a fraction of a down payment. In this respect, the French are no different from Americans: The nicer homes in the better locations cost more—a lot more than shabby quarters in a run-down neighborhood.

Look at the kind of property you might buy: What would it cost? Are such houses readily available in the area, or few and far between? Talk to a salesperson, and perhaps visit some of the offerings. When a house is described as livable, are you likely to be satisfied, or would you want further renovations? If so, at what cost?

This is the sort of information you need to take back with you for serious planning. Perhaps you will establish a rapport with a real estate agent that will prove valuable when you do get serious. On the other hand, you may find agencies to avoid in the future.

So, the rational approach is to prepare yourself carefully, consider all your options, and weigh the pros and cons of each choice, avoiding all the possible pitfalls. Then do what most people do when suddenly realizing that they are looking at the home of their dreams: Forget all the good advice and follow your heart.

Sample Itineraries

TEN-DAY ITINERARY: NORTHERN FRANCE

Days 1 and 2: Paris
On the first day, explore Left Bank *arrondissements* 5, 6, 7, 13, 14, and 15. On day 2, explore Right Bank *arrondissements* 1, 2, 3, 4, 8, 9, 10, 11, 12, 16, 17, 18, 19, and 20.

Days 3 and 4: Paris Environs
On day 3, visit the suburbs surrounding the Left Bank *arrondissements:* Boulogne-Billancourt, Chatillon, Issy-les-Moulineaux, Vanves, Malakoff, Joinville, St. Mandé, and Montreuil. On day 4, visit the suburbs surrounding the Right Bank *arrondissements:* Neuilly, Le Pré St. Gervais, Asinieres, Courbevoie, Levallois, Versailles, and St. Denis.

Days 5 and 6: Normandy
On day 5, explore Haut Normandy: Rouen, Le Havre, Giverny, Les Andelys, Evereux, and Louviers. On day 6, explore Basse Normandy: Caen, Honfleur, Cherbourg, Barfleur, Mayenne, and Alençon.

a typical day in Paris

© Corel/Velocity Stock

Day 7: Brittany
Tour Rennes and the surrounding countryside.

Day 8: East of Paris
Visit Fontainebleau, Coulommiers, Meaux, Yonne, and Sens.

Days 9 and 10: Burgundy and the Rhône Valley
On day 9, explore Dijon, Beaune, Avallon, Autun, Mâcon, Auxerre, Louhans, and Chalon-sur-Saône. Second day, explore Lyon, Roanne, and St. Etiennne.

TEN-DAY ITINERARY: SOUTH OF FRANCE

Days 1 and 2: Bordeaux and Environs
On the first day, visit the city of Bordeaux and the towns across the river: Lormont, Floirac, and La Bastide. On day 2, explore the coast around Arcachon, Cap Ferret, and the towns in or near the great regional park, Landes de Gascogne, such as Sabres and Pissos.

Days 3 and 4: Dordogne and the Gers
On day 3, check out Libourne, Bergerac, Sarlat, and Périgueux. On day 4, tour Agen, Auch, Fleaurance, Pau, and Tarbes.

Days 5 and 6: Toulouse and Environs
On day 5, take a look at the city of Toulouse and nearby suburbs Blagnac, La Balma, and Roques. On day 6, visit the north: Montauban, Albi, and Cordes-sur-Ciel.

Day 7: The Pyrénées
Explore Foix, St. Gaudens, and St. Bernard Comminges.

Day 8: The Mediterranean Coast
Tour Perpignan, Coulioure, Narbonne, and Gruissan.

Days 9 and 10: Languedoc Interior
On day 9, check out Montpellier and the nearby suburbs: St. Jean-de-Védas, Lattes, St. Clement, and Clapiers. On day 10, explore Nîmes and Uzes.

© Corel/Fotosearch

Paris and the Île-de-France

The French capital and its environs, home to about one-fifth of the nation's population, offer a cosmopolitan ambience, employment possibilities, and cultural opportunities. Your French neighbors in this region are urban and suburban folks, better educated on the average than those in rural areas.

This region is the cradle of the French nation. The Franks who lived here gave it their name and language, but it was the city of Paris and the kings who occupied the throne here who gradually came to rule the rest of the country. This remains the case, despite efforts to decentralize the government and allow more regional decision-making. The region also dominates the French economy; many corporate headquarters and the stock exchange are located here, as are the greatest employment opportunities and the greatest concentration of industry and research institutions. While this dominance was once confined to Paris itself, recent generations have brought such growth that the city can no longer contain it all. The departments that ring Paris are playing an increasingly important role.

This is also the region of France where you will find the most Americans. No one knows the exact number, because many of them have no *carte de séjour* (residence permit). Some of them are tourists or students who have found ways to remain beyond their original visas; others have independent means and have not bothered with the formalities of a long-stay visa, perhaps not intending to reside permanently in France. Still others may own apartments or homes here and stay for extended periods without actually moving here. In actual numbers, we can reasonably estimate that we're talking thousands, not hundreds of thousands.

But the number of Americans living permanently in France has never been great; in the past, most have come here with a French mate. Unless you are already acquainted with an American living in France and choose to move in nearby, chances are you will have no American neighbors. That does not mean you won't find any Anglophones, however; scattered throughout France in far greater numbers than Americans are the British. Then add the Dutch, who speak English almost universally, Australians, Irish, Belgians, and Germans, in addition to the French themselves, many of whom speak English, and you have a sizeable English-speaking population.

The Lay of the Land

Paris is densely populated, with 20,000 people packed into each of the 87 square kilometers (33.5 square miles) enclosed by the *périphérique,* the beltway that surrounds the city. That's 52,000 per square mile; if San Francisco were that densely populated, it would have 2.5 million people, instead of 750,000.

Paris is divided first of all by the Seine River—into the Rive Droite and Rive Gauche (Right Bank and Left Bank). The other primary divisions are the *arrondissements,* the 20 districts of the city. Paris is more or less circular, and the lower numbered *arrondissements* in the center also form a rough circle. They are smaller, more congested, and generally more prestigious—with the exception of the 16th—than the higher numbered ones that form the outer circle. Since all Métro lines start at different points around the periphery of the city and weave their way to the opposite side, they tend to cross near the center, giving the inner *arrondissements* the best transportation.

Surrounding Paris, with its more than two million residents, is the rest of Île-de-France, the name of the province comprising Paris and the seven surrounding departments. This region is home to another nine million people.

SAFETY

In any big city today, crime is bound to be a concern. The central *arrondissements* on both sides of the Seine have less crime than the outer districts, but they are also far less densely populated, considering the number of public buildings and parks. The first seven *arrondissements* have significantly lower rates of crime against both people and property. Of the 20,128 crimes against persons committed in 2004, 1,702 occurred in *arrondissements* 1 through 7. Of the 163,728 thefts reported that year, 32,691 happened in these seven central districts.

The *arrondissement* with the highest crime rate is also the poorest, the 19th—which reported 1,862 crimes against people and 10,281 thefts. But the next highest-ranked *arrondissements* were the 16th, with 1,237 attacks on people; and the 17th, with 9,807 thefts.

Paris

Paris is expensive. Think New York, San Francisco, and Tokyo. And as in those other cities, even those who can afford the price tags will find the perfect location is not for sale and will have to make do with something else. The problem is that individual houses seldom come on the market in Paris. In 2004, for instance, about 39,000 pieces of property changed hands, but only 197 were single-family homes. In the past few years, property prices in many districts have increased 10 to 15 percent or more annually, more than five times the rate of inflation.

Apartments, especially if they include a garage or parking space, are also quite expensive, but at least they can be found. Fortunately, a car is not a necessity in Paris, with the Métro going nearly everywhere day and night. In fact, many will find owning a car to be more trouble than it is worth. If you need one, a car can always be rented for weekend excursions or vacations, almost certainly for less than the price of year-round maintenance—and definitely without the aggravation.

For those who wish to rent a furnished house or apartment for less than the normal French lease of three years, but for longer than a one-week to one-month vacation stay, Paris and its environs offer far more choices than other regions. Whatever the reason for your stay—perhaps a change in jobs, research abroad, or simply an extended vacation—you will find a variety of furnished homes available to let or sublet. The owners (or lessors, in many cases) have a desirable residence and do not wish to lose it, so they will rent it furnished. Since this region has the

Paris Transit

Paris and the Île-de-France are well served by public rail transportation. Le Métro, the subway system, opened its first line more than a century ago. Its name comes from La Compagnie du Chemin de fer Métropolitain de Paris, the firm that operated it.

Today, there are 14 Métro lines, some extending well outside of Paris. Perhaps more importantly, the Métro is part of a much larger regional transit network that also includes surburban RER (Réseau Express Régional) trains and the national French rail system, SNCF (Société Nationale Chemins de Fer Français). These three systems combine to provide public transportation for millions of riders daily.

Paris is the densest city in Europe, cramming more than 20,000 people into each square kilometer, 2.5 times as many as in London. Add 2.5 million cars entering and leaving each day, plus 200,000 tons of merchandise being delivered daily, and efficient public transit becomes a necessity.

The Métro system is simple and easily mastered. The various lines are just that—lines with two ends.

The trains shuttle from one end of the line to the other with stops in between, usually connecting with one or more other lines. Maps in all the stations show all the stops and connections. It takes approximately 50 minutes to cross the city by Métro.

Individual tickets are €1.40 ($2.03), but since one ticket is almost never enough, it's cheaper to buy a *carnet* (packet of 10) for €10.50 ($15.23), or one of the various passes available for either tourists or commuters. For around €1,382.70 ($2,004.92), you can buy a *carte integrale,* good for a year in all eight zones that form a series of concentric circles around the heart of Paris. The Métro and the RER trains travel through all these zones and are covered by the *carte integrale.*

Paris also has buses. During the day, the Métro is much faster because it avoids traffic congestion, but the Noctambuses, marked with a yellow owl in a black circle, run from 1:30 A.M. to 5:30 A.M. These are important, because the Métro does not run all night. Depending on the line and where greatest population density,n and it is expensive and difficult to replace good lodgings, people want to hang on to their homes.

Prices for such a rental are always a matter for negotiation. In a sublet, it is unlikely that you will pay less than the price of the original lease, and probably more. Wear and tear or possible damage to the furnishings must also be considered. While you might find a studio or two-room apartment for €650–800 ($878–1080) per month, larger accommodations are likely to run in the €2,500–5,000 ($3,375–6,750) range.

It is the larger apartments, those with four rooms or more, that have

you are, you may not be able to catch a subway train between about 1 A.M. and 5:30 A.M.

The RER speeds passengers to the suburbs via lines A, B, C, D, and E, but these are deceptive, because each of the lines forks off into branches after getting out of Paris. For instance, Line A to the west has three different terminals: St-Germain-en-Laye, Poissy, and Cergy-le-Haut.

SNCF, the national French rail system, also runs lines from Paris. Some of these serve suburban areas, such as the line that goes to Roissy and Charles de Gaulle Airport. These two rail systems complement each other; at many suburban stations, you can transfer from one system to the other in order to reach a particular destination.

The advent of numerous TGV lines in recent years has given many cities, such as Rouen, Chartres, Orléans, and Amiens, a boost. Thanks to the trains, each city is now an hour or so from Paris. Consequently, they have become attractive to middle-class families, who can find better housing available for less than the cost of the commute. To avoid becoming mere bedroom communities, these cities have formed an association, Les Villes du Grand Bassin Parisien, and have begun their own renewal projects.

The problem facing this transit system, however, is that all of these lines radiate from Paris. They are spokes without a wheel. As the Île-de-France has grown, so have its transit needs. By 2000, two-thirds of the traffic, whether passenger or freight, fell within the region. That's 3.5 times more passengers than the number going into or coming out of Paris, and 4.5 times the number of passengers within Paris itself. And the percentage is increasing annually. So, even though public transit to and from Paris is good, public transit around the city is not, forcing many people into their cars to go to work.

To handle the problem, construction has already begun on a series of new tram lines and other projects, such as extensions of Métro lines that will eventually form a beltway around the outer edge of the three departments surrounding Paris. This is a multi-billion-euro project that will take years to complete. But at this point, perhaps what is most important is not when the work will be completed, but the fact that it has started.

residences on the Île St-Louis

shown the greatest increase in price. Studios and two-room apartment prices have risen, but not at the same dizzy rate. The average purchase price of smaller apartments in Paris is now more than €4,850 ($6,547) per square meter, according to one survey.

You are likely to find prices of more desirable residences running closer to €6,500 ($8,775) per square meter. In most cases, the price per square meter is greater in smaller apartments than in larger ones. Paris apartments are generally small, many of them studios or two rooms. A two- or three-bedroom apartment of 100 square meters (1,076 square feet) is, by middle-class standards, a big place.

The actual surface of the apartment is quite important. Consider two nicely furnished three-room apartments for rent within a block of each other on rue Cler, a short, delightful street lined with good food and other shops in the 7th *arrondissement:* One rents for €1,400 ($1,890) per month, the other for €2,300 ($3,105). The less expensive unit has 48 square meters (516 square feet), the other is nearly double that size at 95 square meters (1,021 square feet). Another factor that can affect the livability of a small apartment is a sleeping loft. In a unit with high ceilings, this may be one solution to the cramped quarters often found in Parisian apartments.

Another factor that can affect the rent is the position of the apartment in the building. Given apartments of equal size and quality, a unit on the ground floor (*res-de-chaussée,* or RdC, as it is often abbreviated) opening onto the street will cost less than one opening onto a court-yard. An apartment on the top floor, away from noise and traffic, is worth even more.

As with real estate anywhere, location and quality are the prime ingredients in any purchase. For the best properties in any given neighborhood, the price may be double or more than the average. At the same time, averages are just that: Some properties will sell for less, as well as more. But consider lower prices carefully. The bargain flat may end up costing more than a newer one by the time renovations are completed. Or a less favored neighborhood may have its share of delightful streets.

Many real estate agents began 2005 by predicting a slowdown in the prices of French property, especially in Paris. Only time will tell if those predictions come true, but it is clear that rents have peaked, and in some cases are declining. Faced with a rent increase, many tenants became willing to leave Paris for one of the nearby suburbs; others found something cheaper elsewhere. One expert whose agency only handles rentals said the recent decline has ranged from 5–15 percent. Landlords who rejected reductions saw vacancies of two to three months before new tenants were found.

One rule of thumb is that you cannot tell what a building will be like from its exterior. You may be able to judge the neighborhood as desirable or not, but you must get beyond the front door and through the courtyard to learn about a building, no matter how uninspiring it may appear from the outside. In some cases, the facade may be all that is left of the original building. In others, the building may have been a beauty from the beginning and either well maintained or taste-fully restored.

In the chic and much sought-after 6th, 7th, and 16th *arrondisse-ments* of Paris, the average price per square meter had topped €4,600 ($6,210) by the beginning of 2005. Studio rentals begin at €600 ($810) and go up from there. Sections of other *arrondissements,* such as the 1st, 5th, and 8th, were nearly as high, but these latter ones had some neighborhoods with lower average prices as well. Only in the 10th and the 19th do prices fall below €2,500 ($3,375) per square meter.

THE RIGHT BANK

The first four *arrondissements* are all on the Right Bank, although the 4th includes the Île St-Louis and most of the Île de la Cité, islands in the Seine, with the 1st claiming the balance of the Île de la Cité. Given the historic character of these *arrondissements* and the lack of vacant lots, there is no new construction here.

These districts include such landmarks as the Louvre, Notre-Dame Cathedral, and the George Pompidou Center of the Arts, or Beauborg as it is more familiarly known. The Marais, the ancient Jewish quarter, bridges the 3rd and 4th *arrondissements* and includes the luxurious Place des Vosges. Today, it has become an area much favored by gay visitors to Paris. These districts are also centrally located, with good public transportation and lots of cafés. No less than six Métro lines pass through the 1st *arrondissement,* for instance.

The less pricey apartments in any of these districts are likely to be near a lot of nighttime activity and traffic, and have a somewhat run-down aspect. But even these will be €3,400 ($4,590) or more per square meter. For a better location and perhaps a view of the Seine or the Tuileries Garden, the price can easily double. Studio rents run €500–700 ($675–945); for 70 square meters (750 square feet), expect to pay €1,100–1,800 ($1,350–2,430).

One of the most famous historical points of interest on the Right Bank is the Notre Dame Cathedral.

© Corel/Fotosearch

For the very best properties, which rarely come on the market, the price can exceed €12,000 ($16,200) per square meter. If there are any bargains to be had, they will probably be found near the Place de la République and the border of the 2nd and 10th *arrondissements*, around the Strasbourg St. Denis Métro station, and along Boulevard Bonne Nouvelle. Here you can find buildings in mediocre condition and prices in the €3,500–5,000 ($4,725–6,750) range.

To the north of this Right Bank core lies a semicircle of five more *arrondissements*—the 8th, 9th, 10th, 11th, and 12th—in clockwise order from west to east. These vary considerably. The Avenue des Champs Élysées divides the 8th. Property here is expensive on either side of the avenue, as it is around the Place de l'Opera in the 9th, in contrast with some of the seedier neighborhoods in the 10th. These five districts also contain the majority of Paris's train stations, including Gare St-Lazare on the border between the 8th and 9th; Gare du Nord and Gare de l'Est, adjacent to each other in the 10th; and Gare de Lyon in the 12th.

The minimum price in these districts is about €2,400 ($3,240) per square meter. Most of the apartments at this price level will be found in the 10th. At that price, expect to do major remodeling. But even in the 10th, it is more realistic to expect to pay €4,000 ($5,400) per square meter for better units. Near the Place de la Bastille, which sits at the intersection of the 4th, 11th, and 12th *arrondissements,* and not far from the 3rd, or near St. Georges in the 9th, prices are likely to be closer to €6,000 ($8,100) per square meter for units in top shape, and €5,000 ($6,750) per square meter for those needing some work.

The northern borders of the 8th, 9th, and 10th—marked by the district north of Gare St-Lazare in the 8th, the Métro stops at Clichy between the 8th and 9th, and Métro stop Barbès-Rochechouart between the 9th and 10th, are probably the least expensive in these *arrondissements.* There are lots of Turkish and North African restaurants and shops in the 10th, and some of the boulevards in these working-class neighborhoods have a shabby appearance. But there are also nicer spots near the St. Martin Canal.

Because these are some of the less expensive areas in the city, rents are also lower here. Studios begin around €400 ($540), although in better sections, the going rate is more likely to be €500 ($675) per month or more. Expect larger units of 95 square meters (1,021 square feet) and up to begin at €1,300 ($1,755), and with rents of €2,700 ($3,645) for larger units of top quality.

In *arrondissements* 9, 11 and 12, you can find buildings less than five years old. These sell for almost double what the least expensive units in the same neighborhoods do. For instance, in the 9th around Métro stop Cadet, where you will find old two-room apartments of 40 square meters (430 square feet) selling for €115,000–155,000 ($155,250–209,250), new apartments go for €240,000 ($324,000). In the 11th, between the Belleville and Père Lachaise Métro stops, older five-room apartments range €315,000–520,000 ($425,250–702,000), while new ones start at about €590,000 ($796,500).

An exception is in the 12th around Porte Dorée and the Bois de Vincennes, where there is little difference between old and new; in fact, the new units may be a bit less—€2,900 ($3,915) per square meter versus €3,200 ($4,320) for an older unit. In many cases, this reflects the proximity of the Bois de Vincennes, a public park that includes the Paris Zoo, the Museum of Natural History, a horse racetrack, and flower gardens, as well as the convenience of five Métro lines nearby. The 12th is home to Bercy, the Ministry of Finance. Nearby are the Bercy Sports Palace, the American Center, and the Bercy business park, a very expensive office and commercial area.

THE LEFT BANK

The heart of the Left Bank is certainly the 5th and 6th *arrondissements,* home to the Latin Quarter, the Sorbonne, the Jardin-des-Plantes (arboretum), Luxembourg Garden, École des Beaux Arts, and the Pantheon. Boulevard St-Michel, often abbreviated to "Boul' Mich'," and Boulevard St-Germain are perhaps the two best-known thoroughfares.

Both of these *arrondissements* are stylish, desirable addresses, often the equal in prestige and price to those on the Right Bank. The 5th may get the nod from the intelligentsia, and the 6th from wealthy sophisticates, but there is a good mix in both. Five Métro lines serve the 5th *arrondissement.* As in the first four *arrondissements,* the historic character and lack of vacant land mean there is little new construction.

The 5th is on the average the less expensive of the two. Here you can expect to pay €4,500–8,000 ($6,075–10,800) per square meter for apartments. For newer units located strategically near the Sorbonne or Val de Grâce hospital, the price begins at €10,000 ($13,500) per square meter, with larger units commanding higher prices.

In the 7th *arrondissement,* which contains the Eiffel Tower, National Assembly and many of the ministries, the Musée d'Orsay, and the military academy, as well as the U.S. embassy, prices are equal to the 5th and 6th. In all three *arrondissements* a cost of €9,000 ($12,150) per square meter is not uncommon; the big bargains are anything less than €6,000 ($8,100) per square meter. Newer apartments here range €9,000–12,000 ($12,150–16,200) per square meter.

Naturally, rents in these districts reflect the property values. You may find studios in the 5th for €600 ($810) per month, although furnished units will likely start at €900 ($1,215) per month. Add 10 percent to these prices for the 6th and 7th. Apartments of 95 square meters (1,021 square feet) begin around €2,100 ($2,835) per month.

The heart of the Left Bank is certainly the 5th and 6th ar-rondissements, home to the Latin Quarter, the Sorbonne, the Jardin-des-Plantes (arboretum), the Luxembourg Garden, Ecole des Beaux Arts, and the Pantheon.

As in the Right Bank *arrondissements,* as you move further from the center of the city, prices generally decline. South of the 7th is the 15th, one of three *arrondissements* in the outer ring on the Left Bank. Gare Montparnasse straddles the border between the 15th and 14th, almost where they border on the 6th. The area between Necker Hospital and Montparnasse is perhaps the most expensive, averaging €4,200–6,500 ($5,670–8,775) per square meter for apartments in good condition. In other areas, you may find older buildings in fair condition for €3,200–4,700 ($4,320–6,345) per square meter. Rents in the 15th begin at €500 ($675) for a studio and €1,800 ($2,430) for 95 square meters (1,021 square feet), then rise depending on location and appointments.

The 14th to the east has some very nice streets and a beautiful park, Montsouris. Average prices here run €3,600–5,000 ($4,860–6,750) per square meter, but rise to €6,000–8,000 ($8,100–10,800) for newer, larger apartments in favored locations. Rents will begin around €550 ($742) for a studio. However, larger units cost somewhat less on average than in the 15th, beginning around €1,500 ($2,025) for 95 square meters (1,021 square feet).

The 13th borders the Seine on the east. Here you'll find Paris's Chinatown and Gare d'Austerlitz—it faces Gare de Lyon across the river in the 12th. Place d'Italie, an important Métro transfer point, and the recently built Bibiliothèque Nationale are also here. You can find fair apartments in the €2,800–4,500 ($3,780–6,075)-per-square-meter range, mostly in the southeast corner of the district. But most new or renovated units will run €3,500–6,000 ($4,725–8,100) per square meter.

The *arrondissements* on the outer periphery of the Right Bank contrast greatly. The 16th on the west side is sandwiched between the Seine and the Bois de Boulogne, a 2,000-acre wooded park that was once the hunting ground of kings. Over the years, it became a favorite prowl of prostitutes and their clients; today, it contains two horseracing tracks. With the Arc de Triomphe at its northern border, the 16th also contains the Trocadéro fountains. It is considered the most bourgeois part of the city, not always a compliment in the French lexicon. But it does have many larger apartments; prices here accelerated faster sooner than in many other parts of the city in the late '90s, but slowed to about 13 percent by 2004.

Prices in the district average €5,400 ($7,290) per square meter, with places in the southern end the least expensive at €4,000–5,500 ($5,400–7,425) per square meter. At the lower prices in these ranges, there will be renovation required. Moving north between the Trocadéro and the Arc de Triomphe, prices rise to the €6,000–8,000 ($8,100–10,800) range. Brand-new apartments may be found starting around €10,000 ($13,500) per square meter. Rents begin at €500 ($675) for studios, but push higher than in many other areas. For 95 square meters (1,021 square feet), expect to pay a minimum of €1,500 ($2,025) per month, up to €3,000 ($4,050).

The southern part of the 17th is very similar to the adjacent 16th. However, average prices diminish somewhat as you move north. Around Place des Ternes and Monceau Park, you can find older apartments in the €4,200–6,500 ($5,670–8,775) per-square-meter range. For new units, expect to pay €6,800–7,900 ($9,180–10,665) per square meter. Rents are similar to the 16th.

The northern part of the 17th, separated by the railroad yards leading to Gare St-Lazare in the 8th, is less pricey, but few larger apartments come on the market. Average prices here range €3,800–4,900 ($5,130–6,615) per square meter. Rents decrease about 5 percent for studios, and rise perhaps 10 percent for larger units.

The 18th *arrondissement* surrounds Montmartre, the hill on which Sacré Coeur(Sacred Heart) Basilica stands. Prices jumped an average of 15 percent in this district in 2004. Transportation can be a problem, so it is wise to check for Métro lines. Many immigrants live in this district; the neighborhood along Boulevard Barbès, for instance, is heavily African and very colorful. Montmartre itself commands good prices, €3,600–9,100 ($4,860–12,285) per square meter, with the higher figure for large apartments with a terrace and a view.

But many other neighborhoods cost much less. Older buildings in fair condition average €2,300–4,500 ($3,105–6,075) per square meter, and renovated and newer buildings bring €4,000–5,000 ($5,400–6,750) per square meter. Rents are also less expensive. Studios in the better neighborhoods range €450–1,000 ($607–1,350) per month, reflecting the same discrepancy as sale prices. In the less sought-after districts, prices drop considerably: below €400 ($540) for a studio, and under €1,000 ($1,350) for 95 square meters (1,021 square feet).

The 19th *arrondissement* is the least expensive, but also the most isolated in Paris, so transportation may be a consideration. Nonetheless, prices rose more than 12 percent in 2004, as investors came hunting bargains. The area around the Stalingrad Métro stop on the border between the 10th and the 19th is also notorious for addicts and drug-dealing.

However, the National Conservatory is located in the 19th, as is Paris's largest park, Buttes-Chaumont. Buildings in good condition facing the park bring €4,300–4,900 ($5,805–6,615) per square meter; in other favored locales, such as near Métro stop Jourdain, prices are €200–300 ($270–405) less per square meter. In other parts, prices range €2,800–3,800 ($3,780–5,130) per square meter. Rents also are lower, with studios starting at €400 ($540), and larger units starting at €1,300 ($1,755).

The 20th *arrondissement* contains the famous Père Lachaise cemetery. Most of the neighborhoods are working-class, and there is a mix of races and ethnic groups. The western neighborhoods along Boulevards Belleville and Ménilmontant are certainly coming up, much as the 3rd (Marais) and the adjacent 11th have done. The area around Place Gambetta on the eastern side of Père Lachaise has shown big increases in price recently, gaining an average of 14 percent in 2004. The average price is now about €4,700 ($6,345) per square meter in the neighborhood around Place Gambetta. Apartments in fair condition elsewhere average €3,000–4,500 ($4,050–6,075) per square meter, while new buildings go from €4,000–5,500 ($5,400–7,425) per square meter. Rents are comparable to the 19th.

Les Banlieues: The Suburbs of Paris

The rest of Île-de-France is 12,011 square kilometers (4,637 square miles), about the size of three Rhode Islands. The seven departments form two concentric circles around Paris. The inner ring, or *petite couronne,* consists of three departments. Four more form the *grande couronne.* While in past ages, the Paris basin was rich agricultural land, urban sprawl limits most of the farming to the *grande couronne,* where sugar beets, wheat, and corn are major crops.

There are no real peaks in this region, and none of the few hills tops 1,000 feet in elevation. However, the numerous rivers feeding into the Seine as it snakes its way to the ocean create a series of valleys and ridges covered by many wooded areas.

One thing to note about the Parisian suburbs, unlike American ones, is that they remain small towns.

A regional network of trains called the RER (Réseau Express Régional), whose lines cross Paris and connect with the Métro and the national rail system, serves as the major public transit system. For either commutes or just occasional forays into the city, the RER plays a major role. In addition, many of Métro lines extend well into the departments of the *petite couronne.*

As you might expect, there is a great deal of difference between the various suburbs. Some are wealthy bastions, others have huge public housing developments with concentrated pockets of poverty and unemployment. One thing to note about the Parisian suburbs, unlike American ones, is that they remain small towns. The largest of them, and the only one with a population greater than 100,000, is Boulogne-Billancourt, where the Renault car company was founded.

Most suburban growth has taken place since 1950. Beginning in 1954, France began building very large high-rise complexes with more than 500 apartments. (The first of these, Sarcelles, totaled 2,000 units.) A little more than a decade later, the emphasis changed. New towns with individual houses, smaller apartment buildings, and little shopping streets were created and supplied with transit, libraries, swimming pools, and other civic amenities. These new towns were actually groups of villages and developments, with open land between them and separate identities.

Another decade later, the emphasis changed again, this time in favor of development centered in older towns. As a result, you can find almost any sort of residence scattered through the departments—the worst of it a hodge-podge of unattractive sprawl, but the best of it superb development in this cradle of the French nation.

THE INNER CIRCLE: HAUTS-DE-SEINE, SEINE-ST-DENIS, AND VAL-DE-MARNE

The most favored towns are those just beyond the prized outer *arrondissements* of Paris: the 16th and 17th on the west, the 12th through the 15th on the south, and the 20th on the east. These are the *proche banlieues* (nearby suburbs), with excellent transit connections into the city. The suburbs to the west, south, and southwest lie in the departments of Hauts-de Seine (92) and Val-de-Marne (94).

Suburbs to the north and northeast in the department of Seine-St-Denis are the poorest. They have experienced high unemployment and higher crime and delinquency rates than others. But rising costs in the city, combined with proximity, has resulted in gentrification, with attendant rises in real estate values.

One town in particular, Montreuil, has been successful in attracting young families. Directly east and three Métro stops from Paris, Montreuil (pop. 91,000) is the third largest in the region and culturally active, sponsoring a blues festival and a children's book fair. This sort of community spirit has a price, and in 2004, prices rose 30 percent. Small houses of 80 square meters (860 square feet) with a little garden or courtyard sold for €320,000–350,000 ($432,000–472,500). You might find an even smaller fixer-upper for under €200,000 ($270,000), but larger homes of 110 square meters (1,182 square feet) with a garden range €350,000–450,000 ($472,500–607,500).

Apartments in Montreuil run €1,500–3,000 ($2,025–4,050) per square meter, depending on condition and location. Rents are also noticeably lower than Paris. Studios start below €300 ($567) per month, and 90 square meters (967 square feet) may be found starting at about €900 ($1,215) per month.

Between Montreuil and Bois de Vincennes Park to the south is the community of Vincennes. Here, prices run higher, particularly around the former royal château and facing the park itself. Prices begin at €3,600 ($4,860) per square meter and rise to about €5,500 ($7,425) per square meter for the best. The center of the town is cheaper: €3,500–4,200 ($4,725–5,670) for apartments in good condition, close to the Métro

The Oldest Profession

France, long tolerant of prostitution, decided to get tough when Nicolas Sarkozy became Minister of the Interior. Sarkozy, whose political base was the posh Parisian suburb of Neuilly, heard plenty of complaints from his neighbors and constituents, who often passed through the Bois du Boulogne en route to their homes. The wooded park had become notorious as a wide-open pickup place for prostitutes of both genders. Raucous solicitations often resulted in barely concealed sexual activity.

Also, about two-thirds of the 15,000 to 18,000 prostitutes in France were illegal immigrants, many from former Soviet bloc countries, lured to France with promises of honest work and then forced into prostitution. The 2003 laws made even passive solicitation punishable by prison, and took aim at pimps as well as the prostitutes themselves by offering illegal aliens the right to stay in France if they denounced their procurers.

More than 100 women in Paris and another 100 in the rest of the country managed to step out of life on the street in the first year the law was in effect. "Some of them are now sales clerks, waitresses, and bakers," said Marie-Claude de la Lande, of the prostitute support organization Nid de Paris (Nest of Paris). But others simply disappeared, quitting their work rather than risk prison.

But approval of the law was not unanimous. Prostitute support groups in Lyon and Toulouse say that the law has forced these women into more secluded locations out of sight of the police, making them more vulnerable to aggression. Catherine Deschamps, a social anthropologist who has studied prostitution, notes that Paris has experienced "an explosion of massage salons, and other prostitutes work out of apartments, making their contacts on the Internet."

Jean-Paul Proust, prefect of police in Paris, says he is pleased with a law that resulted in the arrest of 709 procurers in a year; and 80 percent of prostitutes who have been helped by support groups remain off the streets after six months.

and shops. On the eastern edge of Vincennes and in adjacent Fontenay, prices drop further. A square meter costs €2,300–2,700 ($3,105–3,645) if it needs renovation, and €3,500 ($4,725) if it is new.

Between Paris and the west side of the Bois de Vincennes is a small town called St. Mandé that offers easy access to Paris and the park. Here, prices range €4,000–5,300 ($5,400–7,155), with the higher prices along the edge of the park. Closer to Paris and the noise of the *périphérique,* apartments without much charm may be found starting at €3,000 ($4,050) per square meter. Rents begin at €350 ($473) for a studio and €1,150 ($1,552) for 90 square meters (967 square feet).

Along the southern and eastern sides of the park are the towns of Charenton and Joinville. Charenton, positioned between the park on the north and the Seine on the south, is the most attractive; Joinville is separated from the park by the river and *autoroute*. In Charenton, the best properties border the park, and prices begin at €4,000 ($5,400) per square meter. Moving south towards the Seine, which is bordered by an *autoroute,* the price drops as low as €2,500 ($3,375) per square meter when renovations are required.

Joinville offers some small houses, beginning around €280,000 ($378,000), but larger ones up to 120 square meters (1,290 square feet) can run to €450,000 ($607,500), depending on location, the size of the garden, and whether or not it has a garage. Apartments, especially further south towards St. Maur, run €2,000–3,200 ($2,700–4,320), depending on age, condition, and location. Rents in both of these towns are comparable: Studios start around €300 ($405), with the best going for €450 ($608). Larger units of 90 square meters (967 square feet) begin around €900 ($1,215) and rise to €1,500 ($2,025).

Away from Bois de Vincennes, prices drop somewhat. At Maisons-Alfort, older apartments average about €2,700 ($3,645) per square meter, with some going for €2,100–2,300 ($2,835–3,105). The range for new units is €3,800–4,500 ($5,130–6,075) per square meter. Older houses cost about €350,000 ($472,500), while new ones cost €650,000 ($877,500).

Ivry-sur-Seine, an old industrial town nearby, offers lofts at €2,000 ($2,700) per square meter. There are also some prewar buildings to renovate, costing €1,600–2,100 ($2,160–2,835) per square meter. New or newly renovated units range €3,300–4,100 ($4,455–5,535) per square meter.

Further west along the south side of Paris are the towns of Malakoff and Vanves. Prices here are more or less comparable, although Vanves is a bit more upscale. Prices range about €2,600–3,300 ($3,510–4,455); larger units will bring a 10 percent premium in Vanves, and the few available houses found there will generally bring €500,000 ($675,000). Rents are likewise comparable, with studios beginning around €300 ($405) per month and €900 ($1,215) for 90 square meters (967 square feet). Both towns offer new apartments beginning about €4,700 ($6,345) per square meter for 90 square meters (967 square feet).

South and southwest of Malakoff and Vanves are Châtillon and Issy-les-Moulineaux. The latter is bordered on the west by the Seine, and its best apartments offer view of the river or the Paris skyline. Prices for older apartments range €2,700–4,500 ($3,645–6,075) per square meter, and new units begin at €4,500 ($6,075) per square meter, climbing to €6,400 ($8,640) per square meter for larger units of high quality. Prices drop as you move south.

Châtillon lacks views, so more apartments are at the lower end of the scale, starting around €2,700 ($3,645). Small houses are much sought-after, and many of them have been sold and resold in recent years, elevating the price. One such house of 105 square meters (1,129 square feet) sold for €220,000 ($297,000) in 1996. Eight years and four owners later, it sold for €360,000 ($486,000).

New apartments offered in both towns are seldom larger than 90 square meters (967 square feet). Prices for such units begin at €4,400 ($5,940) in Châtillon and €5,550 ($7,425) in Issy, where new construction has been concentrated on more scenic sites. Rents in these two towns are comparable, but somewhat higher than in Vanves and Malakoff. Studios begin about €325 ($439), while prices run €1,200 ($1,620) for 90 square meters (967 square feet).

Across the Seine from Issy is Boulogne-Billancourt, the second biggest city in the region after Paris, with 108,000 people. Best known as the birthplace of the Renault automobile empire, Boulogne gave way to office and apartment buildings in the 1980s. Enclosed on three sides by the Seine and on the north by Paris and the Bois de Boulogne, it is something of an island. Apartments here begin around €3,500 ($4,725) per square meter in the southern end of the city, and move up to €6,000 ($8,100) per square meter in the north. New units begin at €5,000 ($6,750) per square meter. Rents for studios begin at €350 ($473) and move up to €525 ($709); bigger units begin about €1,400 ($1,890) per month.

Adjacent to the entire western side of Paris is the department of Hauts-de-Seine (92). These towns, which are close to some of Paris's more expensive real estate in the 15th, 16th, and 17th *arrondissements,* and which also have the Bois de Boulogne close at hand, command prices higher than many Parisian neighborhoods. These towns, along with the Bois de Boulogne, are contained within a loop of the Seine, between the river and Paris. The Seine arcs through Paris, exiting the city's southwest corner. Almost immediately, it abruptly turns north and finally northeast, creating this exclusive enclave.

Neuilly-sur-Seine, home of Nicolas Sarkozy, former minister of the interior, former finance minister, and possibly the next president of France, is the most chic and expensive of these. The price per square meter here averages about €5,000 ($6,750). But that masks a large disparity between a small ground-floor apartment on a busy boulevard, which might cost €3,800 ($5,130) per square meter; and one near Saint James park, where the going rate is €8,000 ($10,800) per square meter.

New construction in the better neighborhoods begins at €6,000 ($8,100) per square meter, and rental prices for studios start at €450 ($608). For newly constructed larger units, the prices mount to €10,000 ($13,500) per square meter, and rent for a 120-square-meter (1,290-square-foot) apartment begins around €2,500 ($3,375).

Levallois, a town north of Neuilly without its cachet, is nearly as expensive; demand outstrips supply. Older units near the *périphérique* begin about €3,100 ($4,185) but those fronting the Seine begin at €3,500 ($4,725). For new apartments, the price begins around €4,100 ($5,535) per square meter, although prices drop along the northern border with Clichy. Rents in Levallois begin at €300 ($405) for studios and €1,350 ($1,823) for 90 square meters (967 square feet).

In the northwestern part of the department, the vast business park called La Défense dominates another loop of the Seine. The unpredictable river, after curving around Paris to the north, changes direction again. In a 180-degree turnabout, it meanders southwest toward St-Germain-en-Laye.

La Défense lies between these two folds of the Seine. Nearby Courbevoie, which underwent a construction boom in the 1990s, offers older apartments averaging a little above €3,000 ($4,050). Prized units, such as those fronting the river, will top €4,000 ($5,400) per square meter, while new units bring €5,000 ($6,750). Rents in Courbevoie begin at €350 ($473) for a studio and run up to €1,250 ($1,688) for 90 square meters (967 square feet).

Northeast of Courbevoie about five kilometers is Asnières, a town anticipating an extension of the Métro in 2007. Here, prices vary €2,000–5,000 ($2,700–6,750) per square meter. The higher prices are found in the center of the town, where shops and services are plentiful. Older apartments in good condition can be found for around €4,000 ($5,400); new, quality units bring the higher figure. Rents for a studio begin below €300 ($405), while larger, 90-square-meter (967-square-foot) units begin at €1,050 ($1,418).

The department of Seine Saint Denis (93) covers much of the north side of Paris and is sometimes referred to as the "21st *arrondissement*." Despite its proximity to the city, it has not always been considered prime residential area because of the amount of heavy industry concentrated there, as well as the number of the public housing projects. Two towns that are far enough from Paris not to suffer from that reputation are Epinay-sur-Seine in the west, and Le Raincy on the east side of the department. Epinay, where prices rose 21 percent in 2004, has undertaken much civic beautification along the Seine and in the center of town. Small houses here sell for about €200,000 ($270,000). Le Raincy has always been more upscale—apartments range €2,300– 3,000 ($3,105–4,050) per square meter, and houses begin at €2,700 ($3,645) per square meter.

Real estate this close to Paris is undergoing gentrification and rising prices. They are also areas with much new construction, and many of the old industrial buildings are being converted to lofts. The towns much closer to Paris, such as St. Ouen, St. Denis, and Aubervilliers have all seen lots of new homes and apartments built in recent years. In all three towns, new apartments are priced below €3,100 ($4,185) per square meter, and older units range upwards from €1,500 ($2,025) per square meter, with Aubervilliers being the least expensive.

On the east side of Paris, north of Montreuil and just across the border from the 19th *arrondissement,* are the towns of Le Pré St. Gervais, Les Lilas, and Bagnolet. Le Pré has lots of redbrick buildings with apartments and lofts starting around €2,700 ($3,645) per square meter for small units, but quickly rising to €4,500 ($6,075) per square meter for the best of the old and most of the new. Houses in the area known as Villa de Pré range €3,800–4,500 ($5,130–6,075) per square meter. In the north toward Pantin, there are buildings constructed in the 1970s that range €2,200–2,800 ($2,970–3,780) per square meter.

Les Lilas offers older apartments from €3,100–3,600 ($4,185–4,860) per square meter, and new ones from €3,500–5,300 ($4,725–7,155) per square meter. Houses around Place Charles de Gaulle are in the €400,000–500,000 ($540,000–675,000) range. Bagnolet has lots of public housing, but also good Métro access to Paris, and lofts start around €2,100 ($2,835) per square meter. The most sought-after addresses are in the southern end of town, close to Montreuil both geographically and in price.

THE OUTER CIRCLE: VAL-D'OISE, ESSONNE, YVELINES, AND SEINE-ET-MARNE

Once you get out beyond the *petite couronne* (inner circle), the possibilities begin to open up. In nearly every direction are historic names and forested land. St-Germain-en-Laye, birthplace of Louis XIV, lies at the south end of the forest of the same name with its golf course and racetrack. (Note: At the north end of this area is one of the world's largest sewer plants. For years, nearby residents have complained of odor.) Southwest is Versailles and further on, Rambouillet. North is Montmorency and Chantilly; southeast is Fontainebleau. Disneyland Paris is to the east.

South of Paris is Orly Airport, with its nearby TGV line, and Rungis, the vast wholesale market that replaced Les Halles in Paris when the Pompidou Center was built three decades ago. It is also home to a large number of research institutes, think tanks, and schools. An RER line passes through the Chevreuse Valley, and the towns along it are very popular. Another TGV line serves the north side of Paris—Charles de Gaulle Airport and Disneyland on the east.

Development has generally followed transportation, and locating near a rail line or *autoroute* may be a convenience for those who anticipate coming and going with some frequency. It can be a mixed blessing, however, when the *autoroutes* are jammed with commuters and vacationers.

The largest and least expensive department in the province is Seine-et-Marne, covering the eastern 40 percent of the province. East of Disneyland is the old city of Meaux (pop. 63,000), famous for its brie cheese. Houses in its historic sections, caught between the coils of the Marne River, sell for €350,000–500,000 ($472,500–945,000). Apartments are about €2,000 ($2,700) per square meter, falling to €1,400 ($1,890) in some neighborhoods. In nearby towns, old houses in need of repair may be found for about €180,000 ($243,000). For house rentals, the average rate in 2004 was about €8.50 ($11.48) per square meter.

Closer to Paris and near Disneyland is one of the new towns—actually a grouping of separate communes—called Marne-la-Vallée. In the Val Maubée area of town, older apartments go for €1,700–2,300 ($2,295–3,105) per square meter, with new units selling for upwards of €2,500 ($3,375) per square meter. Houses of 90–100 square meters (968–1,075 square feet) with a small garden begin at €150,000 ($202,500).

South from Meaux along the Grand Morin River are villages such as Crécy-la-Chapelle, known as "Little Venice" for its network of small canals, and Coulommiers, another town famous for brie.

Closer to Fontainbleau is the new town of Melun-Sénart, complete with an RER station and a 35-minute train ride from Paris. Apartments range €1,400–2,500 ($1,890–3,375) per square meter, with houses beginning at €230,000 ($310,500). Rents for either apartments or houses hover just above €110 ($149) per square meter.

At Fontainbleau, houses rarely come on the market. Apartments average €2,300–2,500 ($3,105–3,375) per square meter, but prices rise by €500 ($675) per square meter for newer buildings in the center of town. For houses, expect to pay up to €3,000 ($4,050) per square meter.

West of Fontainebleau, and directly south of the departments of 92 and 94 that form the section of the *petite couronne* around the south of Paris, is the department of Essonne (91). Numerous university and scientific research institutes are based here. Well-served by rail and *autoroutes*, with Orly just beyond its northern border, Essonne offers areas relatively close to Paris that are wooded and calm.

Nonetheless, as in other departments of the outer ring, the trip into Paris will generally take 30 minutes or more—and this is obviously a factor to consider when searching for property. Development follows transportation, whether road or rail, and commuters pay a premium to save time. With Paris as the hub, the highways and rail lines radiate outward like spokes; and the further from the hub you get, the greater the distance separating the spokes. If Paris is not a frequent destination on your agenda, you might find suitable accommodations at an advantageous price in the small towns between these arteries. In considering such locations, however, take services into account: How close is shopping? A doctor? Think about your daily life in this kind of location.

Following the transit lines further from the city, you can find less expensive housing. For instance, in Juvisy-sur-Orge and neighboring communities just south of Orly airport, the square meter price of an apartment or house runs €1,700–1,900 ($2,295–2,565). In Corbeil-Essones, another 15 kilometers further from Paris along the same rail and *autoroutes*, older houses and apartments—even renovated ones—were readily available in 2004 for less than €1,700 ($2,295) per square meter. Rentals could be found for €10–11 ($13.50–14.85) per square meter.

The department of Yvelines (78) lies east of Paris and the Hauts-de-Seine (92) and contains three historic towns that were once the homes of French royalty, all with forests and gardens to match: Versailles, St-Germain-en-Laye, and Rambouillet. It is also a department with prices comparable to Paris. Prices have risen more than 10 percent every year since 1999. One reason may be that relatively few properties have been for sale. Another is that with its verdant valleys, massive forests, and a population high on the socioeconomic scale, it is quite a pleasant area.

In St-Germain-en-Laye, new apartments range €3,500–5,800 ($4,725–7,830) per square meter, while older units bring €1,850–3,000 ($2,498–4,050). Rents here start around €300 ($405) per month for a studio, or €1,400 ($1,890) for an apartment of 95 square meters (1,021 square feet).

Versailles has a lot of disparity in prices, according to the proximity to the château and the quality and date of construction. The best of these from the 18th and 19th centuries range €3,800–5,000 ($5,130–6,750) per square meter. These prices nearly match that of the best new construction. Large houses with gardens can approach €1 million ($1.35 million), although smaller ones some distance from the château begin around €500,000 ($675,000). Rents also reflect the cachet of the palace: €350 ($473) for a nearby studio, €300 ($405) for one further away, with similar discrepancies for larger units.

Rambouillet, much further from Paris, had older apartments selling for €2,100–2,250 ($2,835–3,038) per square meter in 2004. Prices for renovated units ran about €2,400 ($3,240) per square meter, and new units began at €2,800 ($3,780) per square meter. Houses sold for about €1,900 ($2,565) per square meter, and rents for both houses and apartments neared €110 ($149) per square meter.

On the other side of the St. Germain Forest, along the banks of the Seine and a half hour by train from La Défense, the huge business park outside Paris, price start to moderate. In Poissy, for example, new apartments in some neighborhoods sell for €1,200–1,900 ($1,620–2,565) per square meter, although the best units in the center of the city will double that higher price. Houses begin at €250,000 ($337,500).

Val d'Oise (95) is the northernmost department in the Île-de-France. It stretches east to west across the top of three other departments. Its southeastern corner, bordering Seine-St-Denis and Hauts-de-Seine, is close to Paris and densely populated.

At Argenteuil, an industrial city of about 100,000, new apartments average €2,250 ($3,037) per square meter, while older, unrenovated units go for €1,300 ($1,755) per square meter. Houses start at €1,800 ($2,430) per square meter, and rents average just over €10 ($13.50) per square meter.

Further north, the more desirable areas of Montmorency, with its forest, and Enghien-les-Bains, which boasts a lake, prices increase. The average price per square meter for older apartments in Enghein range €2,150–2,400 ($2,903–3,240), and for new ones, €4,300 ($5,805). Houses averaged €2,650 ($3,578) per square meter. Apartments rented for an average of €13 ($17.55) per square meters, while houses rented for about €17 ($22.95) per square meter.

In Montmorency, older apartment prices recently fell by about 10 percent, while new ones averaged about €3,100 ($4,185)—the much higher Enghein prices reflecting the luxury units around the lake. The average house price was also much lower, at €2,000 ($2,700) per square meter.

If you get even farther away from Paris to towns like Taverny, prices drop, with the average square meter selling for about €1,600 ($2,160). In the new town of Cergy-Pontoise, new apartments sell for an average of €2,050 ($2,767) per square meter; older units average €1,425–1,750 ($1,923–2,363) per square meter, depending on renovations. Stand-alone houses average €1,425 ($1923) per square meter, while apartment and house rentals run €9–10 ($12.15–13.50) per square meter. In the old town of Pontoise, prices are about 20 percent higher across the board.

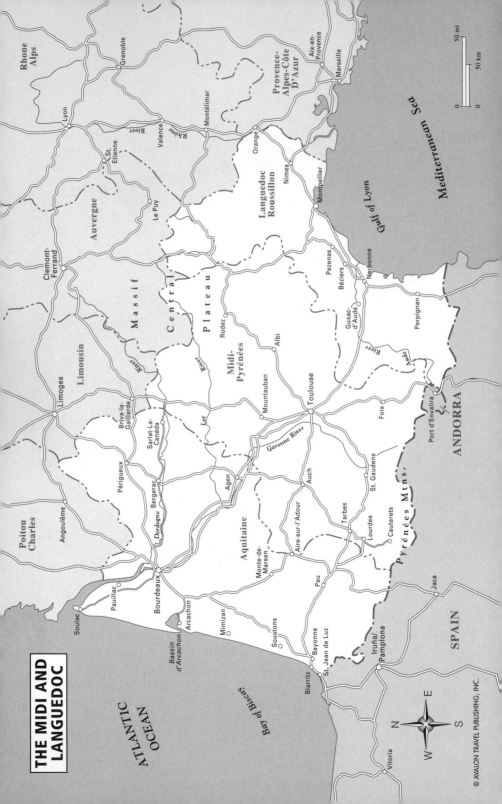

The Midi and Languedoc

Between the Pyrénées and the Massif Central lies an island of high-tech in a sea of wine. Southern France between the Atlantic and the Mediterranean—from the Spanish border along the crest of the Pyrénées as far north as Bordeaux, and the desolate southern reaches of the Massif Central—remains one of the least appreciated yet most attractive parts of the country. Whether you prefer the sun and sand of the Atlantic and Mediterranean coasts, hiking and skiing in the steep Pyrénées, or the wooded hills and river valleys of the Massif Central, this region has everything you might want in France, except Paris. Exploring this region from west to eastwill help you determine where you might wind up.

The Lay of the Land

The westernmost of the three regions that comprise this territory is Aquitaine, with three million people in five departments: Gironde, Pyrénées-Atlantique, Dordogne, Landes, and Lot-et-Garonne. Gironde, with Bordeaux as its heart and soul, is the most populous and fastest growing. While the province as a whole grew 3.8 percent from 1990 to 1999, Gironde grew by 5.9 percent. It was rivaled only by Landes, the department immediately south of Gironde, which grew by an even five percent.

If you love wine, foie gras, armagnac brandy, truffles, cheese, hot summers, mild winters, and stone houses, and prefer to live within easy reach of the big city amenities of Bordeaux, Montpellier, and Toulouse, this region will appeal to you.

Bordeaux is Aquitaine's major city. With its pricey, world-famous wines and historic ties to the U.K., Bordeaux is justly regarded as the most bourgeois area of France outside of Paris' 16th *arrondissement.* In this city, formality reigns, and pedigree is more important than achievement.

Northeast of Bordeaux from Perigueux to Agen, you will find wetter, more rugged terrain and numerous Anglophones, mostly British and Dutch, who have retired here or own second homes. The beaches from Bordeaux south to Biarritz and the pine forests behind them provide a great playground most of the year. The southwestern part of Aquitaine is Basque Country, where the strikingly different language makes it possible to believe you are no longer in France.

South of Bordeaux, in the middle of the territory (hence the region's name: the Midi), lies Toulouse, a great city with a fine university and an industrial base. Boeing's rival, Airbus, builds here, as do the producers of European Ariane rockets. Grapes grow here and there, but are greatly overshadowed in importance by grain.

The eastern third of this vast territory is sparsely populated Languedoc, another great wine-producing area; its southern corner is an extension of Catalonia, while its inland reaches are dry and rugged. Its wide, sandy Mediterranean beaches and similarities to Provence have encouraged an influx of foreigners in the past decade, some of them Americans. They come seeking vacation homes; few have settled here permanently.

The southern part of this territory is dominated by the Pyrénées, standing along the horizon like a wall around Heaven. From them flow rivers such as the Garonne and the Aude, which, along with their tributaries, wind through the plains below. The Pyrénées are as indisputably the southern boundary of France as the Atlantic is its western border.

The northern part of this territory recalls the Pyrénées' rugged terrain without ever competing in magnitude with that range's peaks. The uplift of the Massif Central plateau and bordering hills, such as the Montagne Noir, contribute greatly to the watershed with rivers such as the Dordogne, Lot, and Tarn flowing into the Garonne and the Herault. The Orb brings their waters to the east.

In the center of the region lies a rich agricultural region producing grain, vegetables, meat, and fruit in abundance. But the region's most widely known crop is wine, from some of the most famous and expensive in the world—the first growths of Bordeaux—to *vin de pays* (regional wine) scarcely known beyond the villages where it is made.

If you love wine, foie gras, armagnac brandy, truffles, cheese, hot summers, mild winters, and stone houses, and prefer to live within easy reach of the big-city amenities of Bordeaux, Montpellier, and Toulouse, this region will appeal to you.

RENTING

If you plan to rent while looking for property to buy, you should be able to find a four- or five-room unit of 100–125 square meters (1,076–1,345 square feet) for €500–1,000 ($675–1,350) per month in the cities throughout the region. In smaller villages well beyond the periphery of the cities, you might find houses to rent for half that price. The difficulty may lie in finding a rental for less than three years, the length of the normal lease in France. In small villages, shorter leases may be more likely, although you may have to take a house, rather than an apartment.

The typical rental unit is unfurnished. During off-season, you might find the owner of a furnished vacation property rented by the week in summer willing to take a longer-term tenant at an advantageous price, since otherwise the unit would remain empty. In such an arrangement, however, heating will be a point of negotiation between you and your landlord.

One strategy for finding a rental is to enlist the aid of your real estate agency. Tell them you are looking for property to buy, but want to live in the area for a few months before deciding; can they help you find a rental? Even if you do not buy anything from them immediately, they still stand to profit from the rental finder's fee—and they gain more time to find the right property for you.

Bordeaux

Bourgeois Bordeaux may be known as a haven for the beautiful people, but regular folks live here, too. By French standards, it's a relatively big city, with a population of nearly 250,000, plus another 500,000 in the metropolitan area. Housing choices vary, but there are far more buyers than sellers, and most of the sellers are willing to wait until someone meets their price.

Much of property along the Garonne River in Bordeaux has undergone renovation. Old warehouses are being demolished and building facades restored, especially

Farmhouses and villages line the river valleys and dot the wooded, sometimes rugged landscape.

in the neighborhood of Chartrons. On the river itself, prices climbed as much as 15 percent in six months during 1999. Today, these upscale apartments with a view of the Garonne River and in the Triangle of Gold in the center of the city run €2,500–3,500 ($3,375–4,725) per square meter, with two- and two-room units cheaper than either studios or those of five rooms or more. Expect monthly rents for a studio of less than 30 square meters to be €350 ($473) per month, with prices mounting to the €850–1,300 ($1,148–1,755) range for bigger apartments, depending on size and location. For houses of 120 square meters (1,291 square feet), expect to pay €900–1,500 ($1,215–2,025) per month in rent.

Away from the river and in less expensive neighborhoods, especially on the Right Bank to the east, the price drops. You can find apartments for €800–1,800 ($1,080–2,430) per square meter. Houses fall in the €1,300–1,900 ($1,755–2,565) per-square-meter range, with monthly rents of €700–1000 ($945–1,350). With the tramway now making access to the center of Bordeaux quite easy, neighborhoods here have also begun to climb, especially those on the river itself, with city views.

Little, stone, one-story houses from the 19th century, called *échoppes,* were once the homes of laborers and are much prized today. They represent an important architectural style in the region. Most of these, away from the center of the city, have already passed the €200,000 ($270,000) mark. Bigger houses bring even higher prices, on the order of €350,000 ($472,500). Those searching for an *échoppe* at a lesser price should cross to the less fashionable side of the river, east of Bordeaux, where they are more prevalent and can still be found for about €150,000 ($202,500). The communes of Lormont and Floirac on either side of the tramway have not yet increased to the extent that La Bastide has.

For units on the outskirts of the city, prices fall by 10 to 12 percent. For older units, costs were significantly less—less than €1,000 ($1,350) per square meter for all but the best. Houses likewise decline in price away from the center, although in the nicer suburbs among the famous vineyards, prices climb back up. In those areas, even small houses start around €190,000 ($256,500).

AROUND BORDEAUX

North and east of Bordeaux, vineyards dot both sides of the river. Just above Bordeaux, the Dordogne River joins the Garonne, and the estuary widens and becomes the Gironde. The famous communes of Margaux, Pauillac, St, Julien, and St. Estéphe line the west bank, while the lesser-known Côtes du Bourg lies opposite on the eastern side. To the east of Bordeaux are Libourne and the vineyards of St. Emilion. Southeast of Bordeaux are the vineyards where the sweet wines of Sauternes and Barsac are produced.

Land in these regions is valuable; vines are planted everywhere, and the spacious grounds of châteaux elsewhere in France are often absent. You'll find no bargains these days, with the spiraling prices of wine. In St. Emilion, vineyard land starts at €200,000 ($270,000) per hectare. Even in the lesser region of Entre deux Mers, the price of a stone house with a few hectares of vines starts at €1 million. However, house prices in Libourne, about 30 kilometers (18.6 miles) from Bordeaux, and the small villages surrounding it are much less than those in the suburbs surrounding Bordeaux on the other side of the river. Small village houses begin at €70,000 ($94,500), and larger homes with gardens at €100,000 ($135,000).

East of St. Emilion is the department of Dordogne, which takes its name from the river. This region is beloved by the English who move to France. Its numerous little villages have proved such a magnet for them that the local *chambre des notaires* has been offering its members lessons in English for some years.

Heading along the Dordogne River into the Perigord, the countryside around larger cities such as Libourne, Bergerac, and Sarlat is dotted with small villages. From here to Albi and south to the Garonne, you will find little except farms and small villages in wooded, hilly settings.

Principal towns include Bergerac, Périgueux, and Sarlat. With a population of 30,000, Périgueux is the largest of the three. The entire department contains less than 400,000 people. Water is plentiful, as numerous rivers and streams tumble through the rocky escarpment of the Massif Central. Farmhouses and villages line the river valleys and dot the wooded, sometimes rugged landscape. This is the region of Lascaux and other ancient sites withmagnificent prehistoric cave art, perhaps 17,000 years old.

Because of the influx of foreigners, there are few properties available for less than €100,000 ($135,000), and even the smallest houses with character begin at €220,000 ($297,000). For a house and several hectares of land, the price mounts to €450,000 ($607,500). Many of these properties now serve as bed-and-breakfasts or as *gites* (weekly vacation rentals). To grasp the magnitude of the British penetration of the region, consider that in the first quarter of 2004, 26,000 passengers flew into the Bergerac airport from England. In the summertime, one airline alone brings in three British planeloads daily.

Much of the land from the Atlantic, east, north, and west of Bordeaux, is covered with pine forests, lagoons, and wetlands until you reach the vineyards along the banks of the Gironde. The Bassin d'Arcachon, a shallow bay and marine preserve, is the most prominent feature on the coast. It stands at the northern end of the great regional park, Landes de Gascogne, covering 290,000 hectares (700,000 acres) southwest of Bordeaux.

Close to Bordeaux, Arcachon sits contentedly on its bay, with beaches and boating and all the recreational opportunities of the regional park not far to the southwest. Some are calling Cap Ferret the new Côte d'Azur, with prices to match. There are few houses to begin with, and those are often sold by word of mouth. A price tag of €1.5 million ($2.03 million) is to be expected. South of the bay at Andernos, prices have doubled in the past five years, and now there are sales of €2 million ($2.7 million). But between Bordeaux and the water along route N250 are a number of housing developments where you might find something for about €200,000 ($270,000).

The park is a tremendous recreational area, and much of the land between its western edge and the Atlantic beaches is forested and dotted with lagoons. Towns such as Sabres and Pissos, in the park itself, and Mimizan, Castets, and Soustons, remain comfortably small yet close to larger cities such as Dax and Mont-de-Marsan. In these latter two, house prices begin around €1,200 ($1,620) per square meter.

These towns serve as something of a dividing line between the pine forests of Landes and the uplands leading into the Pyrénées. South from Bayonne, the towns of Biarritz, Hendaye, and St-Jean-de-Luz line the coast shoulder to expensive shoulder along the Spanish border. Inland from the actual coast, Bayonne is perhaps the cheapest of these, with apartments costing €1,850–2,650 ($2,498–3,578) per square meter and houses from €2,100 ($2,835) per square meter. At the high end is St-Jean-de-Luz, where apartments run €3,000–5,000 ($4,050–6,750) per square meter, and houses begin at about €2,500 ($3,375) per square meter.

From St-Jean-de-Luz, you can follow highway D918, the Route du Fromage (Road of Cheese), inland. It leads to St-Jean-Pied-de-Port and, from there, deeper and higher into Basque Country. Basque homes always appear neat and freshly painted—usually white with red shutters, except for the large rectangular stones that form the corners of each wall and are left bare, the shape emphasizing the sturdy square structures of two or three stories.

Moving east, you remain in Basque Country, but enter the region of Midi-Pyrénées. In the foothills of the Pyrénées are Pau and Tarbes, looking onto the fertile plains to the north. These and other cities further east, such as St. Gaudens, serve as market towns for the villages in the foothills. Some of these, such as St. Bertrand de Comminges, are quite lovely and have proved attractive for second homes.

Throughout the Pyrénées are slopes and trails for winter skiing, both downhill and cross-country, and for hiking or cycling in the summer. Most of these spots are one to two hours from cities in the warmer plain formed by the Garonne River and its numerous tributaries.

North of the Pyrénées on the plain is the department of Gers, a rich agricultural area noted for poultry, wine, and armagnac. Between the towns of Auch and Agen lie the villages of Condom, Fleurance, and Lectoure. In this area, you can find houses of 150 square meters on lots of about one acre for around €300,000 ($405,000). Small village houses range €110,000–150,000 ($148,500–202,500).

Toulouse

In the center of the Midi region is Toulouse, *la ville rose* (the pink city), once a Visigoth capital and now the heart of France's aerospace industry. Ariane rockets and Airbus jetliners are built here. The super-jumbo Airbus 380, capable of carrying 650 passengers and representing an investment of more than €12 billion ($16.2 billion), is also being assembled here.

Much of this high-tech industry is built on a well-educated population. The University of Toulouse continues to attract high-caliber students and professors. Some 140,000 students attend the university on campuses spread around the city. Toulouse is second only to Paris as a center of higher learning in France. About 10,500 researchers work in 340 public and private institutes.

Growth in Toulouse surpassed that in Bordeaux during the last decade. Toulouse itself increased by 8.9 percent to 390,000 people; the department of Haute-Garonne, which includes Toulouse, now has a population of more than 1.1 million. It is the fourth-largest metropolitan area in France after Paris, Lyon, and Marseille.

All this growth has resulted in an average annual increase in housing prices throughout the department of 11 percent over the past five years. The prized small, one-story, four-room *toulousaines* houses near the center of the city now often approach €300,000 ($405,000). New apartments in the same areas run as high as €3,200 ($4,320) per square meter. With a garage and a terrace, the price goes up. The price of renovated older units of lesser quality drops to €2,000–2,500 ($2,700–3,375). To the east of the Canal du Midi and west of the Garonne River, prices begin at €1,500 ($2,025) per square meter.

Rents in the center of Toulouse are consistent with the cost of housing. Studios begin at €300 ($405) and go up to €1,800 ($2,430) for luxury five-room units. Houses begin at €1,000 ($1,350) per month.

Toulouse opened a single Métro line a few years ago that cuts across the city northeast to southwest. This configuration gave residents who wanted to live near it a wide choice, and resulted in price increases in housing all along the line. As the transit system expands, those areas in turn are being seen as choicer locations. Les Minimes, Bonnefoy, and La Roseraie have all gained popularity with young families. Small houses with gardens start at €200,000 ($270,000); bigger, well-renovated homes with an attached garage sell in the €300,000–500,000 ($405,000–675,000) range. Apartments here begin about €1,500 ($2,025) per square meter for purchase and €8–11 ($10.80–14.85) per square meter for a rental, while houses rent for €9–14 ($12.15–18.90) per square meter.

Suburbs close by, such as Blagnac, where Airbus and the airport are located, may offer new homes beginning around €150,000 ($202,500) for a duplex and double that for a villa.

AROUND TOULOUSE

Surrounding Toulouse is a rolling plain, with farmhouses dotting the ridgelines and villages tucked away in the folds of the hills. Corn and maize, barley and sunflowers fill the landscape of the Lauragais, as the region is called. Cintagabelle, the home of former Prime Minister Lionel Jospin, is not far from Toulouse. The Ariège River flows through here before joining the Garonne near Toulouse. Many of the villages within 10 kilometers (about 6 miles) of Toulouse have become quite suburban as city growth has pushed outward—you can find houses with gardens starting around €150,000 ($202,500). But beyond them in every direction are villages that have retained their agricultural charm. Prices drop as distance from the city increases. Larger towns, such as Auterive to the south or Montauban to the north, serve as market centers. In Montauban, older homes of 120 square meters (1,291 square feet) range €120,000–190,000 ($162,000–256,500), while new construction for a home that size begins at around €175,000 ($236,250) and goes up to €230,000 ($310,500). Here, you can find new studios to rent for €250–330 ($338–446) per month, and four rooms for €550–650 ($743–878) per month. Older units are generally cheaper.

Following the Garonne and the canal that parallels it northwest from Toulouse, the countryside remains much the same until you gradually come upon the Massif Central. This is Quercy, not a department or province, but the name commonly given to the area covered by the departments of the Tarn, the Lot, and the Lot-et-Garonne. Similar to the Dordogne and Perigord, the region is home to many small farms and villages.

Property prices vary with location and quality. Proximity to an exit off the *autoroute* or a larger city, such as Agen or Cahors, will increase the value. Much of this region is little more than an hour from Toulouse on the *autoroute*. In Cahors, new houses of 120 square meters (1,291

Les Cathares

Throughout much of the Midi between Toulouse and the Mediterranean, you'll see signs announcing, *Vous êtes en pays Cathares* ("You are in Cathars Country"). Even those with a working knowledge of French history may be puzzled by the reference. Who are the Cathars? To the 13th-century northern French Catholics, they were Albigensian heretics, dissenters from Albi who challenged Roman Catholic authority, and they were slaughtered by the thousands in a Catholic attempt to gain control of the region.

The purported heresy—dating to debates by some of the earliest Christians, and appearing in various regions throughout Europe and Asia Minor—began as a denial of the Trinity doctrine promulgated by Rome. It gradually evolved into a sketchy challenge to Catholic ecclesiastical authority. In an era of clerical corruption and great church wealth, the Cathars preached asceticism. They believed that the material world, the world of flesh, was evil and created by the Devil. God's world was the spiritual one, reached only after death. Accordingly, they denied the humanity of Christ and the transubstantiation of bread and wine into Christ's body and blood during Mass—two big theological heresies.

The Cathars' beliefs were particularly strong in the south, brought there by the Visigoths when they ruled the region after Roman authority crumbled in the 4th century. Over the years, some people stubbornly refused to give up these beliefs, regardless of what some group of bishops might have said. And the corruption of the clergy gave plenty of ammunition to those who believed in the intrinsic evil of the flesh.

The success of the crusades in conquering the Near East inspired both French clergy and nobles to consider the possibility of a similar venture in the south, where a complex political situation prevailed. The Count of Toulouse and his vassals, though nominally liege to the king of France, were both independent and attracted to Aragon—the kingdom in the east of what is now Spain—that also controlled Provence. Moreover, within recent memory, Eleanor of Aquitaine had shown how weak the French grip on Toulouse and Languedoc was, after her divorce from Louis VII brought so much of what is now western France under English rule.

In 1210, with the blessing of Pope Innocent III, Simon de Montfort and Abbot Arnaud Amaury, the papal legate, led an army south. Their first conquest was the city of Beziers, near the Mediterranean and south of Montpellier. When thousands of civilians took sanctuary in the cathedral, and the crusaders suspected heretics were among them, the abbot gave the order: "Burn them all; God will know his own." Several thousand died in this first engagement, which set the tone for the next few decades of on-again, off-again warfare. In feudal times, armies generally fought for about six weeks in the summer and then returned home.

The crusaders moved southwest, conquering where they could and leaving islands of resistance in place for later. Many Catholics, as well as Cathars, suffered the fate of those in the Beziers Cathedral. When one southern abbot whose orthodox beliefs were beyond question complained that his family was being deprived of its lands without cause, his abbey and lands were given over to a northern cleric, who ruled in absentia.

Carcassonne was captured after Viscount Roger Trencavel met the crusaders under a flag of truce. They seized him, and he died in prison. In another instance, when a village fell to De Montfort, he killed all but 50 of the men. Forty-nine of them he blinded, and the 50th he left with one eye to lead the band to the next village to urge surrender.

De Montfort was finally killed in 1218 as he besieged Toulouse, but his son took command, and the war went on for several more years. Despite the eventual capitulation of Count Raymond VII of Toulouse in 1229, resistance continued for years in fortified castles set atop rocky crags in the foothills of the Pyrénées. The ruins of these castles—Queribus, Peyrepetuse, Puylaurens, Puivert, and Montsegur, where more than 200 people were burned to death—are important tourist attractions today.

To root out the heresy after the military conquest, Pope Gregory IX ordered the first Inquisition to be conducted by the Dominican friars, whose founder had been instrumental in arousing church action against the Cathars. One of the most zealous inquisitors, Bishop Jacques Fournier, later became Pope Benedict XII.

While the beliefs of the Cathars eventually disappeared from the pages of history, southern resistance to northern authority, both ecclesiastical and civil, remained alive. It was in this region that Protestantism flourished in France centuries later, and where many of the revolutionaries of the 18th and 19th centuries were born.

square feet) in residential areas cost about €200,000 ($270,000), with similar older houses running 5–25 percent less.

Agen, a city along the Garonne, the canal, and the *autoroute* between Toulouse and Bordeaux, once served as the southern port for the region, loading its produce onto barges. *Prunes de Agen* gained their name not because they were all grown in Agen, but because they were shipped from there. Tobacco is another historically important crop in the region.

Rocamadour, the tiny village built into the side of a cliff where pilgrims came to worship at the altar of the black Virgin, is in Lot. Truffles and mushrooms, fruit, walnuts, foie gras, and *charcuterie* (cooked meats) are common products. And, of course, wine: Bergerac, Cahors, Gaillac, and Monbazillac are all well-known names to French wine lovers.

South of the Garonne is the department of Gers. Auch (pop. 24,000) is one of the centers and a desirable place to live. Other towns like Condom, Nerac, and Eauze have populations of less than 10,000. The main products here include poultry, foie gras, and armagnac, the brandy that many find superior to cognac because it is so often the work of small producers, rather than the giant distillers of the rival product.

One little-known crop of the region is *pastel,* a plant of the mustard family that yields a beautiful blue dye called woad, which has been used since prehistoric times. Woad was a source of great wealth in the textile industry centered in Toulouse in the 16th and 17th centuries, before it was replaced by much cheaper indigo from the New World.

Languedoc

The eastern part of the Midi borders the Mediterranean and presents an entirely different face. Dry, rocky, and sparsely populated, but also warm and sunny, with excellent beaches and old stone houses, Languedoc is little known even among the French for reasons both historical and geographical.

A thousand years ago, things were different. Near the turn of the first millennium, Languedoc represented the peak of Western European culture. The Arab occupation had been repulsed in the 8th century, but left behind a residue of learning. The region had suffered little from the Viking invasions that so ravaged the north. Maritime commerce and the cloth trade had enriched it. The poetry of its troubadours, the wealth and refinement of its nobility, and the level of its learning—in literature, architecture, and law—all confirmed Languedoc's superiority.

Later centuries were not so kind. The religious and military crusade against the Albigensian heresy—a belief in asceticism held by a people known as the Cathars—brought the region beneath the Catholic heel of the north. Plague, invasion, and religious persecution all swept across in succession. Additionally, the hegemony of Paris overwhelmed the native languages of Languedoc.

Internationally, the Italian Renaissance, the colonization of the New World, and the Golden Age of the Netherlands all passed beyond its borders. Continental trade routes, well-established after a century of crusades to the Holy Land, passed to the north, and the great pilgrimages of medieval times fell off. Europe turned to face the Atlantic, no longer the Mediterranean, and Languedoc became in every sense a backwater.

The province is now called Languedoc-Roussillon, the hyphenated latter portion in deference to the Catalan culture that dominates the department of Pyrénées-Orientales on the Spanish border. Historically, the border region has had economic and political ties with Barcelona and the kingdom of Aragon. In fact, the frontier between France and Spain was not set until 1659. Today, the European Union regards the Toulouse-Barcelona axis as an economic region, much as it was centuries before nationalism swept the continent.

Geographically, this eastern Pyrénées province is less verdant than its western cousins. Nonetheless, there are prime summer and winter recreational areas—skiing and hiking are the major activities. The lower slopes are dotted with vineyards. Collioure on the coast and Céret in the mountains are villages once frequented by artists like Picasso. Towns such as Limoux, south of Carcassonne, and St. Paul de Fenouillet, northwest of Perpignan, are gateways to the Pyrénées without being high in the mountains. Ceret, a French Catalan town beloved by artists for more than a century, is another.

Perpignan, with a population of about 170,000 in the metropolitan area, is the capital of French Catalonia. Like most of the French cities on the east side of the Mediterranean, it is situated away from the sea itself, less subject to flooding and beyond the inlets and shallow *étangs* (lagoons) that cut the wide, sandy beaches north of where the Pyrénées meet the sea.

Perpignan experienced a slowing real estate market in 2004. The mean price of apartments sold in 2003 was €1,050 ($1,418) per square meter.

Wine on the Coasts

Wine is king in Languedoc, just as surely as in Bordeaux. Every wine lover knows the names of the great wines of Bordeaux, such as Châteaux Margaux, Latour, and Yquem. The châteaux were classified in 1855 into first, second, third, fourth, and fifth growths, according to quality. It was a ranking based on the track record of the wines over the years. These rankings have gone unchanged, though not unchallenged. Yet they have stood the test of time, if only as a superb marketing tool.

As with most systems of inherited nobility, however, a great deal of snobbery and elitism have grown up around these wines, having little to do with their quality and much to do with the wealth of those who own the estates and those to whom high prices and good taste are synonymous.

Languedoc engages in a different sort of wine trade. In place of the grand chateaux of the 17th and 18th centuries, the bourgeois mansions and the international jet set that the last 150 years have produced on the Atlantic coast, you find small domains and chateaux where the owner may work side by side in the field with the hired hands. Here wine may come from a tin-roofed shed attached to small modern house with a child's tricycle in the yard or from huge cooperatives that serve scores of small farmers with machinery and expertise.

It's a different kind of wine too. This is wine that people drink week in and week out; that you can afford to drink every day. It's wine that you can buy by the liter for less than the price of gasoline, delivered by the same kind of hose and nozzle that delivers gas from the pump.

But don't be led astray by the rural charm of Languedoc wine production. Today the knowledge and skills to make wine of excellent quality are universal. Where once the wines of Languedoc were stored in concrete vats, stainless steel tanks and oak barrels are now commonplace. Carbonic maceration, temperature-controlled fermentation and all the other techniques of modern wine-making are used.

Any country, any region hospitable to *vitis vinifera*, has the potential for making world-class wine. California proved that a generation ago. Now it's being proven in Languedoc, where the plebian reputation of the past works to the wineries' advantage.

In contrast, the Burgundy and Bordeaux regions are extremely limited in the grape varieties they can grow under the French *Appellation d'Origine Contrôlée* (AOC) system, if only because the land is too valuable to do anything else. The AOC restricts the wines so labeled to traditional varieties of grapes for that region; wines that do not conform must be labeled as *vin de pays* or *vin de table* and bring a much lower price.

Languedoc is a patchwork of *vin de pays* vineyards and AOC regions, some only a few years old with little recognition. Some of these areas produce Rhône-style wines, themselves blends of half a dozen different varieties of grapes, giving all those varieties legitimacy for AOC wines. Still other areas grow chardonnay, cabernet sauvignon, sauvignon blanc, merlot—all of them grapes known around the world.

Thus the wine growers of Limoux who have long used chardonnay and chenin blanc grapes to make a sparkling wine can also bottle these as still wines and compete with chardonnays from all over the world. When wine lovers in London or Amsterdam or San Francisco pits the bottle from Limoux against that from Napa or Burgundy, they consider the taste of the wine in relation to the price, not just the price.

This is part of the Languedoc advantage. A wine grower need not be concerned with the AOC system. Chardonnay grown in Languedoc, for instance, was being sold in Macon as Pouilly-Fuissé a few years ago. It was a tip from someone in the region, not from any disgruntled customers, that brought about the fraud investigation.

But Languedoc producers don't have to resort to subterfuge to sell their wines around the world. Often marketed as *vin de pays d'Oc* and labeled with name of the grape varietal, they sell well all over Europe and in the States. In fact, there is wine being produced in Languedoc that cannot be purchased there—it is all being exported.

The most expensive *vin de pays d'Oc* is that of Mas de Daumas Gassac near Montpellier. In 1970, Aimé Guibert set about to produce a world-class wine. Advised by the great French oenologist Emile Péynaud, he did so by planting cabernet sauvignon vines selected from an old Médoc vineyard. The gamble—and a lot of hard work—paid off. Today, Daumas Gassac wine sells around the world at top Bordeaux and California prices, when you can find them.

None of this means the traditional AOC wines have been abandoned in Languedoc. Rather, the average has steadily improved as a younger generation of winemakers have taken over, recognizing that mediocre quality is no longer viable economically. Both wine cooperatives and individual growers now routinely produce both AOC wines and *vin de pays* varietals. And their wines are finding a ready market at home as well as abroad, selling out at once unheard-of prices as high as €10 ($12.15) a bottle.

Sales of units priced above €150,000 ($202,500) dropped 20–30 percent in 2004, and some prices were being reduced by 5 percent. Both houses and apartments of decent quality may be found beginning at €1,400 ($1,890) per square meter depending on location and appointments.

On the coast itself, campgrounds abound near the water. Some of these beach towns are only summer resorts with little or no independent life. Businesses close between October and Easter and the streets are empty. Away from the water around Argelès, you may find houses in the €500,000–1.5 million range ($675,000–2.03 million).

Going north from Perpignan, the larger towns are Narbonne, Béziers, Montpellier (the capital of the province), and Nîmes. Between Béziers and Montpellier is the Bassin de Thau, a large bay filled with oyster and mussel beds.

MONTPELLIER

Montpellier, with 300,000 inhabitants in the metropolitan area, is the largest and youngest of the Languedoc cities, dating back only to the 10th century. Once part of Aragon, Montpellier was sold by Jacques III of Mallorca to the King of France in 1349.

Montpellier's university, particularly the medical school, is one of the oldest in France, dating to the beginning of the 13th century. Like Toulouse, Montpellier grew rapidly in the last decade. The city itself gained 8.1 percent in population and the department, the Hérault, increased 12.8 percent.

Despite its growth, Montpellier on the average is less expensive than Toulouse or Bordeaux, lacking the industrial base of the former and the world-renowned vineyards of the latter. In 2004, with an unemployment rate of 15 percent, the increases—and the sales—leveled off, and transactions fell by 25 percent.

Nonetheless, the best large apartments will cost €2,600 ($3,510) or more per square meter. Luxurious studios and two-room units in the pricey center are worth nearly as much—up to €2,500 ($3,375) per square meter, with new construction raising the price to €3,000 ($4,050) per square meter. Visitors from the Paris region or other Europeans are often the buyers of these classy units.

The rapid increase in property values has had its effect on rentals. With many landlords selling their buildings at a good profit, rents rose 11 percent in 2003 and again in 2004. The average monthly rent is now more than €11 ($14.85) per square meter. This means studios range

€10–19 ($13.50–25.65) per square meter per month, while four-room units and up range €6–12 ($8.10–16.20) per square meter per month. Houses generally run around €7–11 ($9.45–14.85) per square meter per month, depending on circumstances.

Houses in Montpellier vary quite a bit. While neighborhoods are important, so are design, quality of construction, and garden. A big house of 200 square meters (2,152 square feet) on a lot of 800 square meters (8,600 square feet) might cost €450,000 ($607,500), while a smaller, less elegant home on a lot half that size would range €300,000–350,000 ($405,000–472,500). In some neighborhoods, small houses constructed in the '50s and '60s with handkerchief-sized yards *(jardinets)* begin at €180,000 ($243,000). In general, houses under €300,000 ($405,000) have little difficulty finding buyers, meaning there is not a large selection, because properties do not stay long on the market.

Moving to the periphery but away from the university, the price of older apartments—often of mediocre quality—drops to €1,050–1,400 ($1,418–1,890) per square meters. In the southwest, you can find homes of 100 square meters (1,076 square feet) with yards of 100–150 (1,076–1,614) square meters for less than €200,000 ($270,000). Close to the university, there are no bargains; you might pay €2,000 ($2,700) per square meter for poor quality and little charm.

Some of the most desirable housing is in the towns just outside Montpellier: St. Jean de Védas and Lattes on the south, and St. Clement de Rivière Clapiers and Castelnau le Lez on the north and northeast. In the southern communities, houses run €200,000–450,000 ($270,000–607,500). The more expensive ones are obviously larger, with more land and perhaps a pool.

Castelnau-le-Lez is close to Montpellier, and a new tramway slated to open at the end of 2006 makes the area even more attractive. Homes in the old village begin at €300,000 ($405,000), with less expensive houses further east. Newer and bigger homes to the north reach €600,000 ($810,000).

Both St. Clement and Clapiers are further from Montpellier. These are bigger, newer homes on larger lots, often with a pool. Depending on size and position, prices begin around €380,000 ($513,000) in St. Clement. In Clapiers, houses of 120 square meters (1,291 square feet) on lots of 350 square meters (3,766 square feet), built in the '60s, sell for €200,000 ($270,000); newer houses of the same size but with more amenities, such as two bathrooms and more land, begin about €380,000 ($513,000).

Septimania

The names of various regions in France often prove a puzzle for newcomers, because they may not now be part of any officially designated geography, but still continue in common use. In a territory with two and a half millennia of recorded history ruled by numerous governments and divided and subdivided countless times, perhaps this is to be expected.

Nowhere is this better illustrated than by Georges Frêche, president of the Conseil Régional du Languedoc-Roussillon, who wishes to resurrect the name of Septimanie for his region. Frêche, the longtime mayor of Montpellier before election to his present post in 2004, argues that the name Languedoc-Rousillon was coined in the '60s, when France formed the modern province in the process of decentralizing its government.

The Romans called the region Gaule Narbonnaise when they established their capital there in 118 B.C. When the region came under Visigoth rule in A.D. 412, it was designated Septimanie because of the veterans of the 7th Roman Legion who had occupied it. "Languedoc was essentially the region around Toulouse, and Toulouse was historically the capital of Languedoc. It wasn't until the 17th century that the area around Montpellier was called Bas-Languedoc," Frêche wrote in a monthly publication of the region. It then included departments further north, the Ardèche and Haute-Loire—today not part of Languedoc-Roussillon, he noted.

Frêche takes to task those who would lump his region into either the Southwest or the Southeast of France. "The Southwest—that's Toulouse, Bayonne, and Bordeaux! The Southeast—that's Avignon, Marseille, and Nice. Our region, Septimanie, with Nîmes, Montpellier, Narbonne, and Perpignan, that's the South. We are the people of the South of France," he proclaimed.

Roussillon, or French Catalonia, equally fails as a name, because the word only referred to the coastal plains and not the Pyénées, he said, noting that the separation of the Occitans and Catalans came in the 9th and 10th centuries with the gradual dissolution of Charlemagne's empire. Septimanie was the name used in the 5th century by Sidoine Apollinaire, a Roman prefect and poet born in Lyon.

"Septimanie is the old Roman territory of Narbonne," Frêche said, noting that it remained the name of the region in the 8th century as part of the Visigoth Empire in Spain, and not as part of the kingdom of Clovis, king of the Franks in the north. Septimanie was also the only part of modern France ruled by Damascus (A.D. 719–749), he said.

"We, Septimans, are the heirs of the grand civilizations of Antiquity, of the Judeo-Phoenicians, Greeks, Romans, and Arabs," he declared, then quoted the historian Marc Bloch, who noted that the "history of France cannot be reduced to the history of the Île-de France."

AROUND MONTPELLIER

Along the western side of the Mediterranean beaches is another sea—a sea of grapevines dotted with villages, cut by canyons and streams, and divided at times by brush-covered hills. From Perpignan to Nîmes, from the Mediterranean to the Montagne Noir, are vineyards with small orchards of apples, apricots, and olives, and fields of melons or asparagus interspersed.

In many of these lesser cities, you will find comparable accommodations for 30 to 40 percent less. In Narbonne, for instance, the average price of new apartments was €1,665 ($2,248) per square meter in 2003. The difference is the cultural, commercial, and social advantages that larger cities offer. Health care and transportation may be other factors; proximity to an airport or TGV train may be more than just convenient if you travel regularly.

The Corbières is a particularly rugged region, with grapes in the valleys and steep rocky ridges above. Its western end, southeast of Carcassonne is mountainous and forested, stopping the grapevines only temporarily, as they commence again in the Aude River Valley leading north to Carcassonne. In the north, the Corbières gives way to the rolling plain of another wine region, the Minervois, cut by the Canal du Midi as it winds toward Béziers and the sea.

Not many kilometers west of Carcassonne, the land becomes more fertile, and the vineyards yield to fields of grain and sunflowers that continue to Toulouse and beyond. To the north, the Montagne Noir, made up of rugged hills and canyons that get much colder than the plains, are often covered with snow during winter. These form the southeastern edge of the Massif Central. Beyond them is the regional park of Haut Languedoc, sparsely populated even in the summer months.

North of the park and northeast of Montpellier, you climb up to a flat plain about 4,000 feet in elevation. This is the area known as the Larzac plateau—windswept and desolate, perhaps, but the thousands of sheep that pasture here provide the milk for Roquefort cheese, all aged in the caves beneath the tiny village of Roquefort-sur-Soulzon.

North and northwest of Montpellier is the department of Gard, containing the province's second-largest city, Nîmes, and the beautiful Roman aqueduct, Pont du Gard. An especially picturesque town in the Gard is Uzès, once a wealthy duchy and now filled with well-preserved and restored stone buildings.

Nîmes is another city where price increases slowed to little more than inflation in 2004. The mean price of new apartments actually dropped 7 percent to €2,228 ($3,008) per square meter. The mean price of houses sold that year was €172,200 ($232,470). Prime neighborhoods include Castanet and La Cigale on the west side of the city, and d'Espagne near the center. Home prices here start at about €1,800 ($2,430) per square meter.

Rents in Nîmes start around €400 ($540) per month for a three-room apartment in the center of the city, but rise to €800 ($1,080) in the north and northwest parts of the city. Houses rent for €7–14 ($9.45–18.90) per square meter per month, depending on location. The northernmost department in Languedoc is Lozère. It is the least populated department in France, with 73,500 people.

Houses in many of the little villages scattered through Languedoc that were relatively cheap in the '90s have experienced the same kind of increases that city houses have, albeit from a less expensive starting point. Several factors converged to produce this effect: A growing willingness of the French to commute; the retirement of the postwar generation, and Ryanair, whose low-cost flights from London and Brussels have brought literally thousands of new home-buyers into this once remote region.

A unrenovated stone village house that might have been worth the equivalent of €10,000 ($13,500) a decade ago, if a buyer could be found, will likely fetch €100,000 ($135,000) today, and twice that if it has a good exposure, a big terrace, or a small garden. Even then, the purchaser is likely to spend another €10,000–50,000 ($13,500–67,500) upgrading the plumbing, electricity, and decor.

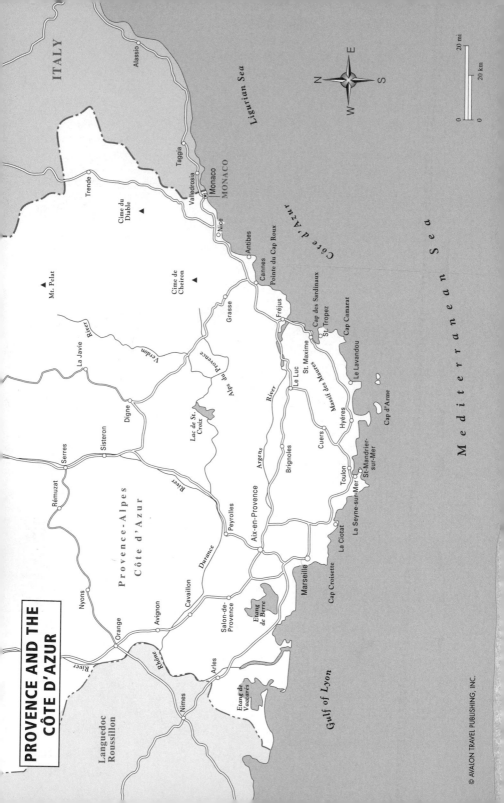

PROVENCE AND THE CÔTE D'AZUR

ITALY

Alassio

Trende

Cime du Diable ▲

Taggia

Valledrosia

Monaco

MONACO

Nice

Antibes

Cannes

Côte d'Azur

Pointe du Cap Roux

Ligurian Sea

▲ Mt. Pelat

Cime de Cheiron ▲

Grasse

Fréjus

Cap des Sardinaux

St. Tropez

Cap Camarat

La Javie

River

Verdun

Alp de Provence

Le Luc

St. Maxime

Massif des Maures

Le Lavandou

Digne

Lac de St. Croix

River

Argens

Cuers

Hyéres

Cap d'Arme

Sisteron

Serres

Rémuzat

River

Durance

Peyrolles

Aix-en-Provence

Brignoles

Toulon

St-Mandrier-sur-Mer

La Seyne-sur-Mer

Mediterranean Sea

Nyons

Orange

Avignon

Cavaillon

Provence-Alpes Côte d'Azur

Salon-de-Provence

Etang de Berre

Marseille

La Ciotat

Cap Croisette

Languedoc Roussillon

River

Rhône

Arles

Nimes

Etang de Vaccarès

Gulf of Lyon

N E S W

20 mi

20 km

0 0

Provence and the Côte d'Azur

Anyone charmed by Peter Mayle's tales of life in Provence will automatically be a candidate for residence in this region. The towns that surround the Parc Régional du Lubéron, such as Cavaillon to the west and Peyrolles-en-Provence to the south, are beautiful places to live.

The Lay of the Land

The modern French region of Provence-Alpes-Côte d'Azur (PACA) contains much more than the Lubéron. The coast from Marseille to Nice includes the wealthy sophistication of Cannes and St. Tropez. Inland, rich agricultural and recreational areas contain villages li

Moustiers-Ste-Marie. The lower Rhône Valley, south of Avignon, has such Roman towns as St-Rémy-en-Provence, full of history and pleasant to visit. From Marseille to Nice stretches France's "gold coast" (not its actual name, but an apt one nonetheless). Part of it is the Riviera, and a much larger portion, the Côte d'Azur, is the Sky Blue Coast. As you would expect in this ritzy region, glamour and the good life don't come cheap.

Nice stands at the eastern edge of the region. About 30 kilometers (18.6 miles) east of this Riviera resort lie Menton, the warmest place in France, and the Italian border, with Monaco nestled in between. West of Nice are the playgrounds of the rich and famous—Antibes, Cannes, St. Tropez. Further west are the great naval base of Toulon and the wines of Bandol, marking the end of the Côte d'Azur. A short distance east of Bandol rise the limestone cliffs called Les Calanques, a plateau separating the great industrial port of Marseille from the rest of this coastline.

As you would expect in this ritzy region, glamour and the good life don't come cheap.

The PACA region consists of six departments and is France's third most populous, with 4.7 million people. Despite the attraction of the weather, it grew only slightly during the 1990s.

PACA is a politically conservative region, with a population of wealthy retired people and military personnel. It is also the stronghold of the xenophobic Front National party, whose demagogic leader, Jean-Marie Le Pen, has made a career of anti-Semitic and anti-immigration views. A split in party ranks and financial scandals seem to have cost the Front National some of its political clout, but it remains influential. It was Le Pen, not the Socialist Prime Minister Lionel Jospin, who garnered enough votes to oppose President Jacques Chirac in the runoff election for the presidency in 2002.

But the region is far more diverse than the reputation the Front National has given it. Cities like Avignon, Aix-en-Provence, Marseille, and Nice are too sophisticated to be limited in such a fashion. For a month every summer, Avignon, not Paris, becomes the theatrical capital of France—and perhaps of Europe—as hundreds of stage productions unfold in a great festival of drama and dance.

North of the coast live thousands of small farmers and artisans—potters, ceramicists, furniture-makers, painters, and sculptors. Industrial Marseille has a large blue-collar base. The influence of Italy next door mixes with hundreds of thousands of tourists from virtually every nation in the world, who throng here each year to create an unforgettable mélange.

Nice

Nice is surely the capital of the Côte d'Azur, as well as the prefecture of the department, with nearly half a million people in its metropolitan area. It is as old as any city in France, but has a modern face. It is also expensive, with property prices that rival Paris, yet it is as far away from Paris as you can get and still be in France. Paris is more than 900 kilometers (558 miles) distant, and Lyon marks the halfway point between the two cities.

Human habitation in Nice dates back 400,000 years, yet for centuries, it was not part of France—from 1388 until Napoleon III won Savoy back for France in 1860. In fact, Genoa and Turin are as close as Marseille to Nice. Much of the city is new. In 1860, Nice had a population of 40,000, and the growth since then has been both industrial and cultural.

Two non-Mediterranean nations have strongly influenced the modern development of Nice. The first is Great Britain. The English had been habitués of the city since the 18th century, when Great Britain was allied with Savoy. The House of Savoy ruled from medieval times until the 19th century. It was an area that ebbed and flowed with the fortunes of war, and at times included what is now Switzerland, southeastern France, Italy's Piedmont, Sicily, and Sardinia. With a strong local colony that has remained constant, the English established what is probably the city's best-known feature, the Promenade des Anglais, the broad avenue fronting the beach of the Baie des Anges (Bay of Angels).

The other is Russia. Beginning in the mid-19th century, wealthy Russian nobles began settling in Nice. They competed to create grand estates. The largest Orthodox cathedral outside of Russia is St. Nicolas in Nice, built by a Russian architect with German brick and Italian tile. Other Orthodox churches include St. Michel-Archange in Cannes and a chapel in Menton.

Housing prices in Nice have risen 10 percent or more annually in recent years, and while future increases seem certain, prices are expected to level off in early 2005. With little new construction and foreigners making up a quarter of the buyers, prices continue in the €2,500–3,500 ($3,375–4,725) range, often determined by views of the sea or neighborhood more than quality of construction. But the choice locations command a much higher price. Houses with a view of the Baie des Anges often go for more than €4,500 ($6,075) per square meter, and studios along the Promenade des Anglais begin at €75,000 ($101,250). On Mont Boron, the hill on the east side of Nice near Monaco, villas with a pool and a view start at €5,500 ($7,425) per square meter. In 2004, a three-room apartment of 72 square meters (774 square feet) with a terrace and parking and an exceptional view all the way to Antibes sold for €505,000 ($681,750).

In less favored neighborhoods, there are more modest apartments in older buildings without elevators, views, and other luxuries in the range of €2,000–2,500 ($2,700–$3,375) per square meter. The lower priced units usually require extensive renovation. However, a new tramway scheduled for operation in 2007 that will run through Nice from west to east is raising prices in some of these neighborhoods. For now, on the east and north sides of the city, you may still find units at €1,400 ($1,890) per square meter.

Rents are also high in Nice. For a studio, €400 ($540) per month is common from September to June, when the apartment tenants are university students; but in the summer, prices triple when the students depart and tourists arrive. For larger units, the price goes up accordingly, rising from about €750 to €1,500 ($1,013–2,025) per month. The world-famous coastal resort towns, such as Cannes and Antibes, are even pricier.

Inland, the department of Alpes Maritimes is far less densely populated, with half of its one million residents in Nice and the surrounding metropolitan area. The *autoroute* parallels the coast, as does highway N7 from the Italian border to Cannes.

North of Nice, perhaps 50 kilometers and an hour's drive into the mountainous Alpes Maritimes to a region known as La Petite Suisse Niçoise—among the little villages around Roquebillière, you can find houses of 100 square meters (1,076 square feet) starting around €80,000 ($108,000), but without a garden or terrace at that price. To the northwest of the region, around Valdeblore, chalets can be found for €150,000–300,000 ($202,500–405,000), depending on terrain and quality. Many people will find these smaller towns near the Mercantour National Park much comfortable for daily life than the crowded, touristy coastal cities.

Cannes-Antibes

Cannes was a small fishing village until the middle of the 19th century. In 1834, England's Lord Brougham was stopped from wintering in Nice by a cholera epidemic. He stayed instead in Cannes, enjoying it so much that he built a home and returned there every winter until his death 34 years later. Other wealthy English followed, along with Russians. In 1939, capitalizing on its reputation as a watering hole for the wealthy, Cannes opened its first film festival on September 1, only to close it two days later for the war. The year after the war, another festival was scheduled, assuring Cannes' place in the world of celebrities and wannabe celebrities. No surprise, then, that housing is expensive here. In the Cannes-Antibes area, prices continue to rise. But there is considerable variation in price, depending on the usual factors of view and location.

In Antibes and the adjacent Juan-les-Pins, prices doubled in the six years prior to 2005. But in 2004, the market hit a wall. Choice villas and apartments took two to four months to sell. Buyers began to negotiate down when they found defects in property. Nonetheless, €1 million ($1.35 million) is the price for even a small villa on Cap d'Antibes, where four-fifths of the residents are foreigners. Apartments here range €4,000–12,000 ($5,400–16,200) per square meter. It is not until you get away from the cape that prices drop into the €2,000–4,000 ($2,700–5,400) per-square-meter range. In Juan-les-Pins, away from the water, prices fall to €2,500–5,000 ($3,375–6,750) per square meter. The average rental in Antibes is about €12 ($16.20) per square meter.

Cannes is more expensive than Antibes. Despite the reputation for youth and glamour that Cannes has earned from its annual film festival, the city is very popular with the elderly: Nearly 40 percent of the population is more than 60 years old. Here, the mean price for an older apartment is €3,300 ($4,455) per square meter, but the most luxurious sell for €6,000–15,000 ($8,100–20,250) per square meter. A minimum price for the rare villa offered for sale in the posh neighborhood of La Californie would be €2 million ($2.7 million). Rentals are equally high. Apartments average €18 ($24.30) per square meter, while houses go for €21 ($28.35) per square meter.

AROUND CANNES
The areas around Cannes are more affordable, while still close to the coast. Leaving Cannes on N85 and driving northwest about 17

kilometers (10.5 miles), you climb into the foothills to Grasse (pop. 42,000), the center of the perfume industry. This picturesque city of steep, narrow streets served as a winter vacation spot for Queen Victoria. The mean house price in 2004 was €300,000 ($405,000), but new apartments were available at €2,500 ($3,375) per square meter. Older units averaged about €1,500 ($2,025) per square meter. Those who like the idea of being near the Côte d'Azur, but prefer a more placid life away from the summer beach throngs, might find this a reasonable compromise.

Those who like the idea of being near the Côte d'Azur, but prefer a more placid life away from the summer beach throngs, might find this a reasonable compromise.

West of Cannes, both N7 and the *autoroute* A8 curve inland while the coastline bows out. N98 is the highway that hugs the coast down to St. Tropez. There, N98 cuts inland, and D559 that heads back to the water for 40 kilometers (25 miles) before rejoining N98 about 17 kilometers (10.5 miles) before that route arrives in Hyères, a town of about 50,000 that is part of the Toulon metropolitan area.

Toulon and its great harbor, two-thirds of the way from Nice to Marseille, was the site of one of Napoleon's early victories. In 1793, as an artillery captain, he seized the city from the royalists who were backed by an English and Spanish fleet. Toulon is much smaller than Nice, with about 180,000 people. The two metropolitan areas also differ in size: Toulon's metro population is about 570,000, while Nice's is more than 900,000. But even without the cultural wealth of Nice, the smaller city nonetheless has a great deal to offer, especially views of the sea. But as the least expensive city in the department of Var, it has seen annual price increases averaging 15 percent since 2001.

Along the coast east of the harbor, what were once small fishing villages, such as Le Mourillon and Cap Brun, have now been engulfed by the city and become prize residential areas. Here, a large apartment with a garage, terrace, and view of the bay runs €4,400 ($5,940) per square meter. Smaller units in less favorable locations will certainly cost less, but not much below €3,000 ($4,050) per square meter.

The average price of houses sold in Toulon in 2003 was €230,000 ($310,500), and you should expect to pay €2,400 ($3,240) or more per square meter. A villa with surrounding garden but no view of the sea approaches €400,000 ($540,000). Away from the coast, prices drop and newer apartments sell for €1,400–2,500 ($1,890–3,375) per square meter, but those at the bottom end of the price scale usually require renovation. North of the city is Mont Faron, with superb views of the harbor. Here, a villa of 110 square meters (1,184 square feet) with a terrace, veranda, garage, and pool will approach €500,000 ($675,000). New apartments of good quality sell for €3,200 ($4,320) per square meter.

Rentals in Toulon vary significantly. Family-sized apartments and homes in the wealthier neighborhoods in the hills with a view of the harbor command up to €1,300 ($1,755) per month. In the old city, comparable accommodations run around €700 ($945) per month.

Between Toulon and Marseille on D559 are two coastal towns worth noting. The first is La Ciotat (pop. 31,000), an industrial town noted for shipbuilding over the centuries, but hit hard by the recession of the 1990s. Along with its modern port, it also has an old fishing port and some very nice beaches. As the port is being rehabilitated, some properties here were considered bargains in 2004, with apartments selling for €1,500–2,200 ($2,025–2,970) per square meter, duplexes for €250,000 ($337,500) and up, and villas from about €400,000 ($540,000). But prices this low are exceptional and will not be easy to find. Rentals run €12–14 ($16.20–18.90) per square meter.

Nine kilometers (5.5 miles) down the road is the smaller of the two towns, Cassis (pop. 8,000) Noted for its excellent white wine, the town has small beaches, but the harbor is filled with pleasure craft. Marseille is 30 kilometers (18.6 miles) away. As in many small coastal villages close to cities, property is expensive, rivaling that of the cities themselves. Plan on spending at least €1 million ($1.35 million) for a house with a view of the sea. Rentals are few and seldom available.

Marseille

"A considerable town," the writer M.F.K. Fisher aptly said of Marseille. It is a big city, the biggest in France after Paris, with nearly half of Paris's population if you compare the actual cities, rather than their greater metropolitan areas. Marseille also feels like a city in a way that Bordeaux, Toulouse, and Montpellier do not, with their much smaller populations and tightly concentrated ancient centers surrounded by modern neighborhoods.

Marseille sprawls, and *autoroutes* snake through it, rather than around; the docks bustle with commerce, and the folds and ridges of the hills on which it is built both shelter and showcase a variety of old neighborhoods: Le Vieux Port, which was *vieux* (old) when Julius Caesar sacked the city in 49 B.C.; the mansions of La Corniche, with their million-euro views; and Le Panier, a popular neighborhood with vestiges of the Greeks, which is now undergoing gentrification.

Marseille does have its unlovely side, too. To the northeast, oil refineries and other industries on the Étang de Berre (a large lagoon adjoining the city) make undesirable neighbors. With its great port, Marseille has all the warts of any large city. As a sprawling, brawling gateway to France and northern Europe for 2,600 years, it has a large immigrant population from North Africa and the Near East. It has been pillaged and conquered, threatened and bombed. It has suffered plagues, no king has ever made it his home, and no religion considers it a shrine. But Marseille has endured and grown, and today is celebrated for its vitality and *joie de vivre*.

The southern part of the city, which rises up from the port like an amphitheater, is the most desirable. This takes in the 7th, 8th, 9th, 11th, and 12th *arrondissements* (districts). Its real estate prices continue to rise. The mean price of a house in Marseille was €2,600 ($3,510) per square meter in 2004, while the mean apartment price of €2,150 ($2,903) per square meter reflected the much greater supply.

The most expensive neighborhoods lie west of the Vieux Port. From near the lighthouse to the entrance of the old port, the Corniche du President J. F. Kennedy runs along the coast for more than five kilometers (3.1 miles), overlooking the sea. Neighborhoods here include Endoume, Bompard, Roucas-Blanc, and Périer. New apartments in this area run €2,500–6,000 ($3,375–8,100) per square meter, depending on location and quality. Older units bring in €2,000–4,500 ($2,700–6,075) per square meter, and a villa of 170 square meters (1,829 square feet) with a small garden costs about €700,000 ($945,000).

Rentals in this area start around €400 ($540) per month for the least expensive two-room apartment, increasing up to €1,500 ($2,025) for a five-room unit.

The fast-paced rise of real estate prices in Marseille has resulted in a spurt of renovation in the areas east and north of the Vieux Port, especially around the train station and city hall. This once slummy area—now three hours from Paris, thanks to the TGV—has taken on new life as buyers have recognized the virtues of the location and spent money to upgrade the buildings.

Some neighborhoods remain questionable. Nonetheless, in the 18th century neighborhood Le Panier (The Basket), you can find newly remodeled units from €2,000 ($2,700) per square meter close to the Vieux Port. A lot of renovation has already taken place in this area, and prices for apartments further from the water and yet to be done up begin much lower. Rents in these neighborhoods begin at €200–300 ($270–405) per month for a studio and increase to €700–1,300 ($945–1,755) for a five-room apartment.

Those looking for suburban bargains might head about 20 kilometers east to Aubagne, birthplace of Marcel Pagnol, Marseille's best-known author. In the west of Aubagne, houses built in the 1970s go for €2,200–2,700 ($2,970–3,645) per square meter, and new construction runs €2,800–3,000 ($3,780–4,050) per square meter. Apartments rent for about €12 ($16.20) per square meter, houses for about €9 ($12.15) per square meter.

If you're seeking a bargain by the seaside, consider Carry-le-Rouet and Sausset-les-Pins, well east of Marseille on the Mediterranean side of the land that encloses the Étang de Berre. Villas here can be found in the €450,000 ($607,500) range, while rentals are in the €14–16 ($18.90–21.60)-per-square-meter range.

Aix-en-Provence

Thirty kilometers (18.6 miles) north of Marseille lies Aix-en-Provence. These two cities and the suburbs between them account for about 1.4 million of the Bouches du Rhône department's 1.8 million people.

Whereas Marseille is a great, worldly city poised at the edge of the sea, the much smaller Aix-en-Provence, despite its academia and sophistication, remains landlocked, one cog in the wheel of a great inland empire. Even so, it's a lively city, full of students, grand mansions, and markets. This was the home of painter Paul Cézanne, who returned here when Paris failed to appreciate his work. In many ways, this is the "capital" of Provence, as it was when it housed the Provençal counts.

By 2004, housing costs seemed to have stabilized, with the mean price of a house in Aix holding steady at €410,000 ($553,000), having increased 23 percent the previous year. The mean price of apartments more than five years old was €2,400 ($3,240) per square meter, while new units averaged €3,250 ($4,388) per square meter. Realtors have predicted that prices will level off at least for the first half of 2005.

Expat Profile: Robert Thorp

Robert Thorp, a 67-year-old former legal editor, and his wife retired permanently to the South of France three years ago. The couple fell in love with the area while on vacation, and now find their friends somewhat envious, their children supportive (despite commenting about parents who "run away from home"), and their siblings "puzzled and perhaps a little resentful that we would want to leave the U.S."

Thorp's biggest shock was learning that there truly are cultural differences between the French and Americans. "Once that was understood," he said, "things got much easier." He explained, "For instance, the French aren't unfriendly, just more formal than we were used to, and their per-ceived unfriendliness was often a reaction to our unintended violation of their cultural rules, such as being too informal too quickly." Continuing difficulty with the language has been and remains his most difficult adjustment.

What Thorp finds most attractive about France is "the attitude that living a good life is more important than making a good living—that there is more to life than higher productivity." His advice to anyone planning on making the move is that they should understand that France *is* the French, and unless you're willing to learn the culture, it's better not to come. "The attitude 'Love France, hate the French' is not a good basis for moving," he said.

In the center of old Aix, where parking places are rare, apartments start about €3,000 ($4,050) per square meter. Moving south, in the area of the hospital and university, prices decline—but only somewhat. You may have to pay approximately the same price, but gain an elevator and/or garage, or perhaps a view onto a garden.

In the most desirable neighborhoods, the very best new buildings begin at more than €4,000 ($5,400) per square meter, while older units start around €3,500 ($4,725) per square meter. Houses start at €2,500 ($3,375) per square meter, ranging upward to €4,500 ($6,075) per square meter.

Rents for studio apartments range €300–525 ($405–709) per month, while bigger four- and five-room places go for €950–2,150 ($1,283–2,903) per month throughout the city.

AROUND AIX-EN-PROVENCE

Aix-en-Provence is the gateway to the region. Many of the towns and villages mentioned below, such as St. Maximin la Ste. Baumes, Brignoles, and Le Luc, are potential places to live. Leaving Aix and going east on the *autoroute* A8 or the smaller N7 that runs alongside it, you are on the overland route to Cannes and Nice. St. Maximin la Ste. Baumes, a town of 10,000 situated in an old lakebed, is 45 kilometers (28 miles) along. Its magnificent basilica was saved from destruction in the revolution by Napoleon's brother Lucien, who turned it into a warehouse and used the organ to play "La Marseillaise" (the French national anthem).

For those seeking a rural or village environment, northeast of St. Maximin are several villages, Chateauvert, Correns, and Entrecasteaux, where you can find 18th century village houses starting from €150,000 ($202,500). North and northeast of St. Maximin, around Barjols and Rian, the pieces drop.

Heading east another 16 kilometers (10 miles) further, you'll come across Brignoles (pop. 12,000), once famous for its plums and the bauxite mined in the nearby hills. Another 25 kilometers (15.5 miles) east is Le Luc, an agricultural town of about 7,000. Grapes and olives are grown throughout the plain of the Var, and Le Luc sits at the intersection of A8 and A57, the *autoroute* that runs down to Toulon and Marseille. From Le Luc, A8 continues east to Fréjus, Cannes, and Nice.

Southwest of Le Luc is the Massif des Maures, rugged countryside with few villages or inhabitants. This oval plateau rises up from the coast and extends from Fréjus to Toulon. The two *autoroutes* border it on the north and west, and the Mediterranean contains it on the south and east. Numerous towns and villages crowd the coast, but there are few far inland in this hilly, difficult terrain.

East of Aix-en-Provence is the Camargue, the flat, watery delta of the Rhône. Much of the Camargue is now a regional park, but the western side is not. In either case, birds and fish abound in the shallow, reedy lagoons. Products includes salt, rice, and reeds, which are harvested for making thatched roofs. The Camargue is a worthy place to visit, rich in natural beauty, but its flat, marshy terrain disqualifies it from consideration as a prime living location.

The dryland parts of the Camargue are France's Wild West, home to cowboys and horses and cattle. The horses are typically white, a particular breed, and the cattle black with curved horns. In times past, they ran wild.

The gateway to the Camargue is Arles. Just above Arles, the Rhône divides into two branches, the Petit Rhône and the Grand Rhône. Arles sits astride the Grand Rhône, the older city on the east side, with its

2,000-year-old arena and the countryside that so delighted Vincent van Gogh. The two forks spread apart, and by the time they reach the open sea some 30 kilometers (18.6 miles) away, they are 60 kilometers (37 miles) apart, creating an immense triangle that is the regional park.

Aix, Arles, and Avignon form another triangle that encloses a charming section of Provence, mostly rolling plains, but with the range of rocky hills called the Apilles more or less in the middle. The Apilles are not high, just peaks of 250 to 400 meters (800 to 1,300 feet), but inspiring in their naked crags.

Arles is the smallest of the three cities, with a population of 55,000. Arles itself is split by the Rhône; the older part on the eastern side is more interesting and intimate than its western sister. Today, Arles is no longer the sleepy Provençal town that Vincent van Gogh knew in 1888, but it remains a city of charm. Here, €2,500 ($3,375) per square meter is the upper end of the market. A renovated house of 130 square meters (1,399 square feet) and a terrace in the old city might sell for €320,000 ($432,000), but sales are few and seldom advertised. In other desirable neighborhoods, the price drops to €1,500–1,900 ($2,025–2,565) per square meter, and a larger home with a garden below costs around €300,000 ($405,000). Rents average €6–9 ($8.10–12.15) per square meter.

About 20 kilometers (12.4 miles) north of Arles, facing each other across the Rhône, are two smaller but no less interesting towns, Tarascon and Beaucaire. Although they lack the cachet of Arles, somewhat lower housing prices may result.

Les Baux, reached from either Arles or Salon-en-Provence via D17 and D5, is absolutely spectacular. The village sits on a massive outcropping of rock nearly a kilometer long and 200 meters wide. All fields below the rock are planted with olives, vineyards, and fruit trees. Jutting more than 100 meters (325 feet) above the surrounding terrain, its sheer bulk dominates the countryside. The beauty is so breathtaking that, in this village of 500 people, there are two Michelin one-star restaurants and one two-star.

Ten kilometers (6.2 miles) north on D5 is St. Rémy-de-Provence, a town of 10,000 about 20 kilometers (12.4 miles) south of Avignon. This modern city stands not far from the ruins of a pre-Roman settlement called Glanum. The remaining ruins include an 18-meter-high mausoleum, baths, and a temple. St. Rémy's tree-lined boulevards and cafés show contemporary life is also alive and well here.

Avignon

Avignon, with nearly 200,000 people in its metropolitan area, is another great Provençal city, and housing prices are lower here than in Aix. The prefecture of the department of the Vaucluse, Avignon is 36 kilometers (22.3 miles) from Arles via N570, and 78 kilometers (48.3 miles) from Aix-en-Provence via N7. Avignon stands beside the Rhône where the Durance River joins it.

In the past, as today, an important factor in building a great, beautiful city was the wealth of the inhabitants. Magnificent buildings, whether mansions or churches, were expensive, and impoverished people could not afford grand constructions. Looking at the Palace of the Popes in Avignon, you can see the wealth that the church fathers had accrued. It covers 15,000 square meters, or nearly four acres. Actually, it is two palaces: Pope Benoit XII razed the old Episcopal palace in 1334 and had a virtual fortress built that is now called Palais Vieux (Old Palace). A mere eight years later, Pope Clément VI found it not to his taste and ordered construction of the Palais Neuf (New Palace). Clement knew how to throw a party. His banquet hall covered a quarter of the area of a football field; the feast marking his election to the papacy required the

© Corel/Velocity Stock

The Pont d'Avignon (Pont St-Bénézet)

The Rustic Best of Provence

Created in 1977, Parc Régional du Lubéron (Luberon Regional Park) covers 165,000 hectares (400,000 acres) enclosing 67 communes. Park headquarters are in Apt, a town of 12,000 in the north-central part of the park. Manosque, near the Durance River on the park's eastern side, is about 40 kilometers (25 miles) from Apt. Cavaillon, near the western edge and famous for its melons, is about 32 kilometers (19.8 miles) away. From north to south, the park's dimension varies greatly, narrowing to 13 kilometers (8 miles) at the western end, bulging to 33 kilometers (20.4 miles) in the middle, and slimming back to 20 kilometers (12.4 miles) on the east.

Within these boundaries lie towns and villages of rustic beauty, such as Gordes and Rousillon, where the colorful ochres—usually warm tones of yellow, rust, and beige—used in Provençal buildings are still quarried. (Ochres are minerals crushed into a powder and used to color the stucco of buildings.) Hiking trails and little roads barely wide enough for one car, let alone two, crisscross the park. The streams that run down its hills empty into the Durance River, which forms the park's southern boundary.

Much of the vegetation in the southern part of the park is *garrigue*, the brush composed of live oak, pine, Scotch broom, and thyme that thrives so well in the rocky, arid soil common to Mediterranean France. In the north, where water is more plentiful, the green forests are oak. The Luberon Mountains, contained within the park, are not high. Le Mourre Nègre, the tallest peak, stands just 1,125 meters (3,750 feet).

Among the prominent features of Luberon Park are the medieval stone villages that cling to the sides and rest on the tops of the hills. As agricultural practices changed in the last century, people

slaughter of 118 cattle, 1,023 sheep, 101 calves, and 914 young goats. The 50,000 tarts baked for the party used 39,980 eggs.

All that medieval wealth has turned into modern splendor. Avignon becomes an immense theater every summer with the best-known festival in France. About 500 plays, dances, concerts, and spectacles of all sorts take place throughout the city during the month of July. Space is at a premium during festival time, whether for sleeping, dining, or presentations. The studio apartments rented to students from September to June for €350 ($473) per month command €350 ($473) per *week* from tourists in the summer. But the festival has made Avignon the most theatrically oriented city in France. Rentals of houses and apartments throughout the city average about €10 ($13.50) per square meter on a long-term basis.

Housing prices in the area between the ramparts of the old city and moved away. Today, that trend has reversed, and many of the stone houses have been restored as second homes. The tourist industry has provided jobs, and the villages are alive again.

Other, newer towns contained within Luberon are also noteworthy. From Avignon, highway N100 runs to the east through the park. But before entering the park, the highway passes through l'Isle sur la Sorgue (pop. 15,000), a town justly famous for its antiques. With more than 150 antique dealers, this city has become a prime stop for anyone interested in old furnishings. Thanks to abundant water, in times past l'Isle sur la Sorgue was an important site for tanning, as well as cloth- and paper-making. Today, many of the old water wheels remain in place, lending to the town's charm.

Apt (pop. 12,000) is by far the largest of the Luberon towns, 34 kilometers (19.8 miles) from l'Isle sur la Sorgue. It is also the liveliest, due to its bustling Saturday market, its site as park headquarters, and its central location. This area is *Le Petit Luberon,* the western part of the park where the peaks of the Luberon Mountains stand less than 2,000 feet.

Southwest of Apt 11 kilometers (6.8 miles) lies Bonnieux (pop. 1,500). It rests between Le Petit and Le Grand Luberon. Rousillon is about the same distance to the northwest, and Gordes a few kilometers further. Saignon, another hill village, is just three kilometers (1.8 miles) southeast of Apt. These are all small villages. With a population of 2,000, Gordes is nearly twice the size of Roussillon.

For a different view of the Luberon, come into the park from Aix, crossing the Durance River on highway D556 into Pertuis. From Pertuis, take D956 six kilometers (3.7 miles) to La Tour d'Aigues, a town of 3,300 that sits amid vines and cherry trees. The waters of the Durance keep things green here. Its 16th-century Italian château now houses a museum of ceramics.

the Rhône have gone up in recent years, doubling in some cases between 1999 and 2004. But sales in the area are relatively few and often not advertised. Nonetheless, when they do occur, many are less than €3,000 ($4,050) per square meter. In the historic neighborhoods, garages are rare, and parking is always difficult.

Prices drop as you move away from the river south and east of the ramparts. Villas of 100 square meters (1,076 square feet) in the hills east of Avignon with a terrace, garage, and garden are generally available for €200,000–300,000 ($270,000–405,000).

AROUND AVIGNON

Northeast of Avignon about 40 kilometers (24.8 miles) lie the slopes of Mont Ventoux, the "giant of Provence," a peak of 1,909 meters

(6,200 feet). It appears so dramatic because it rises as a solitary pyramid, capped with snow in the winter. Several cities around the mountain's western side are worth noting. Traveling from Avignon on D942 for 28 kilometers (17.3 miles), you come to Carpentras (pop. 25,000). This town came into its glory when Pope Clement V decided to settle here before going to Avignon. (The papacy governed Avignon and the surrounding region from 1229 until the revolution.) As church territory, the region became a refuge for Jews when Philip IV expelled them from France.

Twenty-seven kilometers (16.7 miles) north of Carpentras on D938 is Vaison-la-Romaine, a pleasant town of almost 6,000 on the northwest side of Mont Ventoux. An old medieval village occupies the heights, while a modern town stands below, the Ouvèze River dividing the two. The wisdom of the ancients was demonstrated in 1992, when the river flooded and 37 people were killed and 150 homes destroyed. The ancient bridge to the upper village survived, however. Extensive ruins of the Roman city Vasio that once occupied it were also unscathed.

Nyons lies 16 kilometers (9.9 miles) north of Vaison-la-Romaine, with Mont Ventoux to the south. Olives are the big crop here, and groves of trees line the surrounding fields. With a population of 6,300, Nyons is also a center for distillation of lavender and other aromatic plants, as well as home to a truffle market.

The whole region between Avignon and Nyons, on both sides of the Rhône and east to Mont Ventoux, is an excellent area. Roman ruins abound, superb wine comes from towns like Gigondas and Beaumes-de-Venise, and cities like Orange (pop. 26,000) and Valreas (pop. 9,000) provide plenty of commercial activity. Orange is one town where rising real estate prices took a breather in 2004. Apartments now run €1,200–2,000 ($1,620–2,700) per square meter, although the cheaper ones need work. Well-located houses of four or five rooms in excellent condition can be found for €260,000–300,000 ($351,000–405,000). Across the Rhône to the west, more wine is produced in areas such as Tavel. The rugged, sparsely populated Ardèche, with its lengthy river canyons, provides excellent summer recreation.

NORMANDY AND BRITTANY

ENGLAND

BELGIUM

Plymouth

Weymouth

Bournemouth

Eastbourne

Isle of Wight

English Channel

ATLANTIC OCEAN

Calais

Dunkerque

Cambrai

Abbeville

Amiens

Roye

Laon

Nord-Pas-De-Calais

Picardie

Champagne-Ardennes

Sézanne

Burgundy

Île-de-France

Paris

Versailles

Orléans

Vierzon

Centre

Seine River

Les Andelys

Louviers

Rouen

Dieppe

Haute-Normandie

Fécamp

Le Havre

Trouville

Deauville

Honfleur

Bernay

Évreux

Blois

Tours

Loire River

Seine Bay

Caen

Bayeux

Ponte de Barfleur

Cap de la Hague

Cherbourg

Carentan

Basse-Normandie

Avranches

St. Malo

Bay of Mont St. Michel

Gulf of St. Malo

Channel Islands (U.K.)

Argentan

Collines du Normandie

Collines du Maine

Mayenne

Alençon

Le Mans

Angers

Nantes

Pays de la Loire

Rennes

Brittany (Bretagne)

Monts de Bretagne

Guingamp

Morlaix

Monts d'Arrée

Bay of Lannion

Brest

Quimper

Ponte de Penmarch

Lorient

Landes de Lanvaux

Vannes

Bay of Quiberon

Belle-Île

50 mi

50 km

0

N E S W

© AVALON TRAVEL PUBLISHING, INC.

© Corel/Fotosearch; © Gloria Donohoe

Normandy and Brittany

Adjacent regions close to the U.K., Normandy and Brittany are quite different in character. Normandy attracts day-tripping Parisians and British emigrants alike with its rural charm, fresh seafood, and storied past. Brittany is wilder and woollier, at least politically. Its historical push for independence and its conflicts with the central government, both royal and revolutionary, are echoed today in resurgent Breton nationalism, fed by linguistic differences.

The Lay of the Land

The Seine Valley effectively divides Normandy into an upper and a lower region. Haute-Normandie includes the departments of Seine-Maritime and Eure, separated by the Île-de-France. Basse-Normandie encompasses the departments of Calvados, Manche, and Orne.

With the exceptions of Rouen, Le Havre, and Caen, there are no large cities in Normandy, and agriculture remains its primary industry. The lush fields of the Seine Valley and the smaller farms of Basse-Normandie continue to produce grain, produce, and cheese just as they have for centuries. Further south and west, the land becomes hillier and more forested, cut by numerous rivers flowing into the sea. The small towns of these valleys often contain both delightful, unpretentious places and luxurious manors. Basse-Normandie has made a valiant effort in recent years to attract new industry and create jobs by offering subsidies and other enticements to investors.

The beaches remain prime tourist attractions, with hundreds of thousands trekking annually to Mont St-Michel. But the wooded parklands offer equally pleasant recreation. Both because of historical ties and proximity to the U.K., Normandy has long been a favorite destination on the Continent for the British. The opening of the tunnel under the English Channel has only increased this interest. While there are relatively few Americans, there are lots of English-speakers among the population.

Driving northeast from Paris on A-13, the Autoroute de Normandie, you parallel the Seine. The terrain changes slowly, flattening out as you move toward the English Channel. This is the land the Norsemen saw as they came up the rivers in the 8th and 9th centuries: well-forested along the Seine, green, fertile fields, and villages and monasteries rich and ripe for the taking.

And take they did, laying waste to the land and returning to the sea with their treasure. But not all of them left for good. Many Norsemen returned as conquerors, rather than raiders, and settled down. They came to dominate the region, giving it their own name. Within two centuries, they were firmly in control of the countryside and recognized by France, with whom they were allied. In 1066, the ruler of Normandy, William the Bastard, crossed the Channel to become William the Conqueror.

Normandy

Normandy's greatest attraction may be its proximity to both Paris and London, combined with its good beaches, good food, and opportunities for an upper-middle-class lifestyle. Pleasure boats, both sail and motor, abound, as do golf courses and horse farms. Orchards and grazing cattle make every country lane a pastoral scene.

The coastal towns north of Le Havre, such as Fécamp, and those to the southwest, from Honfleur to Houlgate, offer boating, bathing, and easy access to the U.K. The villages and towns along the Seine River are nearly within commuting distance of Paris and Rouen. The inland river valleys between Mont St-Michel on the Atlantic and the Eure on the eastern side are dotted with villages not far from market towns like Alençon, Argentan, Dreux, and Vimoutiers. These villages offer a pastoral lifestyle and the recreational possibilities of the Parc Naturel Régional de Normandie.

Orchards and grazing cattle make every country lane a pastoral scene.

For generations, when Parisians went to the beach, they invariably headed northwest, following the Seine River to the English Channel and the coast of Normandy. The beach resorts, fishing villages, and ports all along the coast, with their tall, half-timbered houses, offered a welcome change from city life. With modern transportation, the journey is scarcely longer than the average American commute, and many people whose work is on the fringes of the Paris area are taking advantage of that fact, positioning themselves at some midway point between the metropolis and the beach.

HAUTE-NORMANDIE

Just across the line from Île-de-France, on the right bank of the Seine, is Giverny, where Claude Monet lived and worked from 1883 until his death in 1926. Today, the Fondation Monet maintains his house and gardens, a very popular day trip from Paris. The beauty of the spot makes it easy to see where the founder of the Impressionist movement drew his inspiration. In fact, many of his paintings were scenes from this very garden.

Across the road from Monet's house and garden is the Museum of American Art, showing the paintings of the many Americans who flocked to Giverny beginning in 1880 to work in the same milieu as Monet himself. The larger town two kilometers northeast is Vernon, on the crossroads of N15 and D181.

Although both departments cover approximately the same area, the Eure has a little less than half the population of Seine-Maritime—less

Le Trou Normand

Normandy gained its reputation as a gourmand's paradise long before *la nouvelle cuisine*. *Leger* (light) is not the word that comes to mind when you look at a typical menu. Reliance on local farms emphasizes butter, cream, beef, and eggs. Aside from today's health concerns, the greatest challenge these meals present is finishing them.

To help overcome the problem, Normans call upon another local product and add a special course in the middle of meal. The pause that refreshes the Norman appetite calls for a neat shot of Calvados, the brandy distilled from apple cider. When looking for good Calvados, remember that age is important—12–15 years minimum, and preferably 20–40.

The common belief is that the alcohol cuts grease; a more scientific answer is that it dilates the wall of the stomach, easing the overstuffed feeling. But whatever the explanation, the result is renewed vigor when the cheese course is brought out.

Cheeses are one of the glories of Normandy: Livarot, Pont l'Eveque, Neufchatel, Brillat-Savarin, and, probably the best known of all,

Camembert. Camembert is actually a modern cheese, unlike many others in France, such as Roquefort and cantal. Its creator was Marie Harel, a Norman cheesemaker who hid a priest from Brie fleeing the revolutionary Terror in 1790. In gratitude, he showed her how to make Brie, and she turned around and invented Camembert. When a rail line from Alençon to Paris opened in 1863, one of her descendants introduced Napoleon III to the cheese. He liked it, and it immediately gained a reputation.

But packaging proved a problem, as the ripe cheese tended to run on its straw pallet. When someone hit upon the round box of thin wood, the famous cheese could go anywhere. During World War I, it became a symbol of France, because it was part of every French soldier's rations.

Ironically, the popularity of Camembert worked against Normandy, because for decades, the cheese could be made anywhere and still be called Camembert. However, in 1993, the best of Camembert was granted an Appelation d'Origine Contrôlée (AOC; verification of origin). Today, Camembert so labeled must come from Normandy.

than 100 persons per square kilometer. The northern part of the department—along the Seine leading from Paris, approaching Rouen, and continuing west to the coast—contains more than half of the population of 550,000.

But the proximity of Eure to Paris has helped it to grow in the last decade. Not only have city folk come seeking second homes, but many of them have arrived intending to become full-time residents. As the metropolitan area of Paris has expanded, so have employment opportunities outside the city, allowing people to live further away without needing to commute all the way into Paris.

On the right bank of the Seine, the town of Les Andelys, population 8,500, offers a panoramic view of the valley. Paris is 100 kilometers (62 miles) away, and Rouen is 40 kilometers (25 miles) away. The town is called Les Andelys, in the plural, because there are actually two of them—Petit and Grand. Commanding the river is Château Gaillard, built in 1196 by Richard the Lionhearted, king of England and duke of Normandy, to bar the French from Rouen. It was in the old market of Rouen where the English, after a five-month trial, burned 19-year-old Joan of Arc at the stake.

On the right bank of the Seine is Giverny, where Claude Monet lived and worked from 1883 until his death in 1926. . . The beauty of the spot makes it easy to see where the founder of the Impressionist movement drew his inspiration.

On the right bank, about 25 kilometers (15 miles) west of Les Andelys and 100 kilometers (62 miles) from Paris, is Louviers, a town heavily damaged in 1940 but very well-restored. Some 35 kilometers (21 miles) south of Rouen, Louviers stands at the head of the Eure Valley. Highway D836 parallels the river, leading to Pacy-sur-Eure and then changing its number to D16 when it crosses the border into the Eure-et-Loir department, then continuing to Dreux.

Due south of Louviers is Evreux, prefecture of the Eure and, with 60,000 people, its largest city. South to Dreux and west to Bernay is thinly populated countryside with small villages. Much of this area is the Pays d'Ouche, a wooded plateau difficult to farm. The town Conches-en-Ouches lies about 20 kilometers (12 miles) southwest of Evreux on D830. This is an area into which those leaving Paris have been moving. Nonetheless, in 2004, it was still possible to find a small house with garden to renovate beginning at about €150,000 ($202,500). Something more splendid starts at €300,000 ($405,000).

The two principal cities of Haute-Normandie, Rouen and Le Havre, both lie in the department of Seine-Maritime. Le Havre, France's greatest port on the Atlantic, was heavily bombed during World War II. It was rebuilt according the plans of Auguste Perret, known as "the magician of reinforced concrete." The population is 250,000. Heavily industrialized, most of the city lacks the charm of yesteryear. Nonetheless, apartments in Perret's buildings often rent for more then the €8–9 ($10.80–12.15) per square meter price of the average Le Havre apartment.

Rouen, the capital of the region and a university city, is the smaller of the two, but sits in the center of a much larger metropolitan area. The population of Rouen itself is 107,000, but when the 33 communes surrounding it are included, the count reaches 400,000. However, the area as a whole has shown little growth in the past decade.

As a result, prices have not skyrocketed the way they have in Paris and some southern cities. The most desirable neighborhoods are on the right bank or near the cathedral just across the river, where quality apartments sell in the €2,000–2,400 ($2,700–3,240) per square meter range. However, in other parts of the city center, prices remain below €2,000 ($2,700) per square meter, although €1,800 ($2,430) per square meter is probably a minimum, unless extensive renovation is required.

It is still possible to buy a house in Rouen with a small garden for less than €150,000 ($202,500); the mean price in 2004 was €128,000 ($172,800). About five kilometers north of the old city, in Mont-Saint-Aignan, the mean price was €201,500 ($272,0258). Rents are also correspondingly lower here, with 40-square-meter (430 square feet) apartments in the best neighborhoods generally available for about €13 ($17.55) per square meter. In other sectors, the average rent is about €8 ($10.80) per square meter. Studios and smaller units range €6–12 ($8.10–16.20) per square meter per month.

In areas on the right bank near the Jardin des Plantes and between Grand-Quevilly and Sotteville, prices are less than in the heart of the city. Here one might pay €1,200–1,500 ($1,620–2,025) per square meter, much less if renovation is required. Houses in Sotteville may be found below €100,000 ($135,000). In general, houses in the immediate suburbs remain equal in price to those in Rouen, but face a lesser tax burden, and are therefore cheaper to own—€115,000–200,000 ($115,250–270,000), depending on size and appointments.

The coast and two great fishing ports lie about 65 kilometers northwest and north of Rouen. Fécamp, once the capital of the French cod fishing industry, is the smaller of the two, with a population of 21,000. Cod fishing as practiced in the past has all but died here, and pleasure craft have replaced many fishing boats in the harbor. Such industry as has survived deals now with drying filleted cod into flat, stiff pieces to be reconstituted by French housewives and made into *brandade* (salt cod purée).

Dieppe, where 7,000 Allied troops staged a reconnaissance raid in 1942 testing German defenses, is the beach closest to Paris. Two hours from the city, it remains an active commercial fishing port, as well as a harbor for pleasure boats and a transfer point for fruit from Africa. It is also the port where the Newhaven car ferry docks. Old houses of four and five stories, their ground floors devoted to commerce, line the waterside.

All of this maritime activity merely continues a long tradition in Dieppe, population 36,000. Some claim that a Dieppois, Jean Cousin, sailed along the coast of Brazil and set foot in the New World four years before Christopher Columbus.

The estuary that forms Dieppe's harbor is created by the Béthune and Varenne Rivers. Near their confluence, about eight kilometers (five miles) southeast of Dieppe on highway D1, lies the village of Arques, population 2,500. It was from here that William sailed to conquer England. Southeast beyond the village the land rises, covered by the Forêt d'Eawy.

BASSE-NORMANDIE

Along the western border of the Eure lie the three departments of Basse-Normandie: Calvados, Manche, and Orne. This is the area that most Americans think of as Normandy. Here are the beaches of D-Day—Omaha and Utah. In France, June 6, 1944 is called Jour-J and the invasion itself is le Débarquement. Here also are the resorts of Deauville and Trouville, so often seen in films, and one of the most photographed sites in France, Mont St-Michel.

Today, except for monuments and memories, much of the land has reverted to its centuries-old pursuits: beef, cream, cheese, butter, apples, cider, and calvados, the brandy distilled from apple cider.

This region's overall population of 1.44 million—less than in 1826—grew very little in the past decade, but some consider that a victory, because numbers had been declining significantly. A large percentage of the population is rural—60 percent in the Orne and Manche, and 30 percent in Calvados—and its decline marked the movement from farms to cities outside the region. Some credit for this decline goes to the strenuous efforts that have been made to bring light industry to the region. There is some foreign investment—Japanese, American, and other European corporations have opened parts distribution warehouses and research facilities in Normandy. Besides location, the lure includes subsidies and tax breaks for the investors, and a lower average wage than in Paris. But most of the businesses in the region are French. Besides producing food products, the area is home to a number of small

Mickey Mouse

William the Conqueror's military success marked the beginning of centuries of warfare and rivalry between France and England. The warfare ended after six centuries, but the rivalry continues today. Oddly, it was the conquest of England that eventually gave the world Mickey Mouse. This is how it came about.

Two knights who sailed with William were Hugues d'Isigny and his son Robert, both from the Norman village of Isigny near the mouth of the Vire, the river that separates Omaha and Utah beaches. The two knights stayed in England, and gradually, the family name was Anglicized—first to Disgny, then to Disney

In the 17th century, some of the family emigrated to Ireland, and in 1834, to North America. In 1901, a fourth son was born to Elias Disney in Chicago. His parents named him Walter.

factories and shops fabricating metal and plastic parts for machinery and consumer appliances.

Caen, the largest city in the region, has a metropolitan population of about 200,000, with slightly more than half that number in the city itself. Located on the Orne River about 12 kilometers (7.5 miles) south of the coast, Caen was heavily damaged during the war, living up to the origin of its name: "field of combat." Less than two hours from Paris, Caen is served by 15 trains daily. A canal built alongside the river in the 19th century has given the city easy access to the sea, and there are docks for pleasure boats.

Caen home prices have risen since 1999, and the better properties have not gone begging. Demand continues to outstrip supply. New apartments in the center of the city run up to €2,500 ($3,375) per square meter, but the average is closer to €2,300 ($3,105) per square meter. Older units average about €1,300 ($1,755) per square meter, with renovated ones in the €1,500–2,000 ($2,025–2,700) range, while the older ones begin at about €1,000 ($1,350) per square meter. The average price of houses was €170,000 ($229,500) in 2004.

The market for houses is on the outskirts and the suburbs, where a home on a golf course will cost up to €200,000 ($270,000). On the right bank of the river, small houses of about 100 square meters (1,076 square feet), built in the 1920s and little changed since the war, sell from about €150,000 ($202,500). In the better neighborhoods of St. Paul and Haie-Vigné, the price for the same size property rises to nearly €200,000 ($270,000).

Those who wish to rent in the center city should expect to pay €300–425 ($405–574) per month for studios, and €400–600 ($540–810) per month for two rooms. Larger apartments begin at €650 ($878) and rise to €1,300 ($1,755). Houses in the city rent for up to €14 ($18.90) per square meter, while those on the edge are available for about €10 ($13.50) per square meter.

At the mouth of the Seine is the charming town of Honfleur, population 8,500. A few kilometers across the estuary from Le Havre, it could not be more different from that industrial center. Honfleur's tiny harbor is surrounded by narrow, colorful buildings five to seven stories high; shops and restaurants line the quai. The elegant new suspension bridge, Pont de Normandie, unites these two faces of France. Following D513 along the coast from Honfleur 18 kilometers (16 miles), you come to at Trouville and Deauville, both popular resort towns.

Samuel de Champlain sailed from Honfleur to found Québec in 1608. Today, just as in 1608, fishing boats dock there to unload the fish and fresh shellfish that is part of the Norman diet. Alongside the port is the church of Ste. Catherine and its bell tower, constructed all of wood. The church was built at the end of the Hundred Years' War. The shipyard workers, all skilled axmen and carpenters, wanted to thank God for the departure of the English. Deciding not to wait for architects and masons, the raised the church themselves with the material they knew best.

In Honfleur, older apartments averaged €1,500 ($2,025) per square meter in 2004. In Trouville, the average was €2,000 ($2,700), while in Deauville, it jumped to €2,500 ($3,375).

At Cabourg, D513 turns inland to Caen, about 25 kilometers (22.5 miles) away. The coast from the mouth of the Orne west are the beaches of D-Day: Sword, Juno, Gold, Omaha, and Utah. D514 hugs the shoreline until the shore itself turns north to form the Cotentin Peninsula.

This area is called Presqu'île du Cotentin because of the low, marshy region that makes it nearly an island and separates it from the rest of Normandy. Cherbourg and its magnificent port lie at its tip. Cherbourg is the second largest metropolitan area in Basse-Normandie, with a population of about 95,000.

To the east of Cherbourg about 27 kilometers (24 miles) on D901 is one of France's prettiest villages, the little fishing port of Barfleur, population 600. Barfleur faces back toward France, somewhat protected from the Atlantic by the width of the peninsula. Its houses are made from granite. The massive church of St. Nicolas dominates the town.

In the opposite direction, about 20 kilometers (12 miles) west of Cherbourg, is La Hague, site of a nuclear waste dump and nuclear fuel reprocessing center. Environmentalists have repeatedly complained that the site is unsafe, a charge vigorously denied by authorities. La Hague was closed a few years ago after its capacity was reached.

The department of Manche, population 485,000, covers the Cotentin Peninsula. At its southwest corner, where the north-south shoreline makes a right angle turn to the west, is Mont St-Michel. This magnificent structure and site draws hundreds of thousands of visitors every year. A mass of granite swept by the tides, the abbey and church that surmount it, and the old 15th- and 16th-century houses at its base, truly deserve the title of "Patrimoine Mondial" (World Heritage Site) bestowed by UNESCO in 1979.

East of Mont-St-Michel Bay, you'll pass through both the department and town of Mayenne on N12. Although Mayenne, population 13,500, belongs in the Pays de la Loire region, this northern part is much closer in spirit to Normandy than to the Loire Valley. The 110 kilometers (68 miles) almost due north from Mayenne to Caen on D23 and D962 passes through the regional park of Normandy and towns and villages such as Domfront, population 4,400, where pears rather than apples are grown and made into cider.

Another village, Clécy, population 1,200, enjoys a central location in what is called Suisse Normandie. The area earned this somewhat fanciful appellation because its massive rock formations, which reach heights of 120 meters (390 feet), recall the Swiss landscape. Clécy is also the center of a great recreational area for hiking in the Orne River valley.

Some 60 kilometers (54 miles) east of Mayenne is Alençon, prefecture of the Orne, third department of Basse-Normandie. Alençon (pop. 30,000), considered the "capital" of the Basse-Normandie région (Caen being the actual capital), is famous for its lace. When lace and lace-making became very popular in France in the mid-17th century, the government feared that too much money was going out of the country to purchase it. Colbert, King Louis XIV's right-hand man, decided to build a lace-making factory in Alençon and forbid imports of foreign lace. The effort was successful, and the beauty and quality of Alençon lace remain legendary.

Alençon also boasts a Notre-Dame Cathedral of its own, built during the English occupation of the Hundred Years' War and well worth visiting. An ornate sculpture by Jean Lemoine adorns the facade, while the windows were created by master craftsmen in the 1500s.

William the Bastard

Argentan is 60 kilometers from Caen via N158. Almost midway between the two cities is Falaise, population 8,000, the birthplace of William the Conqueror. The story of his birth explains why, until 1066, he was called William the Bastard.

William's father was Robert the Magnificent, duke of Normandy, who as a 17-year-old youth became enamored of Arlette, the beautiful daughter of a rich tanner. Robert first spied Arlette as he returned from hunting one day; she was at the *lavoir* (wash house), her skirts pulled up around her thighs as she did the family wash.

From then on, Robert watched from the castle every day as Arlette went to the fountain for water. Robert, who is suspected of having poisoned his brother Richard III in order to succeed him as duke of Normandy, asked Arlette's father if he could take her as a concubine. Her father was enraged, but finally said Arlette could decide for herself. She agreed, but refused to go secretly to the castle. Instead, she waited for the drawbridge to be lowered and entered proudly on horseback. The chronicles of the era reported that "when the time that Nature required had passed, Arlette had a son named William."

About 45 kilometers (28 miles) north of Alençon via N138 and N158 is Argentan (pop. 16,500), the subprefecture of the Orne. Like Alençon, it is a forested area and was noted for its lace. A particular style, quite different from that of Alençon, was developed by Benedictine nuns in the abbey here.

For reference, Rouen lies 150 kilometers (93 miles) north of Alençon via N138; Paris, 200 kilometers (124 miles) via N12; and Chartres, 120 kilometers (75 miles).

Brittany

The town on the east side of the bay of Mont St-Michel is Avranches, population 8,700. From here south on A84, it is 80 kilometers (50 miles) to Rennes, capital and largest city of Bretagne (Brittany). The region grew by 3.8 percent in the 1990s to a population of 2.9 million. Much of the growth took place in Rennes—with a population of 375,000 in the metropolitan area and 900,000 in the whole department—and boosted property prices in the area by approximately 10 percent.

The choicest properties in the center of the city approach €3,000

($4,050) per square meter. However, older apartments in the neighborhoods of Oberthur, Mail, Mabilais, and St. Martin—not far from the center—are less expensive: €1,500–2,000 ($2,025–2,700) per square meter when renovation is required, or starting at about €2,200 ($2,970) per square meter in good condition. Monthly rents here run from about a low of €330 ($446) for a studio and about €900–1,300 ($1,215–1,755) for a house.

The best houses in the center of the city, especially those near the park called Jardin du Thabor cost €450,000–1.5 million ($607,500–2.3 million). Similar prices prevail in the suburbs of Cesson-Sévigné and St. Grégoire. However, many others not far away, especially across the river may be found in the €200,000–300,000 ($270,000–405,000) range. Further into the surrounding area, in villages such as Montauban and Betton, prices drop into the €150,000 ($202,500) range.

Much the same can be said for apartments. Away from the old city and south of the river, older apartments sell beginning about €1,000 ($1,350) per square meter, while new ones are available for less than €2,100 ($2,835) per square meter. Rents are also less: Studios begin about €270 ($365) per month, while houses cost €650–950 ($878–1,283) per month. However, the price of rentals in Rennes is deceptive, because demand is much greater than supply. No matter what the average tenant is paying, if there are few vacancies, your choices are limited.

The city of Rennes has a number of urban redevelopment projects in the works, including both residential and commercial space. As these come to fruition in 2005 and beyond, they could affect housing prices, and prospective buyers would be wise to take them into account.

Once outside of the Rennes area, you can find houses throughout much of the Brittany countryside and in small villages for lower prices. In the 250 kilometers between Rennes and Brest, with the exception of the coast itself, start with a budget of €100,000 ($135,000). In some locations, this will buy little more than a ruin and land, although in many cases, the price of the ruin will be less than €100,000 ($135,000), and the balance can become part of the cost of renovation.

Up the ante to €200,000 ($270,000), and the renovation is complete. In the €300,000–500,000 ($405,000–675,000) range, expect to find large, well-restored granite and slate houses on a minimum of 2,000 square meters (21,520 square feet) of land.

Burgundy and the Rhône Valley

Dominating the eastern-central part of the country, these two regions offer many advantages to those who would move to France. Burgundy and the Rhône Valley are two very different areas bound by the common thread of wine.

The Lay of the Land

The Rhône Valley is really an extension of modern-day Provence. Its architecture, agriculture, terrain, and climate are similar. But despite its lively tourist industry, the Rhône region lacks the seacoast that attracts so many people to the South of France. All the better if you prefer to avoid the crowds! The "capital" of the Rhône region is Lyon, an urban French jewel rivaled only by Paris.

Burgundy lacks a great city like Lyon, but takes no back seat in the charm department. The wealth of the past is easily visible in its well-maintained villages, replete with stone houses capped by slate roofs. The region's proximity to Paris has made it, like Normandy, a favorite weekend retreat for city-dwellers. And, of course, it is famous for its wines. Although those produced in the area south from Dijon to Beaujolais are the best known, grapes grow throughout the region, as do cherries and other fruits.

Outdoor enthusiasts will also delight in the fact that both Burgundy and the Rhône Valley afford easy access to eastern ski slopes all winter long.

The thickly forested hills of Morvan regional park provide both winter and summer recreation. Outdoors enthusiasts will also delight in the fact that both Burgundy and the Rhône Valley afford easy access to eastern ski slopes all winter long.

Burgundy

Living in Burgundy places you about halfway between Paris and Lyon; you can easily keep a lunch date in either city. But it also places you near the unmatched ski slopes of the Alps. For the ski addict with a partner who prefers to live in the lowlands, this may be an ideal compromise.

If the slopes attract you, a good place to live might be a village near one of the eastern towns closer to Lyon, such as Louhans or Macon. If Paris is the draw, finding a place near Semur-en-Auxois would be ideal. You would be close to the Autoroute A-6, the TGV stop at Montbard, and both Dijon and Beaune. Semur-en-Auxios, like Autun to the south and Avallon to the west, lies close to the Parc Naturel Régional du Morvan, with great recreational possibilities. All this comes at a price, though: Count on paying at least €100,000 ($135,000) for even the smallest restored house with land in this region.

The vineyards of Chablis, even closer to Paris, are famous in their own right, with cherry orchards, cattle farms and picturesque villages set in small river valleys.

Transportation is the key to Burgundy and the upper Rhône Valley. The TGV trains and the *autoroutes* have brought Paris and Lyon close together, but both are contained within a narrow corridor. For those who need or want the access they provide, there is a premium to pay. For those who are willing to keep their distance, the countryside has much to offer.

In centuries past, Burgundy was a powerhouse that could threaten the French throne. It was Burgundy that aided the English and bargained away Joan of Arc. "Happy as a duke in Burgundy" is a common saying. Even today, the modern region covers 31,000 square kilometers (19,220 square miles), more than all of Belgium, a land that the Burgundians once ruled.

More recently, the region exists in a precarious state, with its the southwestern parts hemorrhaging population. Cities like Mâcon, Chalon/Saône, and Le Creusot lost 8 to 10 percent of their population during the 1990s. Some see the region as little more than a corridor between Paris and Lyon; wealthy Parisians see it as a perfect weekend getaway—an hour or two from home. Its famous vineyards still produce their liquid gold, but face stiff competition worldwide and lack the possibility to expand production of their best wines.

Burgundy's problem—or, some would say, its saving grace—is that it largely remains a pastoral land in an industrial world. Its rich agricultural tradition continues to provide some of the finest meat (Charolais beef, Bresse chickens), cheese *(langres, époisses, charouce),* and wine (chablis, chambertin) in the world. But, as the monks who have inhabited its many beautiful monasteries would say, "Man does not live by bread alone." He (or she) also needs the employment that the region cannot provide at this time.

Burgundy's two poles are Paris and Lyon, the region stretched on an axis between the two. The northwest corner of one of its four departments, Yonne, borders the Île-de-France. Sens, one of that department's major cities, lies about 115 kilometers (71 miles) from Paris via A5, and 55 kilometers (34 miles) from Fontainebleu on N6. Once a powerful Roman city, Sens today is a pleasant subprefecture of 27,000 people. Its walls have come down; in their stead lies boulevards and promenades.

At the other end, in the southernmost department of Saône-et-Loire, is Mâcon. The prefecture of the department, Mâcon (pop. 37,000) sits on the banks of the Saône River and gives its name to the southern part of Burgundy's wine region. Here begins the transition to the Midi. The climate moderates from northern Burgundy, and the rounded Roman roof tiles appear. Lyon is 75 kilometers (46 miles) further south via A6.

Between these two extremes rolls some very pleasant countryside. Leave Paris on A5, but cross over to N6 at Sens. Following N6 along the Yonne River brings you to Auxerre (pop. 40,000), the prefecture of the department of Yonne. Twenty kilometers (12 miles) east is Chablis, the village of 2,500 that bestowed its name on some of the greatest white wine in the world. Besides grapes, cherry orchards abound along the banks of the Yonne.

Continuing on N6 for a little more than 50 kilometers (31 miles), you arrive in Avallon (pop. 8,600). From a granite promontory, Avallon overlooks the valley of the Cousin River. Remnants of a fortified city, its stone houses with their turrets and chimneys remain an impressive sight. Avallon is the northern gateway to the Parc Régional du Morvan. This mountainous region of granite cliffs, abundant rainfall, and thick forests reaches heights of 900 meters (2,925 feet).

Outside Avallon, pick up A6 (Autoroute du Soleil) to Pouilly-en-Auxois, a village of 1,300 situated at the mouth of the 3,333-meter (10,832 feet) tunnel through which the Burgundy canal passes in transferring from the Rhône basin to that of the Seine. Here, you take highway A38 to go 43 kilometers (27 miles) to Dijon.

DIJON AND ENVIRONS

Unlike most cities in the region, Dijon, Burgundy's largest with more than a quarter of a million people in the metropolitan area, gained population in the 1990s. Its growth was based not only on employment opportunities, but also on the beauty of the city itself. Dijon is known as France's greenest city, because of the number of parks and open spaces.

Moreover, Dijon has done much to conserve its rich heritage from the dukes of Burgundy and French kings. It remains a city of substantial buildings and numerous churches. Some 30,000 students study at its university. Boats and barges dock here, serving Burgundy's excellent network of canals. And it remains the prime place to begin a tour of the region's vineyards. All of this means that housing prices are going up—perhaps not so quickly as in some cities, but rising nonetheless.

Luxury apartments in new buildings in the center of the city sell for about €2,300 ($3,105) per square meter, while older units of good quality go for about €2,100 ($2,835) per square meter. For the few large apartments of 100 square meters (1,076 square feet), prices can reach €250,000 ($337,500). Throughout the city, studios are likely to be the most expensive per square meter, reflecting both the student population and desire of people to maintain a small pied-à-terre in the region.

In the southern part of Dijon, near Colombière park, a calm neighborhood with lots of greenery, prices range €1,800–2,000 ($2,430–2,700) per square meter for older renovated units, and up to €2,300 ($3,105) per square meter for quality units overlooking the park itself.

Less expensive is the neighborhood of Bourroches, near the periphery of the city's southwest sector. Here, apartments built in the 1960s range €700–1,600 ($945–2,160) per square meter, with the lowest prices for units greatly in need of renovation.

Taking the entire metropolitan area into consideration, apartment rentals average €10.50 per square meter ($14.18), and houses €9.30 ($12.56) per square meter. The average selling price per square meter of houses is €1,800 ($2,430), but there is great disparity between older houses on

Dijon is known as France's greenest city because of the number of parks and open spaces.

the east side of the city and those in the suburban hills of Talant and Fontaine.

From Dijon south to Lyon and beyond, the road N74 leads past one famous vineyard and commune after another. Fixin, Gevrey-Chambertin, Morey-St. Denis, Chambolle Musigny, Vougeot, Vosne-Romanée, Nuits-St. Georges—and that's only the first 16 kilometers (10 miles)! Beaune, another 22 kilometers (13.5 miles) south, is a city devoted to wine—wine grapes, wine-making, wine-selling, and wine-tasting—with a little food and a lot of tourism thrown in for good measure. The 22,000 Beaunois have much to celebrate. Their medieval walled city, once the home of the dukes of Burgundy, is impeccably maintained.

In historic Beaune, houses for sale are rare indeed, as in all of these villages famous for their top-quality wines. However, you will find four- and five-room apartments, with about 100 to 110 square meters (1,076 to 1,184 square feet) of space, for about €1,400–1,800 ($1,890–2,430) per square meter. New apartments average €2,000 ($2,700) per square meter, and rents average €7.40 ($9.99).

Outside the historic walls of Beaune, in the more modern sections of the city, housing prices are comparable to those of Dijon. Properties drop in price as you move out into the rural areas to the northwest, southwest, and southeast of the city, well beyond the fabulous vineyards of the Côte d'Or that run south from Beaune.

Although *autoroute* A6 leads south toward Lyon, many roads cross it or branch off to the east and west. Fifty kilometers (34 miles) west of Beaune on D973 is Autun (pop. 18,000), another Gallo-Roman city. The wooded, rolling landscape serves as a gateway to the southern part of the Morvan park, and the TGV stops about 25 kilometers (15.5 miles) away in Le Creusot.

The land west of A6, south from Beaune, is La Bresse Bourguignonne, a *pays* (region) ignored by the nobility in the past and therefore virtually unknown today, standing in the shadow of La Bresse Savoyarde to the south. The more southerly region benefits from its connection to Marguerite of Austria and its capital, Bourg-en-Bresse.

It is in La Bresse Bourguignonne, in Louhans, 37 kilometers (23 miles) southeast of Chalon-sur-Saône on highway N78, where the poultry-producing brotherhood of *poulardiers de Bresse* has its headquarters. But Louhans (pop. 6,140) has more to offer than chicken farms. It is a market town with a street bordered by arcades—the upper floors of the buildings jutting out over the sidewalk and supported by pillars—that may be the longest such street in France.

Chalon-sur-Saône, 70 kilometers (43 miles) south of Dijon, marks the point where *autoroute* A6 begins to follow the course of the river that will join the Rhône at Lyon. A metropolitan area of 77,000, the city lost 8 percent of its population in the 1990s, although the department of Saône-et-Loire lost just 0.3 percent.

These economic difficulties kept the price of housing low. House prices averaged about €1,100 ($1,485) per square meter in 2004 and rented for about €4.50 ($6.08) per square meter. Even new apartments averaged less than €1,500 ($2,025) per square meter, and older ones, whether renovated or not, averaged about €1,000 ($1,350) per square meter. Apartment rents averaged €6 ($8.10) per square meter.

Despite its problems, the city offers streets of beautifully restored old houses with half-timbered facades. Its semiannual market for fur and leather dates back to the Middle Ages, as does the city's *carnaval.* Nearby villages, such as Givry and Mercurey, produce excellent wines.

Twenty kilometers (12 miles) south on A6 is Tournus, the town that stands at the north end of Le Mâconnais, the southernmost wine region of Burgundy. With 6,500 people, Tournus was once an important abbey and today retains some narrow streets and old-stone charm.

Mâcon lies 35 kilometers (22 miles) from Tournus. With just over 34,000 people, it is another Burgundian city that lost population in the 1990s. Nonetheless, it remains a lively, pleasant place, with wine keeping the economy stable, if not growing. Northwest of Mâcon about 20 kilometers (12 miles) via N79 is Cluny, one of the largest and most famous of the medieval Benedictine monasteries.

The average selling price per square meter of houses in Mâcon is €1,350 ($1,823), and rentals go for about €5 ($6.75) per square meter. New apartments go for an average of €1,600 ($2,160) per square meter, and old ones for about €1,100 ($1,485) per square meter. Apartments rent for about €7 ($9.45) per square meter.

Just south of Mâcon are the communes of Pouilly and Fuissé, which give their names jointly to another well-known white Burgundy wine, Pouilly-Fuissé. It is here that the region ends. Across the line in the region of Rhône-Alpes and the department of Rhône, the wine becomes Beaujolais.

Rhône Valley

Historically, the Rhône Valley was an extension of Rome's Provence—known as La Provincia. Roman legions followed the Rhône north from Marseille, and Caesar followed the same river down from the Alps

© Corel/Fotosearch

flowering peach trees in the Rhône Valley

A Question of Taste

Italy gave us the fork, and France taught us what to put on it. On that point, many of us would agree. But how the French nation came to dominate cuisine and cooking in the West remains one of the great, unsolved puzzles of the world. It's not as if no one else had a chance. Everyone must eat, and most of the basic ingredients—meat, poultry, and common vegetables and fruits—have been widely available for centuries, at least in temperate zones. Yet the French have accepted that the transformation of these raw materials into palatable meals is an art form, and they honor it as such.

The French, as a society and a culture, care about taste in a way the United States and many other nations simply do not. As individuals, Americans are just as capable farmers and chefs as the French. But as a nation, we produce tomatoes that have shelf life, not taste—our supermarkets install special lighting to make them appear red. Our daily bread is balloon bread, produced by a few large corporations and sold all over the country. Instead of trying to improve the taste of our food, we cheapen it.

In contrast, the French revel in the taste of things and the subtle differences that individual cooks, or a few kilometers, can make. Is the wine of Paulliac superior to the wine of Margaux? Is the wine of Gevrey-Chambertin better than that of Nuits-St. Georges? These are serious questions for the French, not in the sense of "mine's better than yours," but in the sense of "Can you taste the difference and articulate the reasons for your opinion?" Nuance delights the French.

Contrary to the American notion of "French food," the cuisine of France is very diverse, both in its ingredients and in tastes favored in particular regions. One area uses butter, another olive oil, and

when he came to conquer Gaul. With that conquest, attention shifted northward. The confluence of the Rhône and Saône, not far from the Roman garrison already established at Vienne, proved a natural site; a Roman colony was founded there in 43 B.C. By 27 B.C., it became their capital. In 2,000 years, Gaul has never lost its status as a commercial and intellectual center.

The Rhône River geographically dominates the valley. Most of the region's towns line its banks. But you need only venture a few kilometers east or west of the Rhône to find smaller, quieter villages, populated by French people as they have been for centuries. You won't find a lot of Americans living here year-round, although many own second homes in the region. Today, the Rhône-Alpes is France's second most populous region, with 5.6 million people. Of that total, 1.2 million live in the Lyon metropolitan area.

still another goose fat. In the Alps, cheeses are made from cow's milk, in the Pyrénées sheep's milk, and in Provence goat's milk. Oysters from the Mediterranean are prepared differently than oysters from the Atlantic; cider from Normandy tastes different than cider from Brittany; sausage from Lyon is not the same as sausage from Toulouse.

Further increasing the culinary possibilities, each *pays* (region) has its own version of the regional specialty. Toulouse, Castelnaudary, and Carcassonne—cities only about 30 miles apart—each lay claim to the truly authentic *cassoulet* (a casserole of beans, herbs, and meat). Should a cook use lamb or duck or both? I'll have another helping of each before I answer that, thank you.

The French take *le bon goût* (good taste) so seriously, they educate their children in it. French parents send their kids to tasting classes the way Americans send theirs to tennis camps. And what's

a sophisticated palate for but to savor a meal? A two-hour break at noon is still common, and people go home for lunch on workdays, or they dine out if they live too far away. The big family meal at noon on Sunday remains a tradition.

The taste and quality of good are still matters of great concern to the French as a society; they not only honor the best producers and the best chefs, they seek them out. Michelin's *Guide Rouge,* the celebrated listing of the best in French restaurant cuisine, marked its 100th year in 2000. Every year, a great agricultural show is held in Paris. And every year, both the president and the prime minister attend.

As in any art form, decadence and indulgence occasionally overtake refinement. But always, taste— the taste of the fresh ingredients, the true flavors of the food—reasserts itself, and a new wave crashes onto the old shore. So long as good taste is paramount, the quality of the cuisine will not flag.

LYON

Few would dispute Lyon's title as France's second city. Like Paris, it is so huge and diverse that it seems unfair to single out particular aspects for praise or note. Commerce and trade, the reasons for which Rome founded the city, continue as the city's lifeblood. It was wine and silk in the past, and today it is wine and pharmaceuticals; art and architecture and music and sculpture are just as important today as they were yesterday; transportation and banking—Lyon has it all.

Including cuisine. Lyon is home to famous chef Paul Bocuse, whose family have been restaurateurs here since 1765. It's not just the presence of Bocuse, however, that makes Lyon a capital of gastronomy. It's the whole region—in fact, Bocuse's restaurant is located in a suburb of Lyon. There are the Troisgros brothers in Roanne, 88 kilometers (55 miles) to the west, and La Pyramide in Vienne, 30 kilometers (18.5

miles) to the south, a restaurant where Bocuse himself once plied his trade. A number of excellent Lyon restaurants are named "Mère so-and-so," recognizing Mother as the original chef, or at least the inspiration for so much of the cuisine.

As for the wine, the French like to say that Lyon is watered by three rivers: the Rhône, the Saône, and the Beaujolais. While the Saône follows a wiggly course due south, paralleled by A6, the Beaujolais river of wine comes from the vine-covered hills west of that *autoroute*. The area's vineyards go under the general name of Côtes du Rhône, but the better ones have developed numerous individual appellations, such as Condrieu, Hermitage, and Cornas.

While Lyon stands as a gateway to Provence and the Midi, it also lies at the intersection of routes to Italy, Switzerland, Germany, and Spain, as well as Paris, Brussels, and London. Thus, the population, produce, commerce, and ideas of Western Europe have passed through Lyon over the centuries in one direction or another. These influences, coupled with the city's contemporary verve, account for Lyon's cosmopolitan flavor.

There is a range of housing in Lyon, at a range of prices. The most sought-after areas include neighborhoods like Brotteaux, the old depot near La Tête d'Or park, where prices recently increased 15 percent. Just across the Rhône in La Croix-Rousse and La Presqu'île, the narrow strip of land in the heart of the city between the two rivers just before they join, some new buildings are going for €4,000 ($5,400) per square meter. This price indicates the disparity between costs in the fashionable heart of a great city and the more residential neighborhoods. The average, even in excellent areas, is well below the €3,000 ($4,050) per-square-meter range.

Houses originally occupied by working-class families, running about 90 square meters (968 square feet) with a courtyard of about 30 square meters, sell for €1,700–2,000 ($2,295–2,700) per square meter, even in prized neighborhoods.

Not far south of Brotteaux, where Paul Bocuse runs a *brasserie* (restaurant with bar), around the Part Dieu train station, apartments 20 to 40 years old sold for €1,300–1,600 ($1,755–2,160) per square meter.

In Vieux Lyon, many of the buildings date back to the 15th century, and small apartments average around €1,800 ($2,430) per square meter but go up to €3,000 ($4,050) for well-restored or larger units of 100 square meters (1,076 square feet).

Neighborhoods further to the east in the third and eighth *arrondissements* have gained in popularity, including Monplaisir and Montchat. In Montchat, which has something of a village atmosphere, there are small houses of about 85 square meters (914 square feet) built in the early 1900s that sell for about €250,000 ($337,500), while large houses of 250 square meters (2,690 square feet) sell for about €850,000 ($1.15 million). Here, older apartments sell for €1,500–2,500 ($2,025–3,375) per square meter, while new ones sell for €2,400–3,000 ($3,240–4,050) per square meter.

Rents in Lyon, like the sale prices of property, vary considerably depending on condition and location, from the €300 ($405) studio to the €3,000 ($4,050), 150-square-meter (1,614 square feet) luxury apartment.

Toward the periphery of Lyon, the suburbs on the east side are favored because of easier access to the city. A tramline connects Villeurbanne to Part Dieu. Here, a 70-square-meter (752-square-foot) house with a garden of 150 square meters (1614 square feet) sells for €164,000 ($221,400); and a larger one of 120 square meters (1,291 square feet) with a garden of 423 square meters (4,551 square feet) sells for €236,000 ($318,600).

ST. ETIENNE AND ENVIRONS

Some 60 kilometers (37 miles) southwest of Lyon via A47 is St. Etienne. It might have become the dominant city in the region, had it not been overshadowed by Lyon. With more than 300,000 people in the metropolitan area, St. Etienne has been a city of heavy industry for centuries. It was once known as Armeville, because it exploited nearby coal deposits to become the arms manufacturing center of France, even before the advent of firearms.

In 1746, the royal arms manufacturer was established here; less than a century later, the first French railroad was built here. Manufacturing continues, but times and technology change. In the last decade, the city of St. Etienne lost 10 percent of its population; the department of Loire, of which St. Etienne serves as prefecture, lost 2.4 percent.

Nonetheless, a recent housing boom has not bypassed St. Etienne in the past four years. New apartments in the center of town range about €2,000–2,700 ($2,700–3,645) per square meter, and even the oldest unrenovated ones begin at about €700 ($945) per square meter. Prices vary little in the suburbs, where golf is a popular sport.

However, once you go far into the countryside—90 kilometers (60 miles) north to Roanne, for example—prices drop considerably. Here, the best new large apartments peak at €1,700 ($2,295) per square meter, and houses average €1,000 ($1,350) per square meter. Rents are also much less, with houses averaging €4.40 ($5.94) per square meter, and apartments €5.40 ($7.29) per square meter.

Between St. Etienne and the Rhône lies Parc Régional du Pilat (Pilat Regional Park), a varied landscape. Along the river are vines; just below Vienne lie the famous Côte Rôtie, the "roasted slopes," the oldest vineyards in the valley of the Rhône, and Condrieu, a village of 3,200 famous for the *viognier* grape. Inland, the hills are pastureland and in the uplands, forests of beech and pine.

As the Rhône continues south from Lyon, the highway number alongside the river changes from A6 to A7. The *autoroute* stays on the east side of the river after Vienne, sometimes moving kilometers away to avoid the congestion and the valuable vineyards close to the river.

On the west side of the river is the department of Ardèche, lightly populated with 286,000 people. Near Tournon-sur-Rhône, a town of 9,500 on the east side of the river, and Tain-l'Hermitage, with 5,000 people on the opposite shore, the vineyards widen considerably on both sides of the river.

On the east side of the river is the department of Drôme, taking its name from the river that flows out of the Alps and into the Rhône about 25 kilometers (15.5 miles) south of Valence. Valence, a metropolitan area of about 110,000, is 18 kilometers (11 miles) south of Tournus-Tain and prefecture of the department. The vineyards stop at the Drôme for about 20 kilometers (12 miles), appearing again near Montelimar, where they become Côtes du Rhône, Coteaux du Tricastin, Côtes du Ventoux, and other regions of Provence.

On the west side of the Rhône are the gorges of the Ardèche River, a wonderful recreational area. The river enters the Rhône between Montelimar and Orange. The east side of the river is the plain of Tricastin, filled with vineyards and olive and fruit trees—in direct contrast with the nuclear installations along the banks.

Daily Life

Making the Move

You've finally made the big decision: You're moving to France. Now it's time to roll up your sleeves and get to work. There are many details to take care of before you leave, such as applying for your long-stay visa and deciding what to take with you. Once you arrive in France, you will need to register with the local authorities and set about the process of settling into your new home.

Red Tape

VISAS AND IMMIGRATION

Vacationing Americans need no formal visa to enter France. It is assumed—and legally required—that your stay will last no more than three months. But if you plan to remain in France longer, you are required to obtain a long-stay visa. Once in France, you'll take this visa to your local prefecture to obtain a *carte de séjour* (residency permit). The permit is good for one year and must then be renewed.

After arriving in France, you may register with the consular section of the U.S. Embassy in Paris. There is no requirement for this, but forms are provided, and information about your whereabouts will not be released unless you give permission. Passport details will be noted, making it easier for you to apply for a replacement if your passport is lost or stolen.

Some visas require you to appear at the local prefecture within a specified period of time, as noted above. These include students staying more than six months, who are required to get a student residency card, and those who entered France with an employment contract. People with a long-stay visa must renew it annually at their prefecture.

Long-Stay Visas

Applying for a long-stay visa will be your introduction to French bureaucracy. Fortunately, the regulations are clear and the application process has been streamlined in recent years. If your situation fits comfortably within the rules, chances are everything will go quickly and smoothly. Difficulties generally only arise when applicants seek exemptions or exceptions.

At the time of your initial application, you must be in the United States, and you are not permitted to go to France until the visa is granted. The process, which can take up to two months, may be done by mail, a convenience for those living far from a French consulate (see the *Contacts* of the *Resources* chapter for the office nearest you). The application form itself may be downloaded from the consulate website. Children's applications should be filed with their parents'.

The first requirement for a long-stay visa is a passport valid for at least three months beyond the expiration date of the visa. (U.S. passports may be renewed in France via mail to the American Embassy.) Your application packet must include your passport and three photocopies of it, four copies of the application form, and four passport photos. Your passport will be returned to you with your visa in it.

In the application packet, you must also submit proof of financial independence during your stay amounting to at least $1,800 per month. This can include pensions, verified independent income, rent from a house, etc. An alternative to proof of financial independence would be a notarized declaration from someone in France, such as a family member, that he or she will provide for your support and can prove sufficient income to accomplish that.

The application also requires an address where you will stay in France. If you plan to stay with family or friends, submit a letter from them verifying this arrangement, along with a certified copy of their identification. Otherwise, include a copy of the deed or lease, or the promise of one, on your residence in France.

You'll need to include three additional documents. If you are married and both you and your spouse are applying for long-stay visas, you must submit a copy of your marriage license. Proof of health insurance is also required. Finally, France won't grant you a long-stay visa if you are a criminal; obtain a certification from your local police department that you're not a convicted felon and there are no warrants out for your arrest.

Applying for a long-stay visa will be your introduction to French bureaucracy.

Lastly, include a stamped return envelope for your documents, plus a money order or certified check for about $100 (the exact amount varies with the exchange rate; French authorities will tell you the current fee). Again, once you have started the application process for the long-stay visa, do not plan to go to France until it has been issued. It will not be sent to you in France.

If you have been hired to work in France, there are additional steps to take. First, submit a draft of your work contract to the appropriate French consulate. At the same time, your employer in France—even if it is simply a branch of a U.S. firm—will need to apply to the local employment office for recruitment of a foreign worker. The application is processed and sent to the Office des Migrations Internationales(OMI), which then instructs the consulate in the United States to order you to have a physical examination. Then the visa is granted. For senior corporate managers, approval by the employment office is only a formality; for other employees, justification is necessary, and approval may depend on the particular skills of the individual and the rate of unemployment in France.

After arriving in France, take your visa and medical exam results to the prefecture of the department in which you live to obtain your *carte de séjour.*

Student Visas and Special Cases

There are other long-stay visas that apply in particular cases. These include the student visa, the au pair visa, and one for researchers.

Students staying between three and six months should get a temporary long-stay visa. This is valid for multiple entries into France and does not require the holder to obtain a residency permit. Students staying over six months, however, get a visa that allows them to enter France one time and is valid for three months. During that three-month period, the student must register at the prefecture to obtain a student residency card.

The first type of student visa is much less complicated than a long-stay visa, and it is possible to have it issued in one day if you apply in person. To apply, submit the original plus one copy of the following documents:

- A passport valid for at least for three months beyond the last day of stay in France.
- The application form, filled out completely and signed.
- The *pré-inscription* (letter of admission) to the school or university you'll be attending in France; note that this institution must be accredited by the Ministry of Education.
- Proof of sufficient funds while you reside in France, such as a notarized letter from your parents stating that they will provide you with at least $600 per month in France, a letter from your bank stating that you have a sufficient balance to withdraw at least $600 per month, or a letter from the institution you will be attending granting you a fellowship or a student loan. (This $600 amount could be reduced if you can present a letter from a host verifying that your lodging will be free of charge.)
- Two recent passport-size photographs.

If a student plans to stay less than six months, proof of health insurance is also required with the application. Students under 28 years old who stay longer than six months will be required to join the French student health-care system. Students older than 28 must provide their own insurance.

Students under 18 years old will also need notarized authorization from both parents indicating who will be guardian of the minor and a statement from the host family in France accepting responsibility. Processing this application will take at least six weeks.

Graduate students granted teaching assistantships at a French university follow a similar procedure, but will need the original and one copy of their letter of appointment and their acceptance by the Cultural Department of the French Embassy. Professors and researchers should submit all the necessary documents from the institute where they will work, along with three copies.

Applicants for an au pair visa must be between 17 and 30 years old. They should submit two long-stay visa application forms, two photographs, the original and one copy of their au pair contract (obtained from the family in France for which the au pair will be working), and a letter of admission from a language school.

Moving with Children

If you're relocating the whole family, consider how does each member feels about the move. If you have school-age children, especially teenagers, how will they adapt? Just because you like the idea of living in a foreign country or a small village doesn't mean your children will. Then again, they might view it as the adventure of a lifetime.

Children will have to be registered for school, of course. Placement is up to school authorities, but parents will take an interest in their children's education. While teachers consider themselves the masters of their classrooms, they also need to know something about their pupils. They may have suggestions about ways parents can help their children become acclimated to a different language, culture, and educational system.

Being involved in your child's schooling is also a good way to meet people. Just before noon and again at 5 P.M., parents gather outside the school to wait for their children and chat with each other. In small villages, there may only be a primary school. Pupils will be bussed to *college* (middle school) and *lycée* (high school) in larger towns.

Enrolling your child in sports is a good way to help them make friends, but it's important to know that sports are separate from education in France. (The Sorbonne doesn't have a tennis or a soccer team.) Athletics are organized through the community, rather than the schools.

Soccer, volleyball, judo, tennis, and basketball are all popular for both girls and boys. Players are organized by age into leagues. Another popular game is handball. It is played on a court the size of a basketball or tennis court with a hockey-like goal and a ball the size of a big grapefruit. Teams of players dribble and pass the ball, as in basketball, and score when they throw the ball into the goal. Once the player with the ball faces the opposing goalie, defense is almost impossible—but it's great exercise running up and down the court.

Rugby, the closest the French come to American football, is popular in the south and usually an exciting game to watch, as well as to play. While golf courses remain few and far between, tennis courts and community swimming pools are quite common, even in small villages.

Moving with Pets

Pets are often just as hard to leave behind as friends and family. Fortunately, you won't need to say goodbye to your pet if you move to France. France recognizes that a properly vaccinated animal is no threat to public health. You may bring up to five dogs and/or cats into France, but all must be at least three months old or traveling with their mother.

To enter France, every animal must be identified by a microchip (standard ISO 11784/11785) or a tattoo. If the microchip's standard is different, you must bring your own scanner in order to read the microchip. You'll need to present a valid rabies vaccination certificate dated at least 30 days before the move (30 days is the incubation period for

Although France is a pet-friendly country, some parks don't allow pets—even on leashes.

© Rebecca Freed

rabies), but not longer than one year before. The second requirement is a letter stating the good health of the animal from a veterinarian certified by the U.S. Department of Agriculture within the past four months. However, it is recommended that the examination take place only a few days before departure. Only small amounts of pet food, one or two kilos, may be imported—don't worry, France sells plenty of chow. Birds, snakes, and rodents may also be brought into France with a veterinarian's certificate.

The logistics of transporting your animals should be carefully planned. Check with the airline you're using about its fees and requirements for cages. The cost generally runs $150–125, although some airlines charge extra for large dogs. Contrary to popular belief, tranquilizing is generally not necessary, and may even be harmful to dogs, especially if they wind up sitting somewhere hot for hours. Tranquilized dogs cannot pant—that's how canines "sweat"—and therefore cannot cool themselves. Be sure to consult your vet at home before traveling with your pet to get specific recommendations based on the animal's temperament and medical history.

What to Take

HOUSEHOLD GOODS
Depending on the circumstances of your move, you may want to leave many of your belongings behind. Intercontinental moves of household goods can be very expensive. For instance, Infinity Moving of Bronx, N.Y., estimates a cost of $1,600 to send 150 cubic feet of your prepacked goods from San Francisco to a dock in Paris; that's $10 per cubic foot, with a 150-cubic foot minimum plus $100 for customs documentation.

Larger shipments are less expensive by the cubic foot; a shipment of 420 cubic feet would go for $6 per cubic foot, or $2,520 plus $100 for documentation. If you want the shipment delivered to your residence, the price increases to $9 per cubic foot. These prices are not prohibitive for large quantities of furnishings, but unless you have an employer who is paying for the move, it is better to sell much of what you have before leaving the United States.

Be warned, however, this will not be easy. One of the most miserable days of my life was the day we held a garage sale before moving to France. I watched books and pictures and pieces of furniture that were like old friends go out the door, knowing I'd never see them again. But, unless the objects are quite valuable or irreplaceable, it just does not make economic sense to cart them to France.

Besides, compensation for your sacrifice awaits you when you arrive at your new home. For many people, one of the great delights of their initial years in France is traveling about looking for antiques and *brocante*, the French term for used household goods. You can find great deals on grand old armoires, buffets, beds, and tables, and searching

Taking Care of Business

Making a transcontinental move is never easy. Even if you are fully prepared psychologically, remembering the myriad details and juggling schedules can be physically exhausting. One unexpected crisis can touch off an entire sequence of problems.

That's why some people seek professional help. They decide to handle things back in the U.S., where they are on familiar ground, by hiring assistance in France. To some extent, it's a gamble: Will someone else's arrangements prove satisfying to you, or will it turn out to be a waste of time, and possibly money? Your selection of the relocation service will be the most significant factor in its success. If the move is being handled by your employer, who has hired the service, you probably have some leverage; your dissatisfaction may cost the service futures jobs.

On the other hand, if you are doing this on your own, ask for references and talk to the person who will be helping you before you sign on. Do you feel at ease with him or her? Are you confident that your wishes will be respected? Also, listen carefully to what the person tells you. Not all of your expectations may be realistic.

These services vary. One in the Paris region, called Home Safari, specializes in finding homes for clients. They conduct the search for a monthly fee of €350 ($507.50), then take 2 percent of the purchase price if they find the home you buy. This can be quite a time-saver.

The European Relocation Association is one group of such agencies, and Syndicat National des Professionels de la Relocation et de la Mobilité is a strictly French group.

In the Toulouse region, Mary Rix-Miller's Expat Assistance offers personalized relocation services, including Interpralink, a bilingual telephone service that may be all you need. Interpralink provides clients with the telephone number of a bilingual assistant available around the clock in case of emergencies. When the client encounters a situation that calls for more French than he or she has, the client dials Interpralink and explains the problem, then hands the phone to the French person. After those two have conversed, the client gets back on the phone for an English explanation. Interpralink costs €50 ($72.50) for one month or €180 ($261) for six months.

for them is a wonderful way to explore the countryside, as well as get a glimpse into French life and customs.

Linens are one category of furnishings that should be considered for the move, however. Although U.S. mattresses are measured in inches and French ones in centimeters, American sheets will fit either. A standard double bed in France is 140 centimeters wide and 190 centimeters long—that's 56 inches by 76 inches—very close to the 54-inch by 76-inch U.S. double mattress. The same goes for other standard bed sizes: single, queen, and king.

For many people, one of the great delights of their initial years in France is traveling about looking for antiques and brocante, the French term for used household goods.

The bed itself, along with box spring and mattress, is a debatable item because of the expense of transporting its bulk and weight. These items are certainly available in France, as is a spring system not seen in the U.S. called *lattes*. Lattes are pieces of wood about, 25-inch thick and two or three inches wide that span the width of a single bed or half of a double bed. In their simplest form, they bow slightly upward and are set in a steel frame. A foam or latex mattress sits on top, and the bow in the *lattes* provides the spring beneath the mattress. In more complex and expensive forms, each end of the *latte* is set on a rubber mount to give it exceptional flexibility. Even the simple ones are quite comfortable. The density of the foam mattress also determines the comfort. At least 15 centimeters of thick foam of a minimum density of 28 kilograms per cubic meter should be used in such mattresses, and 18 centimeters of 35-kg density foam is certainly preferable. Pillows in France are sometimes square, rather than rectangular, but the familiar rectangular ones are widely available to fit American pillowcases.

Finally, if you were considering bringing your gun, think twice. France's gun laws are much stricter than those in the United States. For starters, you will need to obtain a permit from *la douane* (customs) to import arms and ammunition. Automatic weapons are banned entirely.

APPLIANCES AND COMPUTERS

What about those appliances you paid so much for over the years? Sorry—forget them. Your washing machine, refrigerator, stereo, mixer, and power tools won't work in France, which uses a 220-volt electrical system. Your computer, may operate on 220 volts, but your printer may not.

If you do bring your computer and other technological gadgets with you, be aware that you are likely to encounter one of the largely unspoken rules of the multinational corporation: Just because the manufacturer sells an item in 169 different countries does not mean it's guaranteed in all of them. Have a problem with that modem you bought at CompUSA for your Mac? The help line is a 1-800 number—not a free call from France, and you won't get a replacement sent to you outside the United States, either. Buy a Japanese camera in the United States, and just try to get it repaired under warranty in France. The list goes on. You're a U.S. citizen who purchased a product guaranteed for one or two years, then up and moved to another country nine months later. Tough luck. Sales are worldwide; guarantees are not.

Fortunately, computer prices have come down considerably in France in recent years; the main difference now between French and American prices is the 19.6 percent sales tax you must pay in France. In February 2005, you could buy a basic Dell desktop for less than €400 ($540). What's more, purchasing a computer in France assures you the guarantee is valid, and you establish a relationship with someone who can later help you when those inevitable computer problems crop up.

Another alternative to purchasing an entirely new system is to go laptop. One word of caution, however: Get a name brand, or you'll have difficulty finding parts. Toshiba, Hewlett-Packard, and Dell are all familiar names in France. You will be able to buy hard drives, batteries and power supplies, modems, and even CPUs for them.

Software is a different story. By all means, bring it along. It's expensive to replace, and besides, the "Help" files in French software are in French, remember? If you leave your computer behind, consider bringing at least the hard drive loaded with your software to be installed in a new machine.

One other computer consideration is the keyboard. The French keyboard is different—annoyingly different, for those of us trained on the QWERTY version. The advantage is that French keyboards include all the accented characters; the disadvantage is that many of the characters, particularly A, W, and M, are not in their familiar places. (Note that the previous sentence has 21 *A*s in it—that's 21 times you might have typed Q and had to erase it.) Fortunately, keyboards are light. Bring yours along.

Language and Education

Yes, French is difficult—but you'd better learn it, anyway. For most of us, learning to speak the language is the most difficult hurdle to cross in living in France. Undoubtedly, sharing a common language is the primary reason immigrants in any country tend to stick together to form national and ethnic colonies. Some might argue that the Chinatowns, barrios, and ghettos of the United States are the result of prejudice, but the United States is replete with examples of Scandinavians, Germans, and other Northern Europeans who are also clustered together and maintain a national identity based on language.

However natural this may be, it presents both a problem and a dilemma for immigrants. The problem is that there are no great clusters of Americans living in France because relatively few have immigrated here. Moreover, much of the food originally identified as American, such as Coca-Cola, ketchup, hamburgers, breakfast cereal, and even peanut butter, is widely available—another reason why an American *quartier* (quarter) never formed.

No matter where you settle, you will find yourself surrounded by French-speakers. Radio and television are in French; many English-language movies are dubbed. While satellite dishes and the Internet make it possible to receive foreign broadcasts, you're not going to get much news about France from other countries.

If you don't learn French, you'll miss out on more than you'll ever know.

But then you should ask yourself this key question: Why move to France if you only want to surround yourself with Anglophones? The perhaps apocryphal tale of the Englishman who retired to France is a case in point. He moved to France, only to tell friends back home he was pleased with everything except that there were "too many bloody Frogs about." The story is greeted by many French people with knowing nods.

Language is a powerful force in everyone's life; it shapes our acquisition of knowledge and our relationships with others. That most of us learn a single language as children and then spend years perfecting our skill in it seems to guarantee that a second language won't be a snap to master. American brains are conditioned to one language, and the natural learning paths available when we were children become narrow as we age. Wordplay, most humor, emotional responses, and attitudes are all conveyed by language; far more than just gathering information is at stake. Moreover, even if you comprehend the gist of what is being said, understanding nuance requires greater depth. If you don't learn French, you'll miss out on more than you'll ever know.

Learning the Language

The English-only speaker can get by in much of France today, especially in large cities and areas where tourists are common. Many middle-aged and younger French people with at least a high school education have studied English for years, along with a third language. As part of their education, they may also have spent time in England or the United States studying English, and many popular songs today have English lyrics. (Movies and television, however, are virtually all dubbed into French.)

Parlez-Vous l'Occitan?

For a country that considers itself ethnically homogenous, France is surprisingly diverse linguistically. As in most European countries, many people speak two or more languages: the native tongue and, often, English. But in France, the picture becomes even more complex. For starters, the native tongue is not necessarily French for some. Sure, dialects of *le français* exist, but many French people also speak a distinctly different language within the borders of the country they share. The main ones are listed below.

L'alsacien: Germanic in origin, this language is spoken by about a million people, principally in Alsace and Lorraine.

Le basque: Basque speakers in France, most of them located in the southwest part of the Pyrénées-Atlantique department, number about 100,000. Across the border in Spain, both Basque and Spanish are recognized as official languages, a status denied to Basque in France. However, Basque is taught in some schools around Bayonne and in the heavily Basque areas of Labourd, Soule, and Basse-Navarre.

Le breton: Spoken by some 800,000 people, Breton is taught not only in the western part of Brit-tany, but also outside the region in Paris, Rennes, and the department of Loire-Atlantique.

Le catalan: The 260,000 French Catalan speakers are found mostly throughout the department of Pyrénées-Orientales. Like Basque, Catalan enjoys strong support across the border in Spain.

Le corse: Corsican, long considered an Italian dialect, today has about 85,000 speakers. The only minority language to enjoy legal support in France, it is taught in Aix-en-Provence, Marseilles, Nice, and Paris.

L'occitan: Of all the minority tongues of France, Occitan has the largest number of speakers, an estimated seven million. But it is hardly uniform. Heard throughout the South of France, it goes by a variety of names according to the particular region: *provençal, auvergnat, limousin, gascon, languedocien,* etc. These variations are widely taught throughout the South.

Les langues d'oïl: These northern French languages, the speakers of which triumphed linguistically as well as militarily over *les langues d'óc,* have virtually died out. Today, *picard, normand,* and *poitevin* are simply regional forms of French.

Nonetheless, it is not uncommon to ask a French person if he or she speaks English, be told no—and, after proceeding in halting French, come to discover the person does speak at least some English, and certainly more than the initial response indicated. Don't take it personally. This is not an attempt to trick you into displaying your feeble French, but merely the understandable hesitancy of any person to converse in a language they're not entirely comfortable with.

For everyday errands and pleasantries such as discussing the weather, most people will pick up the required French vocabulary quickly enough. Merchants with whom you deal several times a week will soon understand your accent and help you make purchases. If you patronize supermarkets, you'll find them no different than in America: All the merchandise is on display, and you select what you want off the shelves without needing to ask for help.

One common mistake many people make is the assumption that once they have moved to France they will be immersed in the language, and it will come quickly enough. But this fails to take into account that they are often living with someone who speaks French no better than they do themselves. The inevitable result is that daily discussions occur in your native tongue. Whether you're chatting about the shopping list, buying insurance, going out to eat, or renovating the house, chances are you and your partner will consult and make decisions in a familiar language, rather than struggling in French. For one thing, neither of you can make authoritative corrections of the other's mistakes.

French friends and acquaintances will be of some help initially, but the need to make continual corrections wears on both tutor and pupil. Moreover, in a social situation—say at a dinner party—people with limited language skills will find they are missing most of what is being said, even with attentive hosts.

FRENCH INSTRUCTION IN THE UNITED STATES

If you are considering a move to France, even if you haven't determined what to do or where to go once there, you would be wise to begin language study in the United States. There are any number of options, depending on time and location.

One of the best places to begin is your local community college. If it has a French program at all, it will have qualified instructors and a choice of courses ranging from a once-a-week informal conversation class up to university-level five-credit courses. Best of all, it is likely to have an audiovisual language lab that enrolled students can use. The cost of these courses is generally less than at commercial language schools, which are also hard to find outside of large cities.

On the other hand, some will find that commercial language schools (Berlitz is perhaps the best known) are a better solution. These schools do only one thing—teach language—and they have to do it well enough to stay in business. Berlitz offers specialized instruction and vocabulary for business, as well as more general language courses. Class size will probably be far smaller than that of a community college, and the instruction will be more concentrated. Moreover, you will find some offering short courses—perhaps all day Saturday—covering particular areas of a language. In addition to its offices in the United States, Berlitz offers instruction in several locations in Paris and a number of other French cities.

A third possibility is Alliances Françaises. This is a worldwide organization devoted to the promotion of French language and culture. It has numerous branches in the United States and sponsors language classes. One great advantage of Alliances Française, if there is a chapter convenient to you, is that the organization offers more than just language classes. It is a gateway to the French community in your area. Check the Alliances Françaises website to find links to individual chapters, as well as many French institutions. Alliances Françaises also conducts classes in five different cities throughout France and holds examinations in Paris, delivering internationally recognized certificates of accomplishment for teachers of French. The organization is a prime contact for anyone interested in France and the French.

Along with formal lessons, consider the possibility of private tutoring. There may be a neighbor, a teacher, or advanced student who can reinforce classroom lessons, explain difficult concepts at greater length, and offer conversation. A tutor's schedule may also be more flexible than that of a school.

FRENCH INSTRUCTION IN FRANCE

If you can take the time, there are more than 100 schools teaching French as a foreign language in France. You don't have to be a university undergraduate spending your junior year at the Sorbonne to learn French in France. Many schools in France offer intensive one-week to one-month courses, so language lessons might be combined with a vacation and exploration of a region. The three main associations of these schools offer a wide range of choice of programs. (See the *Contacts* section of the *Resources* chapter for contact information.)

First is the Association des Centres Universitaires d'Études Françaises pour Étrangers. As the name indicates, these are the university centers for French studies, and as such maintain a high cultural standard. They also have teaching resources, such as language laboratories and multimedia equipment. University credit and diploma programs are offered. For further information about the 25 participating universities, contact the ADCUEFE directly.

Another group comprises the 50 institutions, both public and private, listed as Groupement Français Langue étrangère. Members of the group not only offer language courses, but also pedagogical help for teachers of French from other countries. The participating centers are scattered around Paris and the provinces, including one in Belgium, and the organization's website also offers information about upcoming events of interest to teachers of French.

The third association is SOUFFLE, a professional group of 20 organizations that teach French as a foreign language. Established in 1990, its members are diverse in size, status, and style. By-laws of the group call for independent inspections and set requirements for teacher qualifications. Accommodations and associated programs are also monitored.

While not a group of language schools per se, the National Office for the Guarantee of Language Training and Overseas Stays is a great resource for parents and young people interested in both working and learning in France. Composed of consumer and parent representatives, as well as professionals, it provides guidelines and regulations for those offering au pair positions and other work experiences, plus language classes. The organization's website describes a variety of possible linguistic sojourns, with links to the member agency offering the program.

There are also private institutions for language in most university towns. Even in rural areas, as long as you are close to a town with a *lycée* (high school) or *college* (middle school), you may find courses offered by qualified individual teachers. These usually cost €7.50–15 ($8–16) per hour. In one outlying area, a weekly course in French for foreigners was being offered for about €6.50 ($7.50) per class, with a three-month minimum enrollment required. Many of these tutors seeking private pupils place a *petite annonce* (classified ad) in one of the weekly advertising papers distributed free in each region.

The international organization Eurolingua, which has a French office at Montpellier, offers language-learning vacations in France in which small groups of students spend the morning in class, then have afternoons and weekends off to explore the surrounding area. They also offer a program of one-on-one homestays, where the student lives in the tutor's home for a full cultural and linguistic experience. For those who already speak an intermediate level of French, Eurolingua also offers the possibility of three-month work experiences in France, combined with classes.

Once living in France, you may be able to take classes offered by GRETA (Groupements d'Établissements Publics d'Enseignement), an arm of the Ministry of Education devoted to upgrading the skills and knowledge of residents of the country. GRETA operates in every department, but language classes are only part of their offerings, which include numerous technical courses for employment skills.

FREE UNIVERSITIES

Another educational forum that a French-speaking immigrant might find interesting is the various "free" universities that have sprung up largely as antidotes to the rigid French educational system. That system does a good job of educating young people, but has largely shut out those who do not follow the narrowly prescribed path to a diploma. Along with such traditional subjects as literature and philosophy, you may also find courses in yoga and art history. Perhaps the best known is L'Université Inter-Âges de Paris-Sorbonne, where about 8,000 students sign up for courses each year. Registration is by mail, or visit the school's website for more information. No diplomas are awarded—but then, there are no requirements for admission either.

You don't have to be a university undergraduate spending your junior year at the Sorbonne to learn French in France.

Also in Paris, L'Université de Tous les Saviors (UTLS) offers lecture series on a wide variety of topics, all available through their website.

There are about 50 loosely associated *universités populaires* (adult education courses) around France. The largest by far is the Université Populaire du Rhin in Alsace. The school's website offers information on associated schools around the country and will send brochures on request.

Another group of such schools is the Union Française des Universités Tous Âges (UFTA). These institutions are each linked to an academic university. Originally intended for retired people, they have become increasingly open to wider enrollments.

Caen and Lyon each have a *université populaire*. Caen's has been in existence since 2002, while Lyon's opened at the beginning of 2005. All of these schools have proven quite popular.

A WORD ABOUT ACCENTS

The idea that anyone can speak without a trace of an accent is nonsense. Everyone has an accent, and knowledgeable listeners can often pick out your place of birth and even that of your parents, who may have passed

Tutoyer or Not *Tutoyer*

One confusing aspect of French is its use of two different forms of "you": the familiar *tu* for friends, children, and pets, and the formal *vous,* used to show respect or to address someone with whom you are not acquainted. To complicate matters, *tu* is only singular, and *vous* is plural, as well as respectful. So, even if you were talking to two of your ex-lovers at the same time, you would use *vous*. The practice is confusing even to the French—they have invented the verb *tutoyer* (to address someone as *tu*) just to talk about the situation.

Many other languages, such as Spanish, follow a similar practice. Even English did in the past—remember "thee" and "thou"? Quakers in America still use these terms today. But since the 19th century, the practice has been little used in English, except as a poetic device.

The French themselves appear to be shifting away from it, and few agree on the circumstances under which you may switch from *vous* to *tu*. One university professor reported that many of her students address her as *tu,* rather than *vous,* something she never would have done even as a graduate student.

No absolute rules apply, but there are times when it is always preferred to use *vous:* in speaking to an official or anyone unknown to you outside of a social situation, and in addressing persons older than yourself, such as your friends' parents or relatives. Certainly, it is the polite way to address shop clerks and someone who comes to do repairs.

You will be safe using *tu* to address pets, children, and anyone who tells you that you may.

their own inflections on to you. A Scot speaking his native English can be just as difficult for an American to understand as an Asian speaking English as a second language.

The French are no different. They all have accents and will often argue that theirs is the "correct" one. What's correct in the Midi will be scorned in Paris and Alsace, and vice versa. A French science teacher who comes from the Toulouse area spent six years teaching in California, where his lack of facility in English made life difficult. His joy at being transferred back to a school in Paris was quickly dampened the first time he went shopping. Here he was, back in France, where he would have no trouble saying anything to anyone—and the clerk started mimicking his American accent! He was crushed.

This is not to imply that trying to emulate a genuine French accent is unimportant. Speaking with an accent so poor or so thick that you can't be understood is not speaking the language. But the rhythm of the words, the phrasing, and the emphasis may be at least as important as the accent. Think of the erudite, well-educated people who have come to the United States and speak with a noticeable accent. Two things are more important than an accent: First, can you be understood? And second, do you have anything to say?

Education

Formal education for the French begins at three years old in the *école maternelle,* a preschool with the goal of teaching language and getting children used to working in groups. (Depending on the maturity of the child and space available, a child may begin at age two.) The school is not mandatory and is free. The children remain in *l'école maternelle* until age six.

Foreigners arriving in France with young children will usually find these preschools a great help. Not only do their children learn French and make friends, but parents may also become acquainted with other local parents. Enrollment is a matter of going to the *mairie* (mayor's office) and applying.

At age six, schooling becomes mandatory. The institution is *l'école élémentaire.* It may be public or private, and home schooling is also allowed in France. If the child has not gone through *l'école maternelle,* then his or her parent must go to the *mairie* to obtain a certificate, then go to the school for actual enrollment. This schooling normally lasts three years; however, students may skip ahead a year or be held back, depending on accomplishment.

The next level is the *collège* (middle school). This lasts four years, beginning with the sixth and progressing to the third. After successful completion of *collège,* the student goes to the *lycée* (high school).

High school takes three years to complete. In the first year the student takes a general course and determines which more specialized curriculum to follow—literature, science, or social studies—and in the last two years follows a curriculum oriented to that particular area. To obtain a diploma, the student must pass the national *baccalauréat* (baccalaureate) examination. Failure to pass the baccalaureate, popularly known as *"le bac,"* requires another year of study and a second attempt at the exam.

However, not all *lycées* aim at traditional scholarship. There are many trade schools and a wide variety of certificates and diplomas for technical education—a rough equivalent of an associate of arts degree from an American community college. Typical subjects include agriculture, business, computers, and mechanics, but these trade schools also produce bakers, butchers, and caterers.

With a degree in hand, students are eligible to enroll in a university. The initial degree after two years of university work is called a DEUG and may be followed by a master's degree. Often, the educational level is referred to as a "Bac + 2" or "Bac + 4," with the numeral indicating the number of years of specialized study in a particular area.

The Ministry of Education maintains an Internet portal to hundreds of documents and other websites explaining the French educational system.

STUDYING ABROAD

Many American universities have arrangements with French universities. For example, those who have a basic knowledge of French can enroll in the California state university system for a year of study in either Aix-en-Provence or Paris. But be forewarned: One middle-aged student reported that when the students in her classes—who were from all over the world—socialized, the language they usually spoke was English, because it was common to them all. See www.studyabroad.com for a list of U.S. schools.

A French association that facilitates university-level student exchanges is the Mission Interuniversitaire de Coordination des Échanges Franco-Américains. This group, much more handily referred to by the acronym MICAFA, has liaisons with numerous American universities and colleges, as well as all the medical schools and most Paris universities. Their website is quite helpful in understanding the differences between U.S. and French systems of higher education.

Health

Health care in France is generally good. Doctors are plentiful, and well-staffed hospitals are located throughout the country. Remarkably, many doctors still make house calls. Privately employed nurses visit patients in their homes to administer medication or give care. Health care is generally less expensive than it is the States (although medication may cost more). On the downside, if you're a senior, Medicare won't help you much in France.

Types of Insurance

Americans who come to France to live but not to work (retirees or those on sabbatical, for example) must provide their own insurance and show proof of it before obtaining a residency permit. However, once you have moved to France and established yourself there legally for three months, you become eligible for coverage under the French

Medical Fees

The following medical fees are set by the Sécurité Sociale and reimbursed by health insurance:

Normal office visit to a family physician or dentist: €20 ($27)

Examination of patients with lengthy illnesses: €26 ($35.10)

Examination by a specialist: €23 ($31.05)

Examination by a pediatrician: €28 ($37.80)

Examination by a psychiatrist: €34.30 ($46.30)

House calls by a family physician: €30 ($40.50)

In some instances, specialists are allowed an extra €2 ($2.70) for their fees and psychiatrists an extra €2.70 ($3.65).

Prescribed medicine is generally covered at full cost; however, the price of generics are used to determine the amount. Homeopathic remedies are widely available in pharmacies, and some are partially reimbursed by the health care system.

system. A non-working person (except students under 28) also has the option of maintaining completely independent coverage. This option usually proves more expensive—and if you do need immediate medical attention, it will come from a French doctor, anyway.

PUBLIC CARE

If you are salaried or self-employed, you and your family will be covered by the French health-care system, which is part of Social Security. (The exceptions are Americans sent to France by their companies for periods of less than five years who arrange to continue their American health insurance while in France.) French citizens are covered from birth.

The French health-care system is universal. As of January 1, 2000, full health care was extended to any legal resident of France. At that time, insurance covering 100 percent of medical costs was extended to the poorest 10 percent of the population—those receiving general welfare assistance (RMI, as it is called in France) of €425 per month ($574), and those with an annual income below €6,850 ($9,248). In 2004, the Social Security system racked up a deficit of about €11 billion ($14.9 billion), and at the beginning of 2005, belt-tightening measures were being put in place.

However, those with an income above the minimum must pay according to a sliding scale (8 percent of your earnings above €6,850, up to a ceiling of €150,000 ($9,248–202,500)). Your contribution is determined by your income in the previous year, not your current earnings. Someone who retired with a salary of $100,000 (€74,074), but was living on U.S. Social Security in France, would pay €5,166 ($6,974) for base health coverage, plus whatever complementary plan was elected. This still may be less expensive than health care in the U.S., but it should be taken into account.

The coverage all French citizens have is called the *régime de base.* It covers about 70 percent of the costs of doctors' visits and 80 percent of the costs of hospitalization. Some prescriptions are covered 100 percent, others only 35 percent. Most people buy complementary insurance to cover the balance of medical costs, visits to specialists, and better dental and eye care.

The French Social Security system, which is mostly concerned with health care, rather than retirement, is a hodge-podge of agencies. Which one will serve you depends on your type of employment or occupation. Salaried people have one, civil servants another, and farmers still another. Self-employed tradespeople must enroll in the system and pay for their own coverage. Artists also have a separate system.

For anyone intending to buy complementary health insurance, the simplest path to follow is probably to talk to the agent you bought property and auto insurance from. Chances are the same company offers health insurance, and there may be a savings in buying different sorts of coverage from the same company. The agent should be able to guide you through the bureaucracy. It might be wise to talk to agents from different companies right from the start, getting quotes and letting them understand that you expect this kind of assistance.

For those who intend to stick to the minimum *régime de base,* start with the Caisse Primaire d'Assurance Maladie (CPAM) in your department. This is the local agency that handles health insurance for Social Security. If you are in business, you can also get information from the local Chambre de Commerce et Industrie. Students will get health insurance through their university system.

Under the French health-care system, every medical intervention has a set fee. For instance, a visit to a general practitioner costs €20 ($27). As part of a new reform in effect in 2005, the patient must pay €1 ($1.35) of this. CPAM pays €13 ($17.55), and complementary insurance covers the balance. Fees for a specialist are higher, but under the new system, you must be referred by your primary doctor. Selection of a primary caregiver is now mandatory.

Although most doctors are in the system, it's wise to check first. Some physicians and private clinics do not agree to this schedule of fees. A doctor is free to decide whether to participate in the system or not. If a doctor has not signed an agreement with the health-care system, her fees will be reimbursed at a much lower rate, and the patient must pay the balance. Additionally, some doctors are approved to charge fees beyond the normal ones, and some complementary insurance policies cover this extra charge.

PRIVATE CARE

In applying for your long-stay visa, you are required to provide proof of health insurance that will cover you in France. However, you need only provide short-term coverage; once you're a resident in France, whether as a student, employee, business operator, or retiree, you can purchase French health insurance. Indeed, you will be eligible for coverage by the French system as a long-term resident—in most cases, it is required—and you may find it economically advantageous.

Those who have made an advance trip to France to buy a home or see about setting up a business prior to obtaining a *carte de séjour* (residency permit) may be able to obtain coverage for a limited time from a French company. This will satisfy the health insurance requirement, but you will have to obtain your visa quickly and establish residence in France.

For Americans who must provide their own insurance, at least until they are established in France, there are a number of companies that offer health coverage for expatriates, and others who will be out of the country for extended periods. Usually these companies offer a variety of options—deductibles of various amounts, different percentages of hospitalization costs, and so on. Provisions may also be made for the return to the United States to receive care. Cost varies based on options and the age of the insured.

The prices of health coverage are fluctuating so much that it is impossible to provide reliable estimates. If your current health care is provided by a big, multi-risk insurer like Aetna, for instance, that is a good place to start. If not, then perhaps the agent who handles your U.S. homeowner's or auto insurance also represents one of those companies and will give you a quote. Fortunately, virtually all providers now provide estimates online. Simply by doing a search for "international health insurance" or "expatriate health insurance," you will come up with dozens of sites offering coverage and providing quotes based on your personal situation.

Obviously, age is a factor in the cost, but your location will be also, because the insurer knows that you will be in a country where high-quality care is readily available at a reasonable price. If you are not permanently settling in France or you expect to move back and forth several times a year and intend to keep your U.S. coverage, travel insurance may suffice.

Retired Americans considering a move to France should know that Medicare will not cover them outside the country. However, most people have a supplementary policy covering the 20 percent of their U.S. health-care bills that Medicare does not cover. These supplementary policies often cover 80 percent of the cost of health care when the poli-cyholder is traveling outside the United States. Some expatriates take advantage of this by purchasing minimal policies qualifying for a long-stay visa, then relying on the supplementary policy to cover 80 percent of their health-care costs as "travelers," if necessary.

Doctors are plenti-ful, and well-staffed hospitals are located throughout the country. Remarkably, many doctors still make house calls.

If you choose this option, you'll need to maintain an address in the United States, even if it's not strictly your residence—perhaps your children or another trusted relative will let you "use" theirs. Or you may choose to return to the United States periodically, where you'll be on solid legal ground to make use of Medicare and your supplementary health-care policies.

On the whole, you should not regard a move to France any differ-ently than you would a move from Minneapolis to Phoenix or from Philadelphia to Denver. Wherever you go and whatever your age, you need to find health practitioners in whom you have confidence, and you are going to have to pay for their services. Maintaining a long-distance relationship with your doctor back home may seem like a great way to save money—until you actually need immediate care.

Hospitals and Clinics

France has more than half a million hospital beds, about nine for every 1,000 persons—fewer than in the United States, but above the Euro-pean average. About two-thirds are public, and one-third private. In recent years, the number of hospital beds has dropped slightly, but hospital stays have shortened, so the capability to care for patients has not been sacrificed.

In the last decade, hospital reforms have also tried to better coordinate services and facilities in any given region to avoid duplication and conserve resources. The hospitals in France employ about 150,000 doctors and pharmacists; these are in addition to doctors in private practice who also admit and care for patients in the hospitals as necessary. About 950,000 nonprofessionals also work in the hospitals of France.

University hospitals are huge institutions. The one in Toulouse, for instance, has about 2,500 beds. Patients are transported from a wide region for various treatments and procedures. The advantage is that the professors and their students see large numbers of patients with a particular ailment. Such a hospital may perform dozens of angiograms and angioplasties per week, and the physicians are completely familiar with all aspects of the operation. Furthermore, posts at these hospitals are generally prized and sought by the physicians themselves.

Pharmacies and Prescriptions

In France, you won't find the wide selection of inexpensive over-the-counter pharmaceutical products available in large quantities that we take for granted in the States. Bottles of 1,000, whether vitamins or aspirin, are rare. Even hygiene products, such as toothpaste, usually come in smaller containers than you see in America. The wide array of cold and headache remedies, cough drops and syrups, allergy relievers, and the rest of the acres of patent nostrums you find in any American drug store or supermarket are scarce in France. To be sure, over-the-counter drugs and remedies are available, but the selection of brands and sizes of containers is minimal.

In contrast to the United States, homeopathic remedies are widely available at pharmacies in France, and their prescription and purchase may be included in health plans. As part of its efforts to reduce health-care costs, however, the government has stopped reimbursing all or part of such medications.

Vision Care
Eye glasses are about two to three times as expensive in France as in the U.S. Eye examinations are less expensive, but anyone who needs pre-

scription glasses and does not plan to return to the States for some time might want to get new glasses and/or contact lenses before departure.

Preventive Measures

Before planning a move to France, you'd be wise to get a thorough medical check-up. If you discover a health problem, you may prefer to resolve it before leaving the States—not because the French health-care system is poor, but because you may be more comfortable being treated by a doctor and system you know. What's more, you'll be in familiar surroundings, with friends and family on hand to lend support. Pay a visit to the optometrist and dentist before your move as well. Women should also have a thorough gynecological examination.

The documentation of any conditions you may have will help the health practitioners you may consult in France. With up-to-date knowledge and, one hopes, a clean bill of health, you can undertake your move with confidence.

Whatever Ails You

The French are great believers in the curative powers of water. Dating back to Gallo-Roman times, people have taken pleasure from bathing in the waters of the hot springs that dot the country. In the 19th century, the best of these became famous resorts, such as Vichy.

During this period, spas located beside the sea also became popular, and today offer regular programs of treatment by mineral baths, mud baths, and seaweed packs. These cures are called *thalassothérapie* and may include regimens of drinking particular waters, as well as bathing. Some of these cures may be reimbursed by the health care system.

The latest twist on this theme is called *vinotherapie,* administered at a spa called Les Sources de Caudalie in the middle of the vineyards of Château Smith Haut-Lafitte near Bordeaux. Here, the hot tub is filled with water from an underground source and mixed with extract of grape seeds and organic oils. There are sauvignon massages and crushed cabernet scrubs. Your body may be wrapped in plastic sheets coated with honey, wine yeast extracts, and herbs.

There are different programs available, including one to fight off the effects of aging based on the antioxidant properties of the tannins in grapes. The spa also includes two excellent restaurants and a bar.

VACCINATIONS

In applying for your long-stay visa in France, there are no required vaccinations. Whatever vaccinations you have received in the United States as a child against smallpox and polio, etc., will stand you in good stead. However, after arriving in France and prior to securing your *carte de séjour* from the prefecture, you will have to have a physical examination conducted by the OMI (Office des Migrations Internationales).

Environmental Factors

Environmentally, France is different from the United States and other industrialized nations. Dirty air, polluted water, and industrial and agricultural waste all pose problems in some regions. Perhaps the biggest concern involves the nuclear waste generated by the plants that produce about 75 percent of the country's electricity. Even if the government were inclined to shut these plants—and it is not—disposing of the radioactive material would still be a problem.

Nearly 800 tons of radioactive waste are stockpiled at La Hague, far enough from Cherbourg for safety, but too close for comfort. New shipments are taken to the Aube, near Troyes. There are also tons of slightly radioactive waste at various uranium mining sites in France. Despite the weak radiation this material generates, its mass represents a health hazard.

In June 2000, the national commission charged with studying how France handles its radioactive waste assailed the lack of action in assuring the secure disposal of this waste. It recommended not only more research on improving disposal methods but also far stricter surveillance of what has already been stockpiled. This research is underway, and reports of the results and debates about solutions are expected in 2006.

The parallels between nuclear waste problems in France and the United States are striking. Both countries have produced it as part of their nuclear energy programs, and neither nation has been able to find a way to detoxify it. Both have adopted the disposal method: Collect it in an isolated spot and encase it in material that will shield the public from its harmful effects. Despite assurances of careful maintenance by the governments of both nations, leaks have occurred at sites. Prudence dictates avoiding them. Fortunately, that's easy to do in both countries.

AIR QUALITY

Air pollution consists of all the ingredients of smog: oxides of nitrogen, sulphur dioxide, carbon monoxide, hydrocarbons, and ozone. The internal combustion engine is responsible for much of it, and asthma and other respiratory problems are a major health problem, especially in and around Paris.

As with water pollution, testing of air quality has become increasingly rigorous. The number of air pollution–measuring stations jumped from 1,150 in 1994 to 2,200 in 2005. In times of peak pollution, authorities will order some drivers off the roads, based on license plate numbers and certificates of cleaner-running motors. Outside of Paris and the immediate surrounding area, this has not been a factor to consider.

WATER QUALITY

Maintaining high-quality drinking water is also a challenge. In limited areas, pesticides and nitrates from agriculture have degraded underground water supplies. As contaminated sources are identified, their use is halted. In the heavily agricultural region of Midi-Pyrénées, for instance, while only 7,300 people have water that frequently showed more than 50 milligrams of pesticides and nitrates per liter, another 150,700 have water that has tested between 40 and 50 milligrams per liter. (Adults normally consume more than 100 milligrams of nitrates daily in solid food.) Phosphates are another contaminant, largely from laundry soap. This problem has fallen by 30 percent since 1990, though, as detergent manufacturers have changed their formulas.

Another problem found throughout the country is bacterial contamination. Many small villages have historically relied on sources of water that are not treated and seldom tested. In the department of the Aude, for instance, which is largely rural, some 13 percent of the water samples tested in 1999 failed to meet one or more of 62 separate water purity standards. The vast majority of these failures occurred in villages in which the total population is less than 10 percent of the entire department. The cities and villages where most people live had good records.

Testing of the water supply became more rigorous and frequent in the last decade. This is the key to better water and has done much to clean up the supply. After all, the purpose of the testing is to control any problems that occur. Test results are available in the *mairie* (mayor's office) of each commune. Prospective residents, as well as citizens, can check these records.

Since 2000, water bills have increased annually at the rate of inflation—2–3 percent. The average annual water bill in 2005 was €350 ($490) based on usage of 120 cubic meters at €2.60 ($3.64) per cubic meter.

SMOKING

Smoking remains a public health issue in France, where tobacco has long been grown, and the production of cigarettes is overseen by the government and an important source of revenue. More than 25 percent of the population age 15 and over are smokers, with men outnumbering women 32 to 22 percent—except among the young, where the rate for both sexes is 22 percent. Smoking is also a class issue: 44 percent of the unemployed say they are smokers, while only 32 percent of those working do.

The fight to stop smoking is not as advanced as in the U.S., and you should be prepared to encounter smokers everywhere.

France has passed laws concerning smoking in public places, and the general population is well-informed of the health hazards. The story is told of the minister who was asked why his government, realizing the toll that tobacco took in health costs, did not do more to reduce smoking in the country. "Ah," he replied, "those costs belong to my successors. The costs of reduced consumption, and therefore less tax collected, those costs are mine." Nonetheless, you will seldom see people smoking in a supermarket or other indoor public place, except bars and restaurants. But the fight to stop smoking is not as advanced as in the U.S., and you should be prepared to encounter smokers everywhere.

SANITATION

France produces nearly 650 million tons of solid waste and household garbage annually. The average Parisian is responsible for about 500 kilos, while the rest of the country averages about 350 kilos per person. Recycling is most successful with glass; more than three-fifths goes back. Other products have much lower returns—a little more than one-third of paper, a quarter of batteries, and one-fifth of plastic are recycled. About half of paper products are made from recycled material.

Disabled Access

There is no magic formula that makes life easier for the 5.5 million handicapped people in France. The physically handicapped face the same problems with access to facilities that they do everywhere. And those with mental disabilities will meet with much the same reactions as in the U.S.

A new law due to take effect January 1, 2006, budgets €850 million ($1.15 billion) for a variety of forms of aid, including household help, equipment such as wheelchairs, and lodging modifications. It also establishes a single office in each department responsible for everything relating to the disabled.

For the physically handicapped, there has been improvement in recent years. By law, new construction of public buildings must include provisions for access. Even in small villages, *mairies* (mayor's offices) and other important places like post offices have been retrofitted with ramps for wheelchairs, although you will not find this everywhere. Moreover, curbs and cobblestones, a lack of sidewalks, and cars parked on the sidewalks that do exist may virtually nullify such efforts.

The new law also sets a goal of 10 years for assuring access to the handicapped. Recognizing that rebuilding the Paris Métro, for instance, will not happen that quickly, the law accepts alternative means, such as buses, that will accomplish the goal.

Nonetheless, there is a consciousness among the general public of the need for improved conditions. Often, physical improvements are made after a need is demonstrated. In one village, for instance, a chair lift to the upstairs municipal council chambers was put in place when a paralyzed person was elected to the council.

Shopping centers and other businesses that provide private parking have handicapped spaces for customers with handicapped tags. There is limited enforcement; however, it is probably equal to whatever enforcement of parking regulations exist in a particular community. The public toilets in many commercial centers include wheelchair-accessible stalls. This is not the case in restaurants and hotels, however.

Maison de la France, the national tourist office, maintains a list of accommodations for the disabled on its website, which might be useful as a starting point because it lists by region. But it is by no means comprehensive, citing only those who have applied for the listing.

Because various handicaps can affect such a wide range of activity and life, numerous government agencies are involved, such as work, education, health, transportation, culture and sport. Links to all of them may be found on the website of the Secrétariat d'État aux Personnes Handicapées (Secretary of State for Handicapped Persons).

France has numerous programs offering financial aid and other assistance for people with disabilities. While legislation is national, each department has its own program of implementation dictated by local needs and initiative. In many rural villages, you will find a *maison de retraite* (a community-operated assisted-living establishment and/or nursing home).

The numerous private associations and advocacy groups devoted to either a particular handicap or more general problems are also well-represented on the Internet. Those for whom this is a concern should begin researching the issue in advance and then make contact. Mobility International USA has a database of organizations worldwide searchable by country and disability. Also, the French Yahoo! portal has an excellent listing of sites pertaining to the disabled. See the *Contacts* section of the *Resources* chapter for contact information for all these organizations.

Safety

In France, there are three different numbers to telephone, depending on the type of emergency. To call the police, dial 17; for the *pompiers* (firefighters), dial 18; and for medical emergencies, (SAMU), dial 15. There is a single emergency number to call from a cell phone: 112.

The website of the ministry of health maintains a page called Renseignements Practiques that lists telephone numbers/hotlines for special services, such as suicide prevention (01 45 39 40 00), AIDS (SIDA in French) information (0800 840 800), and rape (0800 05 95 95). The 0800 numbers are free. Also on the site are listings for the Red Cross, homeless organizations, racial discrimination, and drug information.

Police are organized along two major lines throughout France. Most familiar are probably the *gendarmes,* under the Ministry of Defense. The *gendarmerie nationale* operates in every department, with a station in every *arrondissement* (district) in cities and *canton* (small territorial division) in rural districts. They are responsible for maintaining public order, controlling traffic on the highways and investigating crimes.

The ministry of the interior oversees the *police nationale,* a 145,000-person force whose *police judiciaire* perform major crime investigations. The Compagnies Républicaines de Sécurité (CSR) is a national SWAT team that backs up other police agencies as needed during major demonstrations or crises. Uniformed officers on patrol constitute a major component of the force.

The key to organizing these various police units is the prefect of each department. As the ranking local representative of the national government, both the Interior and Defense Ministers fall under prefecture control, and they oversee police coordination.

In case of a serious crime, the procedure in France is very much like that in the U.S.: Call the police on the emergency number, 17. If a phone is not available or it is a minor matter—perhaps an act of vandalism not immediately discovered—go to the local police station or *gendarmerie* to report it. Chances are you will have to go there to report something like a purse-snatching, anyway.

Compared to many U.S. cities, crime is not as big a problem in France. But robberies, burglaries, assaults, and all other crimes known to the human race do occur here. Sex crimes have risen especially rapidly in recent years. Rapes totaled 10,400 in 2004, compared with 7,000 in 1996; police say the biggest increase has occurred within families, as child abuse and spousal rape are now being reported more often than they are being concealed by the victims.

While crimes against persons are most likely more of a problem in cities, homes in the countryside may be plagued by burglaries. Vacation homes left vacant for months on end, even within villages, are subject to break-ins. Sometimes it may simply be vandals or teenagers, but it may also be a well-organized gang seeking valuable furniture. Anyone establishing a home isolated in the country should be especially careful to take all precautions demanded by their insurance company.

© Corel/Velocity Stock

Employment

J ust as in the United States, there are many options for earning
your daily bread in France. Whether you want to start your own
business or become a salaried employee, chances are good you
can find a niche once you navigate the sometimes tricky terrain of
French regulations.

One factor affecting Americans looking for work is the European
Union. It extends greater possibilities of working legally in France
to English, Irish, Spanish, Portuguese, Belgians, Dutch, Greeks, and
other foreigners than it does to Americans. There is a pool of legal
foreigners as well as French people who might be looking for work at
any given time.

Yet there are Americans working legally in France. Many of them are
well-educated people in a technical, though not necessarily high-tech,
field. French salary levels are low compared to American ones, but they
offer benefits, stability, and the chance to live in France.

A rather roundabout possibility for finding employment in France is gaining citizenship in another European Union nation, such as Ireland. It is not necessary to give up your U.S. passport and citizenship when applying for citizenship in another country—and many Americans, either through ancestry or marriage, may be eligible to become citizens of an EU country. As such, they will have access to French employment.

Another possibility to consider is doing a period of professional development in France, called a *stage*. It refers to a stint spent refining your knowledge, or learning particular techniques in your field, or just gaining experience under a master. Pay is minimal, perhaps only room and board if that. This is common in cooking and wine-making, for instance, and the *stagiare* (trainee) is almost certain to benefit upon returning to the United States. It also gives you the experience of seeing what it is like to work in France, and may result in contacts that could lead to employment later.

Self-Employment

STARTING A BUSINESS

Starting or buying a business is a far more complex process in France than in America. Those who intend to come to France and start a business should understand from the start that the process is quite different. Business in France is regulated; you cannot simply decide to put up a sign, open the door, and wait for customers to beat a path to it. In many instances, it is necessary to show proof of education or experience to conduct a business. You cannot simply declare yourself to be a manufacturer of widgets and set about producing them.

This is not to say that it is impossible to establish your enterprise, but rather that the rules are different, and it is best to learn them before drawing up a business plan. The Ministry of Employment and Labor has established the Agence Pour la Création d'Enterprises (APCE) with a website that offers help.

The Chambre de Commerce et d'Industrie, Chambre d'Agriculture, and Chambre de Métiers are also necessary early stops. Unlike in the States, where such organizations are private and voluntary, in France they are governmental agencies that regulate and control most of the business in the country. For example, France Telecom will not put your name or business in the Yellow Pages unless you are registered with one of the chambers. Nor will you be considered professional or commercial

The French Enterprise

In deciding to open a business in France, you should consider the various possible structures, each of which has ramifications for liability and tax consequences. In general, these structures correspond to common forms in the United States.

The simplest form of business is the sole proprietorship, *l'entreprise individuelle*. As the name implies, there is a single owner who is responsible. A spouse who also works in the business is a *conjoint collaborateur*. For a small business unlikely to generate sales in the millions or hire dozens of employees, this structure may be fine. This small business may also qualify for a special tax plan called a *forfait* or *micro-régime* that avoids direct collection and payment of the TVA (19.6 percent value-added tax).

It does have disadvantages, however. The owner is personally liable for business debts and must pay all of his or her own Social Security costs (retirement and health care). What's more, the owner has no worker's compensation coverage if he or she is injured or falls ill on the job. The business ends with the death of the owner and may involve tax levies.

A single owner who seeks limited responsibility and the advantages of a small corporate structure might form an Entreprise Uniper- sonnelle à Responsabilité Limitée (EURL). This is basically a small corporation formed by a single investor who also usually runs the business. No minimum investment is required, but 20 percent of whatever amount is budgeted must be available in cash immediately; the balance is due in five years. Two or more investors (up to a maximum of 100) form a Société à Responsibilité Limitée (SARL). Again, no minimum investment is required, but 20 percent of whatever amount is budgeted must be available in cash immediately; the balance is due in five years.

A Société en Nom Collectif (SNC) is a partnership. The law fixes no minimum investment for its formation, and the partners are responsible for the debts of the business. This operates much like an *enterprise individuelle*, as far as Social Security and health insurance are concerned, but the SNC may not use the simplified tax regimes.

The Société Anonyme (SA) is the formal corporate structure for bigger businesses. It requires a minimum of seven principals and and investment of €37,000 ($53,650) and must employ an auditor. Half of the initial investment must be available immediately, with the balance due in five years.

by other firms and individuals unless you are so registered. For instance, the merchants' association in our village was considering hiring a particular band to play at an annual two-day festival that attracts several thousand people. When someone noticed that the band had no *siret* number (the registration number signifying a legal business), it was immediately dropped from consideration. If you wish to open a business that will attract the general public, you must follow certain steps.

TYPES OF BUSINESSES

Suppose you want to open a cybercafé. Even if you plan to sell drinks only to be carried off the premises, you'll need a license. Perhaps your idea is to guide American tourists around France, booking their rooms or escorting them to historic sites; such a business must abide by regulations, such as hours of operation and pricing. Even a business as simple as renting rooms in your home—a *chambre d'hôte* (bed-and-breakfast)—requires registration with the local Chambre de Commerce et d'Industrie or Chambre d'Agriculture. It is the Chambre d'Agriculture that operates the Gites de France organization, whose members around the country in rural areas rent furnished apartments or houses by the week, or furnished rooms by the night, to vacationers. However, in some departments, agriculture officials may discourage foreigners from participating in this program, and you will find the Chambre de Commerce more welcoming.

Many foreigners think that a B&B would be an ideal business to run in France. It is certainly possible to support yourself from such a venture, but do the math first. You're legally entitled to a maximum of five rooms to rent. When you start out, you're doing well if you can rent each room 60 nights a year at €50 ($68) per night, giving you a gross annual income of €15,000 ($20,250) per year. Double either your occupancy rate or your room rate, and you are up to €30,000 ($40,500) gross. (You cannot expect any business to operate at 100 percent capacity or production in the beginning. After 10 years in the business, our rooms are now fully occupied about 100 nights a year.) Considering the investment and the labor involved, this is not going to make you rich. Someone earning the minimum wage of €7.61 ($10.27) per hour working 35 hours per week earns more than €1,154 ($1,558) per month—and their benefits are paid, and they get five weeks vacation.

Part of the regulation of business in France also involves qualifications—who can do what. Some occupations have educational and experience requirements. Others may be regarded as incompatible; for instance, an accountant or architect may not also be a merchant. Moreover, in French law, a distinction is made between a *commerçant* (merchant) and an *artisan* (craftsperson). Both are self-employed, but they fall into separate categories. Anglers and farmers are also separated, and certain occupations are reserved in principal for French citizens. These include undertakers, insurance brokers, and gambling-casino staff. However, international treaties have begun to modify these regulations lately, and American citizens may qualify for entry into these professions.

Carte de Commerçant

If you wish to legally engage in business in France, you first step is to obtain a *carte de séjour,* the residency permit that permits you to stay in France longer than three months. Your second step is to get a *carte de commerçant étranger* (foreign merchant's visa). Application for this may be made at a consulate in the United States.

A wiser course may be to first visit the Chambre de Commerce et de l'Industrie(CCI) in the department where you intend to locate. The local CCI may have studies of needs in the region, and will be able to tell you the requirements for an application. The CCI is also a good place to test the water: How are you received as a foreigner? How many others in the area operate a similar business—what's the competition?

At the CCI, they can guide you through the application process. They'll explain the various documents you need and tell you about possible subsidies and tax breaks. These last two items are subject to change, depending on the condition of the economy and the policies of the government in power. For instance, in late 1999, the value-added tax (TVA) on labor for home renovation was lowered from 20.6 percent to 5.5 percent to encourage employment of craftspeople. In the spring of 2000, the TVA itself was cut one percent to 19.6 percent. The CCI may be bureaucratic, but those who want to do business in France must come to terms with it. It is the prefecture that will eventually grant the *carte de commerçant étranger,* but you must satisfy the CCI also. With both agencies, patience is a necessary virtue.

Farmers and anglers must work through the Chambre d'Agriculture, and craftspeople through the Chambre des Métiers. It is much the same process. Those who would establish a subsidiary of a foreign company are also placed in a separate but similar category.

The advantage of working through the prefecture and CCI, rather than through the consulate in the States, is that you're a step closer to the results. With the consulate, there is a greater time lag as papers are transmitted back and forth; on the scene in France, you can discuss matters directly with the officials involved. There may be some problems with your initial plan that would not be immediately apparent to a consular official, and you can modify your plan much more effectively when you're in the country at hand.

France, particularly in recent years, has made a great effort to locate new businesses within depressed areas, and to bring young people into the work force.

The CCI is also the source of information concerning subsidies, tax reductions, and other government programs to encourage employment and development. France, particularly in recent years, has made a great effort to locate new businesses within depressed areas, and to bring young people into the workforce. Employers may benefit through direct subsidy, reduced taxes, relaxed work rules, or some combination of these, depending on the industry and locality involved.

Besides your passport, among the required documents for a *carte de commerçant* application will be your marriage license, if you are married; confirmation of a divorce, if applicable; a spouse's death certificate for widows; and a police record. Like any other document you are required to submit, these will have to be translated into French by a specially qualified translator. Either the local prefecture or the consulate to which you apply will have a list of translators whom they will accept.

While legal translating is a specialty, it underscores the need to gain fluency in French. Imagine trying to operate any sort of a business if you cannot understand your customers or your suppliers! There are degrees of fluency and areas of specialized vocabulary, of course—but finance, insurance, and legal matters in the United States are difficult enough for the layperson fluent in English to comprehend. You may well be able to hire someone to translate for you, but the price is often high for professional help: One translator quoted a price of €100 ($135) per hour. Nonprofessional translators may not be knowledgeable enough about business affairs to provide the level of help you need.

Social Security and Business Taxes

Once you have gained *commerçant* status and permission to open your business, you can start paying taxes—not income taxes, they come later—but Social Security and health insurance, which are mandatory

Expat Profile: Philip Gyuling

Philip Gyuling is a 39-year-old software engineer from San Francisco who made what became a permanent move to France in February 2003. This was not his first time living in the country. He met his wife in Paris when they were both studying for their MBAs. She had lived in France for several years and considered it her second home, but after completing their studies, they returned to the U.S.

Living there, they both missed France. "The cuisine, the quality of life really suited us more than the U.S.," said Gyuling, who holds both U.S. and EU passports. Employed in the U.S. by Streamserve, a Swedish software company that has offices in France, he was able to arrange a transfer. "The fact that I have dual citizenship also made the transfer much easier, as I did not need to apply for a *carte de séjour* (residency permit), thereby eliminating a lot of the red tape associated with relocations of this nature."

Gyuling said the most difficult part of the switch has been the language. "Despite the fact that I had lived and studied in France prior to this move, studied French in high school and in college, and spoke French with my wife for seven years," he continued, "needing to work and express myself in a foreign language has been the most challenging adjustment. For us, the administrative issues of relocation were very simple, as we had both lived in France previously, therefore, we knew very well the processes involved."

The Gyulings live in Aix-en-Provence and find life in that city delightful. "There are always interesting events to attend organized by the city: concerts, plays, festivals, wine tastings," he said, adding that they also enjoy being able to go to have a *café* or a cocktail and simply take in the aliveness of the city. "There are always people out and about enjoying the city, the open markets, and the wonderful Provençal cuisine."

and part of the same system. These are based on the income of the business, but since the business will have no track record, they will be fixed provisionally for a small business at €3,100 ($4,185) the first year and €3,700 ($4,995) the second year. After that, actual revenues will determine these charges.

The French Social Security system is not as unified as the American one, although it is evolving in that direction. Different economic sectors have separate plans managed by different agencies. For instance, salaried employees fall under one set of rules, farmers under another, merchants under still another. Benefits vary somewhat according to the nature of your business. Businesses are required to enroll in a particular plan. It is not a free choice.

The French tax rate on companies—a EURL (Entreprise uniperson-nelle à responsabilité limitée) or a SARL (Société à responsabilité limi-tée), for instance, grossing less than €7.63 million ($10.3 million) per year—is 33.33 percent on operating profits. For larger grosses, this in-creases to 41.6 percent. Fortunately, there are numerous ways to reduce the tax. The first two years of such taxes are exempted for companies opening in certain locations, followed by a diminishing percentage over the next three years. Firms creating new jobs or hiring the unemployed will find benefits that will largely offset the new salaries. Profits that are reinvested are also taxed at a lower rate, as are long-term capital gains on specific fixed assets. However, France differs from all other EU nations in that it does not tax corporate profits earned outside of France. Corporate tax situations—whether involving branches of U.S. corporations or the establishment of a subsidiary—are a matter for ac-countants and other tax experts.

The Job Hunt

The days of Americans heading off to France and supporting them-selves with a day job while writing a novel or painting a masterpiece are long gone. Novels may be written and masterpieces painted, but your chances of picking up a job as a clerk or a receptionist on the side are nil.

For the American job-seeker, there are two hurdles: First and fore-most, long-stay work visas are issued only to those who have already been hired by a French employer, or to those whose foreign employer has a position for them in France. The second hurdle is the continuing 10 percent unemployment rate.

There are Americans working in France, often at a fairly high level of education and/or particular skills, the kind of people who would be holding similar jobs if they had remained in the U.S. In some cases, these people went to school in France or another European country, learned the language, and gained a particular skill. And they almost certainly made some personal or professional connections while in school.

However, it's still extremely difficult for foreigners to qualify for pro-fessions such as medicine, law, architecture, and accounting in France because of educational requirements. You need only imagine the diffi-culty a French physician or attorney might have practicing in the United

States to understand the hurdles involved. Though such transatlantic transplants do exist, they are exceedingly rare.

While doctorate degrees from American universities are recognized as the equivalent of the same degree from a French university, they are the only such degrees. Below a Ph.D., there are few parallels for transfer of credit. Each dossier is handled on a case-by-case basis, depending on the schools involved. Anyone who wishes to join that elite group of professionals who were educated in the United States but practice in France should begin by applying to the Ministry of Education.

Aside from expertise in some high-tech areas, many of the jobs for which Americans might qualify involve teaching or using English, as well as French. Unfortunately, there is a great deal of competition, because large numbers of Brits, Irish, and Scandinavians—all European Union citizens with the right to work in France—possess the same skills. Perhaps the best opportunity for someone who wishes to live in France, has no special skills, and does not wish to go into business but needs to earn a living, is to work as an au pair.

Sometimes personal connections make it possible for a person to live and work in France. An au pair may find her employers helpful at a later date; friendships made during a year as a university undergraduate may later be renewed in graduate school. An American with a French partner gains legal status, is entitled to health care, and can work.

But don't despair: Finding a job is not limited to Americans with advanced university degrees. For example, one of the agricultural schools offering training as a shepherd reports that its graduates have no problem finding jobs that pay €1,000–1,500 ($1,350–2,025) per month. Even if shepherding isn't your thing, France offers opportunities for learning trades and skills that may lead to a job offer in the future. It is a form of apprenticeship not too different from that of an intern in the U.S. There is no guarantee of a job following such training, but it will teach you local tricks of the trade, and you are likely to make some useful connections.

Younger people who want to live and work in France should think of it as a long-term project requiring a certain investment of time and money to achieve. One often hears of an American without proper credentials who worked here or there in a restaurant or bar or on a farm, but in such instances, it is usually for a limited time—the summer season, a harvest, etc. This is not a situation you can build a life upon.

There are other ways to earn money in France. If you buy a property and later resell it at a profit, write a novel and sell it to a publisher, own a house and rent it to someone, or trade stocks on the Internet through a U.S. brokerage—these are all things you can do legally, as long as you pay the proper taxes and obey any other regulations.

USING THE INTERNET

For job-seekers, the Internet is a great advantage. Not only can you use it to search for jobs in France, many of the employment sites offer a place to post your curriculum vitae (CV), the term usually used in France rather than résumé. Email also cuts the waiting time for replies. The CV in France is really no different than the résumé you prepare in the U.S. It provides your educational and work history and your qualifications for the post you are seeking. It should be neat and professional in appearance, with a brief cover letter introducing yourself.

You can look for jobs at expatica.com, a site for foreigners living in Europe and associated with the *International Herald Tribune.* Or go the French page of 4icj.com (4International Careers & Jobs), where you will find various categories to search, such as job boards or headhunters. Almost invariably, the agencies listed state that they are accepting CVs from anyone "holding a working visa."

The American Chamber of Commerce in France also publishes a directory of all the U.S. firms that operate in France. It might be used as a source list for sending out applications.

"WORKING BLACK"

Forget coming to France and finding work as a grape-picker or dishwasher. George Orwell might have been able to do it 75 years ago, but if you've read *Down and Out in London and Paris,* you know it wasn't an easy life even back then.

The French call it *travail au noir* ("working black"). It has nothing to do with race and everything to do with paying taxes. Illegal workers don't pay into the Social Security system, nor do their employers. And illegal workers do not pay income tax; many of them are collecting some form of welfare at the time. Others are legitimately employed in a trade—have the skills and insurance already—and do jobs on the side to increase their net income.

While an established member of a community, a native with friends and family and support, may be able to pick up odd jobs of some sort, it is very difficult for a stranger to come into some town and do the same. Many people are willing to turn a blind eye to the activities of a person they grew up with or have lived near for years, but they may regard it as their civic duty to denounce a foreigner doing the same thing. For one thing, unemployment was about 10 percent in 2005. In a country with a skilled, well-educated population, there were no good jobs going begging.

Non-payment of taxes is serious. Employers are unwilling to take a chance on someone they do not know—or someone they do know who bears a grudge—keeping quiet. Moreover, there are numerous benefits to the employer to work within the system, such as tax relief, apprentices, and salary subsidies. The result is that while a homeowner might pay the cousin of a friend to paint his house, this sort of gainful employment comes neither easily nor consistently to a foreigner, although in cities it may be easier to find some kind of casual employment, especially after you have begun to make friends.

Forget coming to France and finding work as a grape-picker or dishwasher.

What's more, you are unlikely to make much of a living at it. Some French people work in this fashion, of course. They have friends and families, and many receive some sort of public assistance, such as unemployment insurance or RMI, the general welfare aid extended to citizens with no other means of support. In some instances, the French who "work black" also have a regular job in the same field. They already have health insurance and other benefits and work on the side as means of increasing their income without increasing their taxes. Yes, it is illegal for them to do this, just as it would be for you. And it is not advisable.

Consider the bigger picture. Unlike in the United States, health care and Social Security are the same system in France. Whoever pays into Social Security through employment or self-employment is also enrolled in the national health plan, as are those who are born in the country or have gained legal residency in a fashion that entitles them to it, such as by marriage or as dependent children.

Americans who receive long-stay visas have had to show both sustainable income and proof of health insurance, so there is neither a need nor a provision for them to become part of the French Social Security system. But the foreigner who arrives in France as a tourist and decides to stay illegally encounters the catch-22 of the French system. They can't be hired without being eligible for Social Security, and they can't be eligible for Social Security as an illegal alien. Unlike their American counterparts, French employers have too much to lose—maximum penalty is the years in prison and a €45,000 ($60,750) fine—and too little to gain in hiring illegal foreigners. By linking employment, health care, and welfare in a single national system, France has limited its illegal immigration problems.

The point is that to build a life for yourself within a French community, you must do so within the confines of the French legal system. It is certainly possible to live in France on income from the United States; that is what the *carte de séjour* (residency permit) allows you to do. But to try to live and work in France without the proper credentials is a gamble that cannot pay off in the long run.

Labor Laws

Labor and farmers are strong in France. They make their needs known to the politicians at the public's expense, usually enjoying widespread support. No other nation shares France's reputation for strikes and demonstrations. Travelers find flights cancelled, commuters can't get to work, the mail doesn't get delivered, garbage piles up, and *autoroutes* are blocked by angry farmers dumping produce.

The minimum hourly wage in France is €7.61 ($10.27) per hour, which works out to a monthly salary of €1,154.18 ($1,558.14) for a 35-hour week. Full-time workers will also receive five or six weeks of vacation plus basic health care.

WORKER'S RIGHTS

France is organized: Its workers, farmers, teachers, and civil servants all have *syndicats* (unions) to look after their interests. When a factory closes, a corporation faces bankruptcy or a takeover, or farmers are told to accept lower prices for their produce, union representatives arrive on the scene to demand that jobs not be lost or living standards lowered.

Three large *syndicats* dominate the labor movement. The *Confederation Générale du Travail* (CGT) was dominated by the French Communist Party for years. More recently, this relationship has begun to break down, and the CGT no longer automatically supports positions the Party takes. Force Ouvière, the second *syndicat,* grew out of schism in the CGT after World War II. Membership of each is estimated at 700,000. The third major *syndicat,* the Confederation Française et Démocratique du Travail, began as a Christian alternative to a Communist union, but dropped the religious affiliation in the 1960s.

As for representation of farmers, rivaling the three large industrial unions in size is the Fédération Nationale des Syndicats d'Exploitants Agricoles. In France, the largest agricultural producer in Europe, agriculture continues to engage a sizeable—though shrinking—percentage of the French population. Even though farming no longer employs so many people, the younger generation is not far removed from the land, and allegiances remain strong.

In the United States, weak labor law enforcement, anti-union legislation, and lack of organization over the decades have resulted in a population generally acquiescent and docile. Not so in France, and French politicians ignore this at their peril. Perhaps this is why the French are such accomplished diplomats: When displeased, the people take to the streets and create a crisis officials must resolve by compromise.

When the right swept to victory in the National Assembly in 1993, followed by the election in 1995 of President Jacques Chirac, the party enjoyed a large majority. But the policies of Prime Minister Alain Juppé—including a two percent increase in the value-added tax (TVA) and resumption of nuclear testing—proved so unpopular that a series of strikes through the winter and spring of 1997 brought the Socialists back to power by summer. But in 2003, Chirac's party regained full control of the government and immediately set about nullifying the changes the Socialists had made, such as the 35-hour work week. In 2004, elections were held for the provincial councils, the equivalent of state governments in the U.S. The left swept all but one of the 22 provinces. However, the point is not one of left versus right, but of the electorate's readiness to impose its will upon its government.

Finance

One caveat: Don't move to France to reduce your cost of living. Item by item, French prices equal or exceed their counterparts in the United States, if only because of the 19.6 percent value-added tax (TVA) added to labor and materials. Insurance is also taxed in this way. But even without the TVA, many items, such as gasoline, are more expensive—and these discrepancies offset savings on any items that might cost less.

Yet you will almost certainly lead a different lifestyle in France than in the United States. These differences can simultaneously lower some of your expenses and enhance your quality of life. It's not really paradoxical when you consider what drives up the cost of living in the States.

Cost of Living

At roughly $2.25 per gallon, gas is comparatively cheap in America; in France, it will run you €4.50 ($6.08) per gallon. But cars are larger and distances greater in the States: A commuter driving an SUV 30 miles or more each way to work, averaging 18 miles per gallon, will spend at least $6 a day. In France, 20 kilometers is considered a long commute; driven in an average French sedan, it costs about €2.50 ($3.38) a day. What's more, there are far fewer two- and three-car families in France. Even so, the cost of operating a car in France is estimated at about €6,000 ($8,100) per year.

Rest assured, you don't have to be a millionaire, or even close to one, to live in France.

Along with gas, food is more expensive pound for pound in France than in the States. But many French people grow fruits and vegetables for their own consumption, increasing their quality of life while cutting down on their food bills. Indeed, the backyard vegetable garden now so rare in America is still part of life in rural France. Even in villages where the houses are built one on top of the other, residents trek to the edge of town to tend gardens on small patches of ground they rent or own.

Housing is comparable to what you'll pay in the States, with some exceptions. Your housing costs will depend, of course, on where you live and what you live in. French houses and apartments, especially older ones, are typically smaller than you'd find in the States. Even in new construction, two- or three-bedroom/one-bath houses are common. Yards are often diminutive compared to those on American suburban lots. But what you sacrifice in square footage, you gain in savings.

Not surprisingly, you'll find the most expensive housing in Paris and its suburbs. If you hail from a pricey city like San Francisco, you won't be shocked at all, and other parts of France may seem like bargains to you. But if you're from Maryland or suburban Atlanta or Houston, where homes fetch far less than they do in California, you'll find housing costs in France either comparable or more expensive. Moreover, prices are rising—more than 7 percent annually in recent years.

In the provinces (generally understood to mean everywhere but the Paris metropolitan area), you can find a decent home for less than €150,000 ($202,500). Whether it's your dream home or not is another question. Prices in the provinces are increasing, both in and around the larger cities offering employment opportunities, and in the countryside, where both French and foreign buyers are driving up the values of the more desirable properties.

Outfitting your home in France will probably cost more than it does in the States. Major appliances are more expensive in France. Side-by-side refrigerators (the style is called *americain* in France) can cost €2,000 ($2,700). Smaller refrigerator/freezers, measured in liters rather than cubic feet, cost €550–900 ($743–1,215). Brand-name washing machines cost €550–1,100 ($743–1,485).

Dell Computer advertised its Inspiron 8600c laptop for €1,200 ($1,620) and its Dimension 5000 desktop with 17-inch flat screen for €800 ($1,080) early in 2005 in France. A Hoover or an Electrolux canister-style vacuum cleaner costs €200 ($270). Television prices have declined in the last decade, but for brand names, you'll pay more than in the States.

Likewise, clothing and household linens are more expensive. Although list prices of such items as brand-name running shoes, jeans, and bedding may be comparable, you'll seldom find the sales, markdowns, and discounts so common in the United States.

Utility prices are more difficult to compare with those in the States because they vary widely in both countries. But telephone service, for one, is somewhat more expensive in France. You'll pay a monthly charge, plus a fee for every call. Water rates vary, but have generally risen in recent years to pay for new sewage treatment plants. Electricity rates vary according to time of day, but users pay a flat monthly fee based on the size of their service, plus usage at €.09 ($.12) per kilowatt-hour (KWH), reduced to €.049 ($.066) per KWH during hours of low demand, TVA included.

So, what *is* cheaper? Wine—as long as you don't demand classified growths from Bordeaux châteaux. Some foods are also real bargains. Pork is the least expensive meat, with boneless pork shoulder available for about €3 ($4.05) per kilo (2.2 pounds) and boneless loins for about €3.50 ($4.73) per kilo.

You can buy a fresh baguette for less than €.75 ($1.01) and treat yourself to a delicious croissant for about €.50 ($.68). A dab of fresh goat cheese costs about a buck, and fresh oysters in the shell go for about €3.50 ($4.73) for a baker's dozen. And you can savor an excellent five-course meal at a nice restaurant for about €22 ($29.70).

BALANCING YOUR BUDGET

Beware, "sticker shock" may strike when you start pricing everyday items in France. After you calculate that it just cost you nearly $67 for 11 gallons of gas, you'll realize this is no cut-rate country. Goods and services, including insurance policies and utility bills, come with a whopping 19.6 percent value-added tax. The French regard a trip to the United States as a chance to buy merchandise at bargain prices. With the decline of the dollar that began in 2003, these price differences have been greatly magnified.

France is a wealthy country. Its workforce is well-educated and well-paid, with a strong sense of social responsibility. It maintains its infrastructure and preserves its *patrimoine* (national heritage), reflecting 2,000 years of historical development. None of this comes cheap, and the French are willing to pay the price (even though they may grumble about it). Inflation continues to be low, averaging around two percent; unemployment remains high at 10 percent. During the 1990s, many common expenses—auto repairs, restaurant meals, personal services—increased at almost twice the rate of inflation, largely due to rising wages and higher taxes.

A consumers group, in an extensive price comparison involving 785 supermarkets around the country, found prices increased an average of 12.2 percent between 2000 and 2004—about twice the rate of inflation. The group attributed much of this to the effect of the euro, since the new currency provided an opportunity to raise prices.

But rest assured, you don't have to be a millionaire, or even close to one, to live in France. You can buy and furnish a comfortable three- or four-bedroom house for $150,000. Cars cost about what they do in the United States. And although gas prices are higher, you probably won't use as much fuel, because you won't drive so far. Good thing, too, because gas prices reached record highs in early 2005 due to the soaring cost of crude oil. At that point, a liter of gasoline cost $1.50, and a liter of diesel fuel cost $1.35. Fortunately, medical costs are far less expensive than in the States—a visit to the doctor costs about $30.

Household and yard help costs about €8–9 ($10.80–12.15) per hour, a reasonable rate that enables many working French women to hire someone to clean their houses. Although domestic workers often prefer to be paid in cash (for obvious reasons), you can also use a *cheque service.* It works like this: With special checks obtained from your bank, you pay the employee the agreed-upon rate. When the employee deposits the check in his or her account, the bank deducts the amount due for Social Security tax—approximately 50 percent of the wage—from your account. At the end of the year, you may deduct the entire amount from your taxable income. If you are not earning income in France, you don't need the deduction.

Here is a monthly budget for a couple in a two-bedroom house or apartment:

Expense	Cost
Rent:	€1,100 ($1,485)
Food/household supplies:	€400 ($540)
Utilities:	€200 ($270)
Auto (fuel, insurance, depreciation):	€650 ($878)
Health insurance:	€350 ($473)
Clothing:	€200 ($270)
Recreation:	€200 ($270)
Total:	€3,100 ($4,185)

These categories are averages—for example, a house in a rural village may rent for €500 ($675) per month, rather than €1,100 ($1,485) in a city. If you buy a house outright, you'll strike that expense from your monthly budget. Heating bills increase in colderregions and larger houses. One point to bear in mind if you buy or rent an unfurnished house or apartment: You'll bear the large, one-time expense of appliances and furniture. Budget a minimum of €20,000 ($27,000) for this, possibly more, depending on your tastes and the size of your bank account.

Look at the categories and consider where you might want to splurge or, conversely, economize. Perhaps €200 ($270) per month for clothing is insufficient for a fashion plate like you. Perhaps it's too much if you're the type who delights in trips to *le frip,* as the French call used clothing markets, where you can pick up a nearly new sweater for about €8 ($10.80). You may choose to economize even further by waiting for the semiannual January and August sales. If like to you eat out several times a week (and you may be tempted to do so in this culinary capital), you may want to budget more for food per month. If you're a gardener, like so many of the French, you may opt to "grow your own" and cut down on your food bills. Living in a town, you may not want a car. You may also find that some of the monthly bills you pay in the States have vanished: no cable TV, perhaps; no daily newspaper subscription or membership at a gym; no gardener, because now you do it all yourself.

The requirements for a long-stay visa call for a minimum monthly income of $1,800. This is sufficient for a couple. A student can get by on less, depending on the particular program, living arrangements, etc. Keep in mind this is a *minimum* and will require careful budgeting. In the longer term, it may not be sufficient to let you live as comfortably as you wish. The luxuries you allow yourself and the ways you economize will finally determine just how you live.

Banking

Banks in France are not much different than their American counterparts. They offer credit and debit cards, checking and savings accounts, safety deposit boxes, and personal, business, and property loans. They also make change and sell insurance.

The large French banks—such as Crédit Agricole, Société Générale, BNP (Banque Nationale de Paris), and Banque Populaire—have branches in most cities and many villages. ATMs have become common. Another option is *la poste*. In France, as in other European countries, the post office functions as a bank, offering checking and savings accounts and credit cards.

In general, French banking rules are stricter than those in the States. Writing a check without sufficient funds is grounds for termination of the account, and other banks may refuse to open a new account for those who have done so. Also, you can't cash a check outside of a bank or cash a third-party check; checks made out to a person must be deposited in his or her bank account. Nor can you postdate a check. A merchant who allows payment in installments may demand a check for each payment, dated the day it is written, but only to be deposited when the payment is due.

If you buy travelers checks in euros, make sure that they say "payable in France" on the face. Otherwise, a French bank will charge 3.5 percent of their value for cashing them. Because of this charge, many merchants will not accept travelers checks.

One similarity between American and French banks: Neither likes to loan money without security. If your assets are outside of France, borrowing from a bank may be difficult. The process for borrowing money is just like it is in the United States, but with tighter limits. If you are seeking a personal loan, you must have the income necessary to make the payments and still have enough to live on.

If you desire a loan to buy property, expect to come up with a down payment of 30 to 40 percent and to repay it in 10 years or less to get the best rates. Thirty-year mortgages are not unheard-of any more in France, but the norm is 15 to 20 years. For the French themselves, a variety of special financing arrangements complement the traditional mortgage. These allow young couples to buy a home. However, they usually are tied to employment or savings previously accrued.

CURRENCY

Just for the record, one euro currently equals 6.55957 francs—and while you can no longer spend francs, you'll still often see prices in both francs and euros. For those familiar with what something cost in francs, it's quite helpful in making comparisons. Euro coins come in denominations of 1, 2, 5, 10, 20, and 50 cents—which people may still refer to as "centimes"—and 1 and 2 euros. Some people favor discarding the one- and two-cent coins, as Finland has already done, and simply rounding up or down. So far, the government has refused, although there was no coin smaller than five centimes when francs were the currency.

Bills come in 5-, 10-, 20-, 50-, 100-, 200- and 500-euro denominations, each with its own size and color for easy identification. Although the theme of the bills' design is European architectural heritage, the images are symbolic, rather than representative of any actual structure or monument. The front side of the bills displays windows and gateways, symbolizing openness and cooperation in the European Union. The back depicts different bridges, connoting communication among European nations, and between Europe and the rest of the world. The faces of the coins are uniform, and the backs bear designs representing individual countries, so national symbols have not disappeared entirely from the monetary system.

Exchange Rates

In early 2005, one euro was worth $1.35. With the U.S. deficit mounting and no concrete plans to curb it, analysts do not expect the decline of the dollar to end. The European Central Bank continued to call for a stronger dollar and resisted calls for lower interest rates. Nonetheless, French unemployment remained just under 10 percent, and Brussels announced suspension of its action against France for excess deficits

The New Euro

The franc converted to euro in 2002 and the change was also adopted in Germany, Austria, Belgium, Spain, Finland, Italy, Greece, Ireland, Luxembourg, the Netherlands, and Portugal. Still refusing to join are the United Kingdom, Denmark, and Sweden.

While the different currencies in Europe hindered economic growth, the euro opened up new opportunities. For example, Europe might have been a potential market of 300 million people, but what business could it cultivate across borders, when producers were unable to predict the costs of their materials from one nation to another?

Before the euro, 12 different currencies seesawed in value—not just in Europe, but vis-à-vis the United States and Japan—every day in response to elections, strikes, scandals, economic statistics, and inflation. The euro can and does fluctuate in relation to the dollar, the yen, and the pound, but the franc, florin, lira, and mark no longer exist.

The euro stabilizes economic exchange. For example, if a German supermarket chain agrees in April to buy wine in October from a French producer for €3 per liter, it knows that wine will cost €3 per liter, not some volatile price based on fluctuations of the franc and mark.

To make the single currency work, participating nations had to align their economies and work to keep them in alignment. This meant controlling inflation and insuring price stability. By 1998, inflation in the euro nations was under 2 percent. Inflation in France for 2004 hovered at 2 percent.

Because unemployment remained high, the creation of jobs and the lowering of government deficits through economic development rather than taxation became important goals. Structural reform and discipline were also required in national budgets to prevent the factors that traditionally created discrepancies in exchange rates. This meant more balanced budgets and government deficits within a 3 percent limit. The EU created a central bank to oversee the individual nations' central banks.

Aside from the threat of inflation, the euro and the economic umbrella it represents have also produced political stress. Any

when they saw the national budget for 2005—with a mere €45 billion ($60.8 billion) deficit.

Transferring Funds

Moving money from the U.S. to a French bank account can be accomplished in several ways, depending on your circumstances. If you are in France, the simplest and cheapest way for relatively small amounts, say $1,000, is to use your ATM card, withdraw the cash, and deposit it nation's currency is symbolic of its history and identity. To give up a national currency is a serious step away from nationalism.

The need to adopt fiscal and budgetary policies in order to produce statistics allowing EU admission has also placed a political stress on member nations. Governments had to curb spending, limit inflation, and divest publicly owned shares of corporations. In many European countries, these economic strictures required political action that governing bodies and their constituencies found not only distasteful, but also contrary to long-held philosophies. Yet, despite more than a half century of increasing unification and individual member nations' fears of eroding identity, the European Union remains a collection of sovereign nations, each capable of taking some drastic step in a different direction.

These reforms have not come easily, and few have been fully realized. Nonetheless, they seem well rooted. What remains to be seen is whether the members can maintain their political will in face of greater adversity over the long haul.

When the euro was initially introduced, it traded for about $1.15, but gradually fell throughout the spring and summer of 2002 until it reached approximately $0.90 in value. Initially, EU economists showed little concern; the weak euro would ensure the competitiveness of European products on the world market and stimulate recovery from the recession.

But with the rising price of oil tied to the dollar, a weak euro lacked purchasing power, and inflationary pressures began to increase. So far, the threat has not become reality—but government deficits in France and Germany brought about by rising unemployment, lack of economic growth, and the cost of other social programs, such as medical care, are certainly real.

In 2003, the drastic decline of the dollar began, followed by even greater increases in the price of petroleum. Instead of €0.90, or even €1, on par with the dollar, the greenback kept slipping. Suddenly, European goods were not so competitive, and a slow economic recovery slowed even further. The decline of the dollar made not only American goods cheaper on the world market, but also China's, because the yuan is tied to the dollar. European manufacturers found themselves competing at home as well as abroad not only with U.S. products in Europe, but also with cheaper Chinese goods.

in your French account. And you can always bring cash to a currency trader in a large airport or bank in a city like Paris, where they are willing to make such an exchange.

If you are in the U.S., you can do a wire transfer from your U.S. account to your French one at a cost of $25–50. Your U.S. bank will need two pieces of information to route the funds: the International Banking Account Number (IBAN) and the Bank Identification Code (BIC). Your U.S. bank determines the rate of exchange because they are using your dollars to buy euros. Your French checkbook will have this information as a special page called a Relevé d'Identité Bancaire (RIB).

An alternative to the wire transfer is to purchase a check or money order in euros either from a bank or currency exchange agency. Usually, they charge a flat fee for this service. Just be sure that the check you get says "payable in France," or your French bank will deduct a commission and credit your account with the balance.

Exchange rates are always problematical. First of all, the rate you see published is not the exact rate you are likely to get, because rates change continuously. However, currency trades are carried to four decimal places, and a drop of more than one cent in a day is not that frequent; usually the dollar loses or gains a tenth or a hundredth of a cent. When you are trading blocks of $100,000, this makes a difference. But for $1,000 the difference is pennies. Second, you won't get the published rate if you are trading relatively small amounts of money, anyway.

However, if you are considering a major purchase in France, such as a home, you can follow trends and try to learn if the dollar is stable, fluctuating only a few cents one way or another as it did during the last months of 2004 and early 2005. In such a case, on an exchange of $500,000, you stood to gain or lose about $8,300, depending on whether you changed money at $1.33 or $1.36 to the euro.

The longer term is much more financially significant. Suppose you had arrived in France in 2002, when the exchange rate hovered around $.90 to €1, with your income fixed either by your U.S. employment or by retirement benefits. During the course of two years, as the rate of exchange rose to $1.35 to €1, our purchasing power would have been cut by one-third.

If you have property, whether real estate or any other you are considering liquidating before or after a move to France, consider the long-range situation. In early 2005, financial experts were forecasting a still weaker dollar based on the growing U.S. deficit. On the other hand, very few experts back in 2002 said for publication that the dollar was going to drop so drastically. Perhaps the best investment is in a crystal ball, if you can find one for sale.

OPENING AN ACCOUNT

Many Americans coming to France will need no more than a checking account. To have obtained a long-stay visa, many of you will have shown sufficient income to live without working while in France. If you are eligible to work or open a business in France, you'll be in a better position to borrow within the country, if necessary.

Opening a bank account in France requires a similar process to opening one in the U.S. You'll have to prove who you are—with a valid passport, for example—and prove where you live. For this, acceptable documents are recent bills for utilities, such as water, gas, electricity, or a telephone. If you wish to open a joint account, the other person will also have to appear at the bank. An initial deposit of €100–150 ($135–203) will be required; the amount varies from bank to bank. You do not need a long-stay visa to open an account, but you do need a fixed address.

Keeping tabs on your American bank account is easy via the Internet.

One difference between U.S. and French checking accounts is that in France, there are no third-party checks. In other words, you cannot take a check you have received and endorse it to someone else, who then deposits the check in their own account. You can only cash a check by depositing it in your account, then wait seven days for it to clear before you can use the funds.

Even without a long-stay visa, Americans owning property in France can open checking accounts that permit them to transfer funds from home and pay bills in France. In many cases, bills such as insurance and electricity may be paid by direct deduction from the account. In other instances, you send along to a creditor a *relevé d'identité bancaire,* or RIB, several of which are included in each book of checks, filling out the date and amount. For many Americans, living in France, the greatest difficulty paying bills is spelling the amounts in French.

If you are retired or living off income in the United States, you should probably keep your American bank account and simply transfer funds into a French checking account as needed. Wire transfers are often expensive, however. One solution is to increase the daily limit on your ATM card attached to your U.S. account to $1,000 or more. This will allow you to withdraw sizeable sums per week. For larger sums, such as for the purchase of property, international firms that specialize in currency trading, such as American Foreign Exchange, will write a check drawn on a French bank for a fee.

Keeping tabs on your American bank account is easy via the Internet. Many U.S. banks maintain websites that allow you to review your account activity and make payments online. And you can always make payments and handle other financial arrangements the old-fashioned way—through the mail.

CREDIT CARDS

The Visa and MasterCard credit cards issued by French banks are quite expensive by American standards, carrying an annual fee of €90 and €120 ($122 and $162) for a gold card. Even a simple debit card can cost €25 per year ($34). The annual percentage rate (called TEG in French) is pegged at just below 14 percent. The cards come with travel insurance: repatriation in medical emergencies, money for meals, lodging in case of cancelled flights, etc. The other reason to have a French credit card, or at least a debit card, is to access the service station pumps that are open at night and on Sundays. Your U.S. card, lacking the *puce* (computer chip) that lives on all French cards, won't work.

In late 2004, Brussels—that is, the European Union—was studying complaints that French banks were involved in a secret deal to stifle competition in offering cards. However, two supermarket chains, Carrefour and Auchan, were offering Visa cards at half the price of the banks. In the meantime, if you don't want to pay those fees, your U.S. cards will work everywhere except at the gas pumps.

Taxes

The French generally consider taxes to be an onerous burden, and certainly they are heavier than in the United States. But American taxpayers, despite all their complaints, pay less in taxes than the French.

FRENCH TAXES

First there is the 19.6 percent value-added tax, or TVA. It works like a sales tax, but unlike a tax on retail sales of merchandise, it is added to labor and less tangible products and services, such as insurance. Each time someone transforms something (adds value to it) for sale, the tax is imposed. And it is the consumer who pays: Businesses deduct the TVA they pay from the TVA they add to their products and services.

The extent to which the TVA helps finance the French government is easily visible in the national budget for the year 2004. While income tax revenue brought in €53.4 billion ($72 billion), and corporate income

The Taxman Cometh

Tax time is a headache in any language. When the day comes to deal with *le fisc* (tax system), anyone facing a packet of unfamiliar forms in a foreign language prepares for an ordeal that may stretch into days of nervous consultations with the dictionary, trying to decipher bureaucratic language and regulations.

In recent years, the government has been trying to reduce the number of these civil servants and close some of the offices around the country. To this end, the Ministry of Finance has set up a website where you can make your annual Declaration of Revenue and pay online. But as with most personal visits to the local tax office, the online communication must be conducted in French.

French fiscal authorities are willing to consult and assist newcomers. After all, their job is to collect taxes, and correctly filed forms work to their benefit. Following this logic, authorities near Bordeaux decided in 2005 to convoke a meeting of some of the 5,000 Anglophones living in the Dordogne region to offer explanations of the forms in English.

The meeting proved a success, with the local Monbazillac wine being served. Bernard Peiclier, head of fiscal services in the region, agreed there was a "real demand" for it, and promised to have at least four English-speaking agents available through the April 4 filing deadline. With more than 200,000 Anglophones now owning homes in France, its a practice that seems likely to spread.

tax produced another €39 billion ($52.7 billion), revenue from the TVA was €121 billion ($163.4 billion). This is out of net total receipts of €265.5 billion ($358.4 billion).

There is movement afoot to lower the TVA. In 1999, the TVA charged for home improvements and renovations was lowered to 5.5 percent. In April 2000, the overall TVA was lowered by one percent, from 20.6 to 19.6 percent. Small businesses may now opt for a system of taxation that bypasses the bookkeeping involved with collection and payment of the TVA; medium-sized businesses grossing up to €762,000 ($1.03 million) may also choose a simplified reporting and payment system.

In addition to the TVA, the French pay property taxes. Their rates vary according to locale and are updated annually for inflation. Property taxes come in two different levies: *taxe foncière* (property tax) and *taxe d'habitation,* the tax owed each January 1 by the person occupying a property, either the tenant or the owner, even if the latter has another residence. The criterion is that the property is habitable; the owner of a barn without a roof or of a house without electricity would not be expected to pay this tax. When property is sold, these taxes may be prorated, although this must be negotiated.

Then there are taxes on the money you make. People earning an income in France are required to pay income tax, capital gains tax, and sometimes wealth tax. Probably the most critical factor in all of these taxes is your domicile, or principal residence. The wealth tax is levied on the worldwide holdings of anyone domiciled in France—one of the reasons some of France's wealthiest citizens have moved out of the country. Not only is their wealth taxed, but those in the highest income bracket are taxed at 54 percent. All of these taxes can add up.

AMERICAN TAXES

If you're planning to move to France, examine your situation carefully to see how you will be affected. Although U.S. citizens can exclude up to $80,000, the Internal Revenue Service imposes certain tests, one of which is physical presence in the country for 330 days of the year. Meeting this test may mean that you are subject to French taxes. However, for the nonresident (that is, the person not domiciled in France), only income earned in France is subject to taxation, and at a lower rate than the resident pays. The amount withheld from a nonresident's earnings is regarded as satisfying his or her tax liability, whereas residents are taxed on worldwide earnings.

Americans not working or operating a business in France, especially retirees, are probably better remaining domiciled in the United States. For one thing, retirees can take advantage of Medicare when in the States, thus cutting down on the amount of health insurance they carry. What's more, you're familiar with the U.S. system; at the point of retirement, you know pretty well how it works and what to expect. You don't need the aggravation and uncertainty of a new and different tax system, at least as complicated and arbitrary as its American corollary, and surely even more difficult to navigate in a foreign language.

INCOME TAX

Foreigners who live and work in France will inevitably fall under the French income tax regime. While a tax convention with the United States prevents double taxation, rest assured you will be taxed by one of them. If you are a long-term salaried employee, whether for a French or American firm, you have no choice under the law: You will be taxed in France and must seek credit when filing taxes in the United States.

For the American who does business in France, there is the question of domicile, or residency. If you are domiciled in France—not necessarily the same thing as owning a house in France and having a *carte de séjour* (residency permit) or *carte de commerçant* (merchant's permit)—you are obliged to pay taxes in France on your income worldwide. Moreover, France, like other European nations, assesses a wealth tax; that is, it taxes an individual on his or her net worth above a limit of approximately €720,000 ($972,000).

For tax purposes, several criteria determine whether you are considered to be domiciled in France. The first criterion is if your main residence is in France; second, if you earn income in France, whether salaried or self-employed, unless the activity and earnings are incidental; third, if your center of economic interest is in France. The tax is assessed on the basis of the household: the total income of spouses (or unmarried partners) and children.

Those not domiciled in France are taxed only on income from French sources, including:
- Income from real property located in France, or from rights connected with such property.
- Income from French movable property and any other stocks and shares invested in France.
- Income from *exploitations* (business concerns) located in France.
- Income from professional activities, whether employment or not, carried on in France or from for-profit transactions carried out in France.
- Capital gains on the transfer, for financial consideration, of property or rights of any kind and profits derived from transactions, in particular those carried out by real estate brokers when such profits are connected with *fonds de commerce* (businesses) operated in France, as well as real property located in France, real property rights connected therewith, or shares in unlisted companies whose assets mainly consist of such property and rights.
- Capital gains on the transfer of corporate rights resulting from the transfer of rights pertaining to companies having their head offices in France.
- Compensations, including salaries, in consideration of artistic or athletic performances provided in France.

Taxpayers domiciled outside of France who receive income from French sources, or have one or more homes at their disposal in France, must normally file a tax return. However, the convention against double taxation may well negate any taxes due in France. There is also a minimum income provision that exempts anyone whose income after deductions is less than approximately €7,500 ($10,125)—the figure is adjusted annually—and €8,200 ($11,070) for those 65 or older.

Social Security

France's Social Security system differs from that in the States in several significant ways. First of all, it is not uniform; various occupations have different plans. Farmers, salaried employees, craftspeople, shopkeepers, and civil servants all participate in different plans. Yet the system is by no means chaotic. It's been compared to a set of Russian dolls, the ones that look alike but come in graduated sizes, one fitting inside the other. And steps are slowly being taken to bring the various sectors into conformity.

The French system is facing a major influx of new retirees. Until recently, it has taken in about 110,000 new pensioners a year. Starting in 2006, as baby boomers retire, that number will more than double to 250,000. Furthermore, these folks will live longer on the average than their predecessors, putting a further strain on the funds. The demographics are staggering: Today, there are 10 active workers for every four retirees; by 2040, the ratio is expected to be 10 workers for every seven pensioners. The strategies for solving this problem are limited. The U.S. solution has been to increase the age of retirement. Others include higher taxes on wages, financing from another source, higher wages, and, of course, diminished benefits.

The important thing for Americans to know is that France and the United States have a treaty covering Social Security, as well as taxation. This treaty allows citizens from both nations to work in either country, pay into either system according to their employment and eligible age of retirement, and receive credit for their total number of years. Years of work in one country will not be lost in the other. Nor will you have to pay into both systems. Again, depending on the situation, you will be eligible—and required—to pay into one or the other, but not both.

Those who have paid into Social Security in both countries may be eligible for benefits from one or both countries. If you meet the basic requirement for either country, that country will pay you. The United

States will begin reduced payments at age 62; France will begin payments at age 60. Those who do not have enough time in either country alone may qualify by combining their credits from both countries.

The system is somewhat complicated, but France will compute benefits based on French credits alone, and then on French and prorated U.S. credits, and pay whichever is greater. The U.S. may reduce your benefits if you are receiving some from France, so it is wise to determine the various options before making a decision.

One thing the treaty does not include is health care. The U.S. Social Security system will not extend Medicare benefits outside the United States. Retired Americans with Medicare coverage who are stricken outside the country cannot be treated under Medicare except on home turf. Say you're on a two-week vacation abroad and you have a heart attack. You may have paid thousands of dollars into Social Security and Medicare, but you will not be reimbursed by Medicare for any treatment you receive in a foreign country. If you have health insurance that covers the portion that Medicare does not, it may cover the Medicare portion when you are abroad.

Investing

In recent years, one of the best investments in France was real estate. With real estate prices rising an average of 11 percent annually nationwide, many people have bought property as an investment, either a principal residence or a vacation home. Others renovated or added to existing homes as an investment. French and foreigners alike have bought old homes in rural villages and renovated them for resale or rental, the profits providing them with an income while continuing with a new project.

In general, France offers the same type of investments as the U.S. There are savings accounts, stocks and bonds, and mutual funds. The CAC 40 is the French equivalent of the Dow Jones Index for U.S. stocks. Life insurance is perhaps the most popular form of saving for retirement.

Communications

The industrialized world is wired, and France is an integral part of it. Aside from the language barrier, you'll find it no more difficult to communicate in France—both within its boundaries and beyond—than you do in the United States. Forget the horror stories you may have heard about French phones and service. Vast improvements have been made in both. Telephone service was separated from the post office years ago and privatized, although the government still held 43 percent of the stock in 2005. There is brisk, swiftly changing competition for your telephone dollar, including via the Internet. From email to *la poste* (mail), you'll find it easy to stay in touch while you're in France.

Telephone Service

Many people have heard horror stories about phone service in France, or remember when businesses commonly used teletypes for communications because the phones were so unreliable. A hangover from those times is that most businesses today have a separate *telecopie* (fax) number, as well as a phone number.

You no longer have to go to a *tabac* (a shop or bar-café where cigarettes are sold) to get a *jeton* (token) every time you want to use a public phone. Those days are gone. Instead, *tabacs* sell phone cards—the size of a credit card and good for a certain number of message units. These are used in many public phones. Some public phones will also accept credit cards such as Visa or MasterCard, and a few still take coins. However, with the boom in popularity of cell phones, many pay phones have been removed from service.

From email to la *poste (mail), you'll find it easy to stay in touch while you're in France.*

Today, the French telephone system is the equal of any, with call-waiting, call transfer, and all the other extras that phone companies like to tack on. France Telecom, the national phone company, was separated from the postal service some years ago. More recently, it was privatized. To remain competitive, it dropped its rates and continued reduced rates during off-peak hours, such as evenings and weekends. The rate structure is complex and changes frequently, often because of competing telephone services. While France Telecom remains the largest single supplier of phone service in the country, other providers may be less expensive in given situations.

However, in France, the monthly bill for telephone service does not include any calls, even across the street or next door. In 2005, the monthly charge for telephone service was €14 ($18.90) and scheduled to increase €1 per year in 2006 and 2007. The Autorité de Régulation des Télécommunications granted France Telecom this increase in return for a proposal that would lower rates for calls by at least 26 percent by 2008.

Despite the recent lowering of French long-distance phone rates, for transcontinental calls you may want to subscribe to one of several services that operate from U.S.-based computers. Here's how it works: You dial a U.S. number, connect with a computer, and hang up. The computer locks onto the French phone number and calls back—at a cheaper U.S. rate. You then answer the return call and dial a U.S. number, or a number in any other country, and wait for the party to answer. As technology changes or as Internet phone services become widely available, these systems may drop out of existence.

SOS Hotline

The French call it *mal de pays,* but to us, it's just plain old homesickness. At some time or another, everyone who lives far from home is likely to experience the impulse is to call a friend and talk. But when that friend is in a time zone six to nine hours away, that's not always convenient.

Sometimes, the situation is more serious, and that's where SOS Help comes in. SOS Help is a crisis hotline for Anglophones in France. You can telephone (01 46 21 46 46) any afternoon or evening and talk to a friendly person. "Whatever the problem, we are there to take your call," is their motto. The Paris region hotline is staffed by trained volunteers who offer practical advice, as well as handle emotional crises. SOS Amité, a French language hotline, sponsors the organization.

The volunteer listeners are selected after two interviews, one with a professional psychotherapist, who assesses their capacity to be warm, empathetic, and nonjudgmental.

Training for listeners is assured by three professional psychotherapists and starts with an all-day group. After the introduction day, the training continues with a course of approximately three months, consisting of two-hour weekly meetings. Topics include communication skills and interpersonal interaction, as well as such issues as grief, bereavement, and suicide.

The organization also needs supporters who don't answer the phones, but contribute their time and energy to keep the project afloat with administrative skills, helping to pay the €500 ($725) monthly rent and traing of phone volunteers.

The website for SOS Help also provides links to other groups that offer helping hands to expats. The Association of American Wives of Europeans, for instance, notes that "our concerns on citizenship, bilingualism and dual cultures bring us together. Our need for friendship and American heritage keep us together."

Area Codes

Whereas Americans are used to dialing just seven digits to reach a friend or business associate in the same area code, you'll dial 10 in France. In 1998, the country was divided into five areas, with two-digit area codes tacked onto the traditional eight-digit phone numbers. Paris is 01, the Mediterranean coast 04, the northeast 03, the southwest 05, and the northwest 02. When calling from outside the country, you use France's country code, 33, and drop the initial 0 from the area code. Inside the country, you must dial the 0, even when you're calling from within that same area. So, if you're calling a friend's home on the other side of Paris, you would dial a number that looks like this: 02 00 11 22 33. From anywhere else in France, you would dial the same number. And if you're calling that same friend from the U.S., you would dial: (01 33) 2 00 11 22 33.

LAND LINES

One of the first appliances to get when you arrive is a telephone. You have the choice of buying one from the phone company, supermarket, or electronics stores. If you bring one from the United States, be prepared to find an adapter, because the French system does not use the familiar little clear plastic jacks. Instead, they have a much larger plug about two inches long. Adapters are simply the French plug with a little hole in the bottom for the American-style jack. They are inexpensive and can be purchased at your local electronics shop.

Phone Companies

Telephone service in France was formerly a state monopoly, and France Telecom, though now privatized, owns and maintains the telephone lines throughout the country. It remains the chief provider of telephone service. However, there are numerous competing services that say they offer cheaper rates, such as 9 Telecom, Tele2, Teleconnect, OneTel, and Cegetel—and in many instances, they do. However, these claims are based on when and where you are calling: locally, nationally, internationally (Europe, North America, Asia), to a cell phone in France, to a cell phone in another country, and so on. And France Telecom itself offers a variety of different rates. In 2005, this was a very fluid market, with new offers and promotions appearing almost monthly from one telecom or another.

For example, Cegetel offers a rate of €.013 ($.018) per minute anywhere in France; Tele2 offers a rate of €.01 ($.014) per minute for all calls within your department and €.034 ($.046) per minute nationally; France Telecom offers unlimited calls anywhere in France for €33 ($44.55) per month, or to particular numbers for even less. There is even one service, ComparaTel, that for a fee of €10 ($13.50) per month will direct your call through the cheapest available provider for that particular call and provide a single monthly bill for all your calls.

Some of these services must be accessed by using a different number in place of the initial 0 in French phone numbers. But when you wish to order their service, they all ask for an existing telephone number. France Telecom charges €55 ($74.25) to install a new phone, and the basic monthly rate in 2005 was €13.99 ($18.89). In other words, no matter which telecom you choose, you will have to pay €55 ($74.25) for installation and €13.99 ($18.89) per month, plus whatever your chosen service bills for the calls you make.

The good news is that there is now an alternative to this hodge-podge of rates, if you have a computer and also want access to the Internet. France Telecom and a number of the other telecoms, including Cegetel, Tele2, OneTel, and 9 Telecom, offer telephone service via an ADSL computer hookup. The rates vary depending on the speed of the ADSL connection, but usually runs €15–40 ($20.25–54) per month. France Telecom provides the service via Wanadoo, its Internet service provider. Another such provider is Free. This is the same service that also brings television channels over your telephone line. A router—France Telecom rents theirs for €3 ($4.05) per month—determines whether the signals are telephone calls, computer-related, or television programs and directs them to the appropriate appliance. In early 2005, this telephone service was limited to France; international calls would be charged in the normal fashion.

The Minitel
A once handy but now outmoded aspect of French telephony to which you may see occasional references is a device called the Minitel, a specialized computer and modem that accesses phone company data banks. Both slow and expensive by computer standards, they are the computer equivalent of rotary dial phones.

CELLULAR PHONES
Cell phones are readily available and widespread in France, just as they are in the U.S. In fact, there are now more cell phones than fixed phones in France. Cell phone numbers begin with 06 everywhere in the country. There are pitfalls to avoid, however. First, make sure that the phone will work where you want to use it. Despite what phone companies say about their coverage, a village need not be very remote for a cell phone to be useless inside a house, or even in the street. Coverage has been improving, but asking your neighbors how satisfied they are with their own service is probably a good idea. You have the option of a year-long contract for a fixed sum for a fixed number of minutes per month, or you can buy a card to use at will. The latter will probably be more expensive per minute, but cheaper in the long run if you do not spend much time on the phone.

There are three providers of cell phone service, and they have a bewildering variety of rates that changes frequently. The largest provider is Orange, operated by France Telecom. Next is SFR, and third is Bouygues.

The rates depend upon the type of service. The most expensive cell phone service per minute is the card: Buy a card for €10 ($13.50), and you can talk for 20 minutes during the next 15 days; buy one for €75 ($101.25), and you can talk for three hours and 35 minutes during the next six months. If you talk more than your time limit, buy another card. Sign a one-year contract for €18 ($24.30) per month, and talk for one hour each month; two hours per month will cost €35 ($47.25) per month. Then there are the special plans for weekends, nights, etc.

Email and Postal Service

INTERNET ACCESS

France was much slower than the U.S. in adopting computers as a basic household appliance, but they have now gained wider acceptance. By the end of 2004, more than 15 million people were online in France, and two-thirds of them had broadband. With *haut debit* (broadband) Internet access already available to more than 80 percent of the country, the government's target is to extend that to 95 percent by the end of 2005.

For email alone—remaining in touch with family and friends in the U.S.—a computer is worthwhile. The six- to nine-hour time difference between France and the U.S. often makes phone calls inconvenient in either direction. Nothing strains a relationship like answering the phone at 4 A.M. to hear someone say they just called to chat. And with telephony software improving all the time, you can use the Internet to make inexpensive calls as well.

Fans of Apple and Macintosh computers should be careful, however, since their products are not well supported in France, where PCs rule—and Windows rules PCs. Linux accounts for a bare one percent of operating systems, and Windows 95 percent.

French *domaines* (Web designations, such as .com, .org, and .edu in the United States) are often designated by .fr, but .com is actually more common. The website of the French national rail system, for instance, answers to either .com or .fr, as does the France Telecom site. Whether the language police like it or not, dot-com is firmly embedded, although often the French version is point-com, with "point" being a dot or period.

The rapid expansion of broadband access throughout the country—

most of it occurred in 2003 and 2004—has radically changed the system of *fournisseur d'accès Internet* (Internet service providers, or ISPs; the French acronym is FAI). The ADSL service offered by providers such as France Telecom, AOL, Free, and others comes at a flat rate per month and can include television and Internet phone service, as well as normal access to the Web. A typical offer in early 2005 was unlimited ADSL access at two megabits or more for €30 ($40.50) per month.

LA POSTE

Mail service in France is generally good, certainly comparable to that in the States, although somewhat more expensive. Letters and postcards up to 20 grams (five sevenths of an ounce) cost €.53 ($.72) within France and €.55 ($.74) within the European Union. Letters to North America cost €.90 ($1.22). The costs go up proportionally for heavier letters.

La Poste (the Postal Service) offers such familiar services as *poste restant* (general delivery), Chronopost (express mail), *lettres recommandées* (registered letters), and money orders. Of course, mark your airmail letters *par avion*. Just as in the States, the post office sells a limited selection of boxes for mailing packages. In recent years, Federal Express and DHL have both established themselves in France, opening up an era of competitiveness.

One big difference between French and American post offices is that La Poste offers banking services. You can open a checking or savings account at the post office, a great convenience if you happen to live in a village without a bank. They will also sell you prepaid phone cards and provide Internet access.

As for receiving mail and packages from outside of France, be aware that shippers are required to list the value of the package's contents. This is duly noted by customs officials. The moral: Don't expect to avoid paying the 19.6 percent TVA by ordering merchandise from the United States. Your goods will be delivered, followed in short order by a bill for the tax due.

SHIPPING OPTIONS

Shipping packages is expensive whether you use La Poste or a private carrier, such as UPS or FedEx. Moreover, private carriers have very few offices in France; just getting your parcel to one of them could cost more than shipping it via the slightly more expensive but much more convenient local post office.

La Poste charges €200 ($270) to send a parcel weighing 10 kilos (22 pounds) from Paris to the U.S. DHL charges €168 ($227) for the same weight, but its offices are few and far between. From Nice to Bordeaux, there are just six DHL branches. UPS, which has two offices in Paris and five others in France, wants €165 ($223) to send 10 kilos to New York and €195 ($263) to San Francisco. Federal Express, with three offices around Paris, charges €177.20 ($239) for 10 kilos to the U.S.

Media

NEWSPAPERS AND MAGAZINES

The first newspaper to appear on the streets of Paris was *La Gazette* in 1631. It began a lively tradition that continues today. French newspapers are very different from American papers in that they do not contain anywhere near the volume of advertising. Many are tabloid-size and thin, about 32–48 pages. The two-pound Sunday edition laden with color sections, preprinted advertising, and supermarket coupons is unknown here.

The first newspaper to appear on the streets of Paris was La Gazette *in 1631.*

Le Monde, one of the most respected of the handful of national dailies, prints a combined Sunday-Monday edition. Its nod to U.S. journalistic practices is to include a tabloid section listing radio and television programming for the coming week following its much smaller news section. *Le Monde* also publishes separate, specialized periodicals that are sold independently, such as *Le Monde Diplomatique.* Other national papers include *Le Figaro, Liberation,* and *Le Parisien/Aujourd'hui.*

France has one weekly newspaper unlike anything known in the U.S., *Le Canard Enchaîné,* a satirical journal that often breaks real stories. Its black humor is always antiestablishment, but based on real facts and events. Its best scoops are usually repeated in more sober terms by the mainstream media.

The *International Herald Tribune* continues doing yeoman service interpreting Europe to Anglophones. Despite its ownership by *The New York Times,* it seems more than ever an independent, authentic voice offering a truly European view of current events, rather than a pale reflection of American interests. It is widely available at newsstands throughout the country.

Comics and Culture

When it comes to culture, there are no higher highbrows than the French. So, it may come as a surprise to Americans that they are passionate about the lowbrow comic book. But, of course, they've managed to elevate it to an art form.

The French comic book—called a *bande dessinée*—is no cheaply printed product of a few dozen pages designed to be rolled up and stuck in your back pocket. Instead, it's a hard-cover, coffee table–sized album of about 100 pages that typically costs €10–15 ($14.50–21.75). Supermarket book sections provide plenty of shelf space for these titles.

Subject matter ranges from juvenile to adult in all the genres of fiction, and most of them offer carefully crafted artwork. Some of these books have become cultural icons recognized far outside of France, such as *Tintin,* the red-haired reporter, and *Asterix the Gaul.*

Along with the Musée d'Orsay and the Louvre, the Ministry of Culture also supports the Centre de la Bande Dessinée et l'Image in Angouleme. Housed in a building that began life as an abbey in the 6th century, the center welcomed a 20-ton collection of Marvel comics from America in the summer of 2004. It also hosts an annual international festival of comic book art that draws national television coverage, as well as coverage in the national press.

The small-town daily papers common in so many U.S. cities, with circulations of 10,000–30,000 covering one or two counties, are not known here. Instead, regional dailies cover particular areas of France with lots of editions. The different editions permit coverage of numerous villages and their very local news: births and marriages, photos of an athletic team of 12-year-olds lined up in a row, an amateur theatrical group presenting a performance, six-year-olds in costume going to a party.

Magazines are also an important part of the French press. *Paris Match,* the provocative color weekly, combines *People*-style celebrity coverage with reportage as serious as anything appearing in the *The New York Times* Sunday magazine. Most French magazines are aimed at specific audiences. *L'Express, Le Point,* and *Nouvel Observateur* are popular news magazines. Both *Time* and *Newsweek* publish European editions. *Elle* and *Marie Claire* cater to women.

One type of publication in France is quite different from its American counterpart. *Bandes dessinées* (comic books) are a serious art form in France. There are many for children, of course, but others boast historical or adult themes and story lines. Comic book artists like Hugo

Pratt are considered cultural figures in France. Many of the books are published in hardcover in large formats. Among the better known series are *Asterix,* about a Gaul in Roman times, and *Tin-Tin,* tales of an adventurous young reporter.

TELEVISION

Much of French television is public—the opposite of the situation in the States. Owners of television pay an annual tax of about €120 ($162) to help underwrite this programming. Public channels also sell advertising to support themselves, just as private channels do. In this respect, the major difference between the two seems to be that public channels do not interrupt movies with commercials, while private channels run a single "intermission" to broadcast a number of commercials.

The two public television channels serving the general public are France 2 and France 3. France 2 is the flagship, with correspondents in major world capitals and full coverage of international events. Its programming is the same throughout the country and throughout the day.

More limited in worldwide coverage, France 3 concentrates on France. Its programming changes depending on the region, with telecasts from 13 locations around the country. Some two dozen news bureaus attached to different stations often work with the local press to cover stories of less than national interest. Part of France 3's programming also includes material in regional languages.

Both channels broadcast syndicated shows, movies, and reruns from around the world, all dubbed into French. However, they also include prime-time discussions of serious subjects, as well as major sporting events like the Tour de France bicycle race and the French Open tennis tournament.

Two other public channels play a lesser role in French television, sharing Channel 5 on the dial: La Cinquième, from 3 A.M.–7 P.M.; and Arte, a French-German collaborative effort, during the remaining hours. La Cinquième runs many of the shows that are staples of public TV programming in the United States: language lessons, nature shows, and documentaries on foreign countries, along with panel discussions of issues and interesting old movies.

Arte often uses its prime time to explore a particular theme during an entire evening. For example, it might open with a documentary on a topic such as suicide, show a feature film involving suicide, move to

Spectator Sports

The French are just as avid sports fans as Americans. Professional football—or soccer as Americans insist upon calling it—is played at night during prime time. The channels bid for broadcast rights and the winner usually walks away with the biggest audience that night.

Throughout the year, certain sporting events receive the kind of coverage similarly devoted to the World Series in the U.S. One of these events is a tennis tournament the French call the *Roland Garros,* the name of the stadium where the French Open is held. (The stadium is named for an heroic French aviator killed in World War I.) For two weeks at the end of May, afternoon telecasts include the tennis matches and the best moments are recapped on the evening news.

In July, there is the **Tour de France** bicycle race—which includes three weeks of daily coverage.

The great sailboat races such as the **Route du Rhum, Globe Vendée,** and the America's Cup also draw daily coverage on the news shows. And although she came in second, Ellen MacArthur became a national celebrity in France as both the youngest person and fastest woman to sail solo around the world.

Rugby, far more popular in southern France than in the north, is relegated to Saturday afternoons, while ice skating is late evening fare on television. Two minor sports that also sometimes make the regional evening news are volleyball, handball, and basketball—now that there are a few European players in the pro ranks.

During the Olympics every four years, you'll see a lot of coverage in sports where the French excel, such as fencing and judo.

a roundtable discussion of the issue, and end the evening with one or two more documentaries. It also repeats films at different times during the week.

Perhaps the most popular television station in France is privately owned TF1, at least during prime time, which begins just before 9 P.M. Both France 2 and TF1 conclude their evening newscasts about 8:45 P.M. and follow with about 10 minutes of commercials before launching into the evening's entertainment. TF1 often garners 25 to 40 percent of the audience, although its programming is not unlike that of France 2 and 3, with feature films, reportage, made-for-TV movies, sports, and music shows.

One curious difference between French and American television: Feature films—those that have appeared in the theaters—may not be shown on Wednesday or Saturday nights. The first is the traditional night films open at a theater, and the second is the favorite night for dates and entertainment. The policy stemmed from the French audio-visual council's efforts to support the French movie industry. The irony is that the most popular films being shown in French theaters these days are not French, but American.

The second private channel is M6, aimed at a younger audience. It carries lots of syndicated shows about teenagers—*Buffy Contre les Vampires (Buffy the Vampire Slayer)* has been a Saturday night main-stay—music videos, and telefilms. Recently, it has become more aggressive in showing documentaries and films, but remains the intellectual lightweight. These channels are all available with an ordinary antenna. Quite common, however, are small satellite dishes for antennas. These dishes, if aimed properly at other satellites, will bring in foreign language programming—English, German, or Arabic, for instance.

France's pay channel, Canal+, which for years sent out its daily serving of entertainment and sports over the normal airwaves to be unscrambled by the boxes of its subscribers, continues that programming. It now also offers Canal Satellite, with various packages of premium channels available for additional fees. Its competitor, TPS, features similar offers.

Cable television was slow to arrive in France, and today exists primarily in large cities and nearby suburbs. About six million homes get a total of 20 cable networks. But technology has already provided another solution. The same telephone wire that brings ADSL to your computer will also bring cable TV—for an additional monthly fee, of course. Both TPS and Canal+ offer their satellite programming in this fashion.

RADIO

French radio is a national affair, with a handful of networks, public and private, covering the country. Puzzling to many is where to find them on the dial. The same program will appear at one frequency in Paris, another in Strasbourg, and yet a third in Lyon. The Internet has provided the solution to this, since all the networks have websites that will provide their frequency in your area, as well as a list of programs.

Radio France is the overall name for the various publicly financed radio networks: France Inter, France Info, France Musique, France Culture, and Radio Bleue. There is also a public network that offers regional programming, its broadcasts differing from area to area.

Three big private radio networks broadcast on both AM and FM:

Europe 1, RTL, and RMC. Local radio programs are offered in the private sector by networks NRJ, Europe 2, Fun Radio, and Nostalgie. All of these stations, both public and private, also broadcast over the Internet and are available on TPS and Canal Satellite as well.

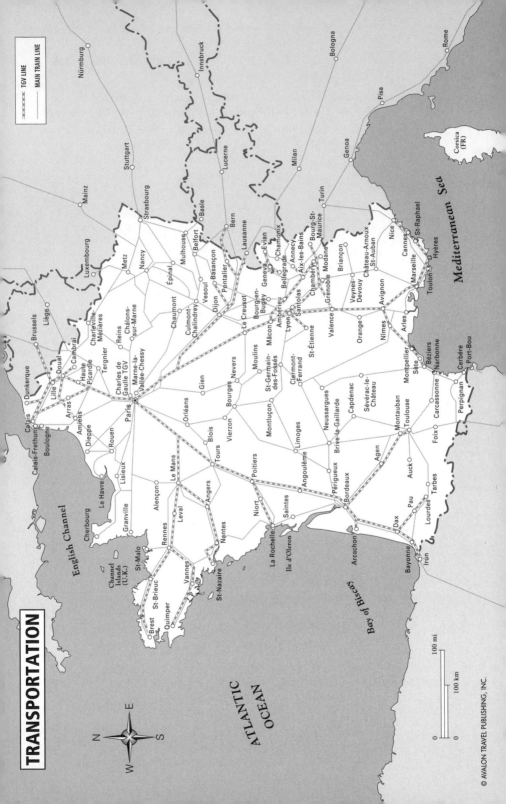

TRANSPORTATION

TGV LINE
MAIN TRAIN LINE

Travel and Transportation

I n the past, you could say of French transportation that "all roads lead to Paris." But during the 1990s, that truism began to give way, although the city remains a transportation hub in France. Today, you can climb off an Airbus in the morning at Charles de Gaulle airport, catch a high-speed train to Lyon, and arrive in time for lunch without ever entering Paris. The same is true of automotive travel. In the past, roads inevitably took you through the most congested areas; today's limited-access highways skirt the cities. Although Paris is still the touchpoint for French and American air travel, other European carriers use their own countries as hubs, flying into various provincial French airports from Amsterdam, London, Brussels, Barcelona, and Frankfurt, among other cities. In short: Fast trains, regional airports, and good roads make travel easy in France, although not inexpensive.

By Air

For air travelers, France offers a network of regional international airports, in addition to the main Paris gateways. Given the distance across France and to neighboring European cities, these airports offer great convenience. While the train takes you quickly enough from Paris to London, Brussels, or Geneva, getting to any of those cities from Bordeaux, Nantes, or Nice by rail is a lengthier proposition, more or less an all-day affair—and may even cost more than the flight. But day trips to Paris or other European cities from Toulouse, Marseille, or Nice—impossible even with direct connections on the TGV—are easily accomplished by air. Frequent flights are offered throughout the day at prices competitive with train travel. This ease and affordability have contributed to a doubling of air passenger traffic in recent years.

Many of these provincial airports (those outside Paris) also feed passengers to other hubs around Europe for flights to the United States. For instance, you fly Lufthansa to Frankfurt, then to the United States; KLM takes passengers to Amsterdam, Sabena to Brussels, and British Air to London for transfer to U.S. flights. Air France, of course, sends its North America–bound passengers through Paris.

The big change in European air travel has come from low-cost Ryanair. Its preferential deals with French cities such as Strasbourg have brought complaints of unfair competition from Air France. Ryanair flies into France from London, Dublin, Liverpool, Frankfurt, and Brussels with numerous flights daily. Its flights from London to the South of France are credited with bringing in hundreds of thousands of visitors each year, thousands of whom have purchased homes.

Within France itself, Air France is the dominant airline, offering far more domestic flights than any other airline. Even a small airport like Montpellier sends half a dozen flights to Orly alone before noon. Airfares change constantly, but Air France maintains a certain number of flights with at least some reduced-fare seats. People age 60 or older, families traveling together, including grandparents with grandchildren, and couples are all likely to find discounts off the regular fares.

Unfortunately, for air travel within the country, you must often as not go through Paris to reach another provincial city. So, what might be a five-hour train ride involving one transfer becomes almost exactly the same duration by air. For example, someone traveling from Toulouse to Biarritz by train leaves Toulouse about 10 A.M. and arrives about 3 P.M., with a transfer at Bordeaux. By air, you leave Toulouse at 10:15 for Roissy (as Charles de Gaulle Airport is popularly known) and catch an 11:55 flight to Biarritz, arriving at 1:10. Add the travel to and from the airports in Toulouse and Biarritz, and the time is nearly the same, but the cost is greater.

By Train

Trains in France are operated by the Société Nationale Chemins de Fer Français,or SNCF, as it is usually called. The emphasis today is on passenger trains, as freight traffic has slowly diminished over the years, with less call for rail transport of coal, iron, and oil. For more than two decades, SNCF has been building up its fleet of high-speed TGVs (Trains à Grande Vitesse), increasing their number and extending the tracks and roadbeds that permit them to clip along at 270 kilometers per hour (167 mph) to top speeds of 350 kph (217 mph). These trains account for more than 25 percent of all passenger service in the country. Competition from both air travel and automobiles has meant train travel has grown more slowly than it might have otherwise.

These fast, luxurious trains link London with Paris, Brussels, Geneva, and the rest of the Continent via the "Chunnel," the tunnel constructed under the English Channel for just that purpose. Such a train travels the 1,200 kilometers (744 miles) from Lille to Nice, for instance, in 10 hours. Connecting trains make the trip down the Rhône Valley to Marseille or Montpellier even faster. Another line leaving Paris passes not far from Orly Airport headed toward Tours, Bordeaux, and Spain. The 600 kilometers (372 miles) from Paris to Bordeaux take about three hours on the TGV.

The high-speed trains not only crisscross France, but also extend throughout Western Europe, often rivaling airplanes for speed and ease of travel. While someone on a tight business schedule is more likely to fly from Toulouse to Paris in the morning and return in the evening, many travelers find the five- to six-hour trip by train in a spacious car with wide seats to be quick and comfortable. For many routes, the TGV has made overnight sleeper trains a relic of the past.

Reservations are required for the TGV and optional on other trains. From the Paris hub, TGVs leave with great frequency, making most French destinations less than an eight-hour trip away.

SNCF has a complicated fare schedule that involves discounts for large families, frequent travelers, annual vacations, children and seniors, students and apprentices, advance reservations, and other factors. Often a limited number of discounted seats is available, and discounts are not available on every train at every time. The various discounts run from about 25–50 percent, so they are worth seeking out.

The high-speed trains not only crisscross France but also extend throughout Western Europe, often rivaling airplanes for speed and ease of travel.

For those who enjoy train travel, the two plans of greatest interest are age-related: the Carte 12–25, aimed at students, and the Carte Senior. The former costs €49 ($66) and the latter €50 ($67.50). Both are good for a year and confer discounts of 25–50 percent. For the youth card, you must be age 12–25; seniors are those 60 years or older. Adults age 25–60 may benefit from a variety of SNCF promotions, including advance purchase of tickets to a given destination at 25–40 percent off, and a special sale every Tuesday for specific destinations in the coming week.

The Senior Card entitles the holder to a 50 percent fare reduction in France, and at least 25 percent in other European countries. It also confers other benefits: a discount on baggage service, car rentals from Avis, and a reduction in the cost of transporting your car by train.

Here is a comparison of different fares (as of spring 2005) for the three-hour trip from Paris to Bordeaux. All prices are for second class; on the TGV, the difference between first and second class may not be worth 50 percent extra, as second class is quite comfortable.

Full fare: €60.40 ($81)
8-day advance purchase: €45.00 ($60.75)
30-day advance purchase: €35.00 ($47.25)
Carte 12–25: €36.00 ($50.40)
Senior Card: €29.70 ($40)

Since passenger service is the majority of its business today, SNCF does a lot to attract customers. Families, for instance, can get their own compartments, complete with a nearby changing table and bottle warmer for babies. Arrangements can made for the care of children between four and 13 years old traveling alone during school vacations. Baggage can be picked up at your residence and dropped off at your destination. Travelers in wheelchairs are accommodated. (The SNCF website includes special pages for the disabled.) Even pets are allowed, as long as they do not bother other passengers.

By Bus

With such an excellent rail system, long-distance bus service is rare in France. However, most cities have bus systems, and secondary systems serve the environs and small villages. These often double as both a commercial passenger vehicle and the local school bus. You might see commuters riding on the same bus with schoolchildren being transported to a middle school in another village, and older students headed to the *lycée* (high school) in the city.

While helpful, these buses are quite limited. Generally, they run from a particular group of villages to a hub city in the morning, and back from that city to the same villages in the afternoon—getting pupils to school before 9 A.M., and returning in the late afternoon to take them home. So, in most cases, you cannot make a connection to go elsewhere. Mostly these buses are valuable for a trip from a village to the nearest train depot—but not on Sundays or holidays, when they remain in the garage.

By Car

The question of whether or not to own a car in France depends on personal preference and where you live. Certainly, an auto is not a necessity in Paris; for many, it would be nothing more than an expensive nuisance. The same might be said of any of the larger cities with narrow streets and limited parking. In general, these same cities will also have the best public transit.

On the other hand, if you plan to live in a suburb or small village, are eager to get to know the countryside, and want to take frequent trips, a car is very desirable. There are many places you will be unable to reach by train or bus, or the trip may entail lengthy waits for connections.

Although public transit is generally good for going to work and school, the convenience of the automobile cannot be denied, and four out of every five French households have at least one car. Two factors have contributed greatly to this trend. The first is the rise of large supermarket chains in suburban malls and the subsequent decline of the small, independent shops in cities and villages throughout France. Thousands of butchers, bakers, grocers, and other small merchants have closed their doors in the past two decades.

The other factor is the rise of commuting and families with two working adults. As the distance between home and work increases, and schedules get squeezed by the need to do the same amount in less time, the automobile has become a solution. While the number of air and rail passengers has risen only slightly in recent years, travel by private automobile continues to grow at a faster pace, as has the number of vehicles on the road. France now has one car for every two people, well behind Italy, but still above the European average. (The United States has one vehicle for every 1.3 people.)

DRIVING

Fortunately, French roads are generally excellent and well-maintained, with appropriate signage. They exist in a hierarchical system, with A roads, denoting *autoroutes*, at the top; followed by N, or national routes; and then D, or departmental highways. The *autoroutes* are limited-access toll roads that make regional travel fast and comfortable, albeit expensive: Tolls hover around €.08 ($.11) per kilometer. And at legal speeds of 130 kph (80 mph), the extra fuel burned at €1 ($1.35) or so per liter also adds to the cost.

Most *autoroutes* have been built since the mid-1960s by private companies that raised the necessary capital for construction. Radiating from Paris, the four-, six- or eight-lane divided highways connect most of the larger French cities. Bypassing towns and most cities, they often provide scenic routes through the countryside. Slower traffic should keep to the right on *autoroutes*—a sometimes difficult proposition, since trucks are limited to 90 kph (55 mph) on these roads and often clog that lane. However, with the legal limit of 130 kph (80 mph) often little more than a convenient fiction for impatient drivers, it doesn't do to dawdle in the faster lanes.

Autoroutes are also an important link in the whole European Union transit scheme, since goods from other European countries must often pass through France to reach their eventual destination: produce from Spain to Germany, electric appliances from Italy to England, and so on. Heavy trucks, which now carry more than half of all freight in France, are required to use the *autoroutes* unless making local deliveries. The tolls help pay for the upkeep of the *autoroutes,* and their absence on other roads lessens the maintenance necessary and eases traffic.

National routes often parallel the *autoroutes.* Although some are divided highways, they are not limited access and may go through the center of towns. On divided national routes, the speed limit is 110 kph (68 mph). On two- or three-lane routes, the limit is 90 kph (55 mph) in the country, but lower in towns and cities.

> *Fortunately, French roads are generally excellent, well maintained with appropriate signage.*

Departmental (county) routes vary widely. Most of them are two-lane roads of greatly differing widths—anything from lanes generous enough to accommodate the largest 18-wheeler to country lanes barely wider than a single car.

Driver's Licenses

Your valid American driver's license will be recognized in France, but the length of time it remains valid depends on residency status. Americans arriving in France with a long-stay visa have one year to obtain a *permis de conduire* (French driving license). Students are the exception to this rule, and may use their valid U.S. license for the duration of their studies.

For some, it is a relatively simple matter of exchanging their U.S. license for a French one. People coming from Colorado, Connecticut, Delaware, Florida, Illinois, Kansas, Kentucky, Michigan, New Hampshire, Ohio, Pennsylvania, South Carolina, and Virginia may make this exchange because their home states offer French citizens in the U.S. the same privilege of exchange.

Whether making an exchange or applying for a new license, you must go to the *préfecture* (police headquarters) to do so. French driver's licenses are issued for life and require a physical examination, along with a test on laws of the road. The *préfecture* will require certain documents, such as a passport, photos, and proof of residence, along with a valid U.S. license. After approval by the prefecture, there is a one-month waiting period to take the written test. After passing the written test, candidates must wait at least two weeks to take a driving test. The driving test must be taken in a dual-control vehicle, making it necessary to have enrolled in a driving school.

Driver's licenses and vehicle registration are handled by the *préfecture* of the department in which you live. (There is no Department of Motor Vehicles in France.) The last two numbers on French license plates designate the department in which the vehicle is registered. The plate stays with the car as long as it remains registered in the department, even if ownership changes hands.

Just as you would in the States, make sure you have your license with you when you drive. If you happen to be stopped by a *gendarme* (police officer) and can't produce it, you could be arrested on the spot. For the same reason, you should always carry two documents in your car: the *carte grise,* as the gray title is called (no pink slips here), and proof of insurance. Rather than patrol highways, as they do in the States, French police set up roadblocks to stop motorists. They will demand to see these two documents, along with an operator's permit, and the absence of any of them can mean immediate arrest. Moreover, upon discovery of a safety violation, such as bald tires or burned-out headlights, they may forbid you to drive the vehicle untilrepairs are made. It's best to keep your papers in order and your car in good shape.

Rules of the Road

French rules of the road vary little from those in the United States. The French drive on the right side, stop at stop signs, pass on the left, and generally follow the same practices American drivers do. Two notable exceptions are that you cannot turn right after stopping for a red light, and at intersections without signals or signs, you yield to the driver on the right. This can be disconcerting when you are on a through road, and a driver suddenly pulls out from a side road because he has the right of way.

Another practice that unsettles many American motorists in France is the propensity of French drivers for tailgating. However dangerous, it is often the only way a motorist can get in position to pass slower vehicles on a two-lane road. Leaving a safe distance between yourself and the car ahead becomes an invitation to the motorist behind to zip between the two of you.

Probably the biggest problem American motorists in France will face is a familiar one: congestion. The American experience is being replicated in France. As more people turn to cars as their primary mode of transportation, the roads become overcrowded; as the highway system expands, so does the number of vehicles, and the congestion continues. Consider the truck traffic alone coming from Spain into France. In

Death-Defying Drivers

French traffic can be a killer, especially on those long weekends. Happily, the trend is moving toward considerably fewer fatalities—and that's no accident. In May 2000, after two very deadly holiday weekends over Easter and May Day, Transport Minister Jean-Claude Gayssot vowed to stop the carnage on French highways.

During the four-day Easter weekend, 90 people were killed and 2,119 injured on the highways of France. On the May 1 weekend, the number of deaths increased to 98. That was an increase in Easter fatalities of 14 percent from 1999, another four-day weekend when 79 people were killed. Comparing the May 1 weekend fatalities to 1998, another four-day May 1 weekend, they were up 15 percent. In comparison, the United States counted 393 fatalities on the four-day Memorial Day weekend in 1998. Considering the U.S. population is nearly 4.5 times greater and a smaller percentage of the French drive, the French carnage is impressive.

Gayssot was out of office before solving the problem, but his successors continued the effort. Their solution was radar: roving squads of police armed with radar set up speed traps, and automatic machines were set up alongside the road to photograph speeding motorists, who were then sent citations.

The crackdown was effective. Traffic deaths dropped from 7,242 in 2002 to 5,250 in 2004. More than 36,000 drivers lost their licenses in 2004, compared to fewer than 21,000 the previous year. By the end of 2005, about 1,000 radar units will be in place. Penalties were increased for driving without a seatbelt and for driving under the influence. These drastic measures did not go without criticism. More than one of the automatic radars has been put out of operation. Members of the National Assembly caught speeding protested loudly about repressive measures—so far, to no effect.

Part of the problem is the French attitude toward driving and traffic laws. In a 1997 survey, one-third of French drivers said everyone should be free to decide how much he or she could drink before getting behind the wheel. In a survey taken in May 2000, 93 percent of French drivers rated themselves as very good drivers who obeyed the law. However, the same survey revealed that half of those polled routinely exceed the speed limit on the highway, and one-third do so in towns.

About two-thirds did not know the penalties for running a red light (a fine of €760 and license suspension for up to three years), drunk driving (a maximum of two years in prison, a fine of €4,500, and license suspension for five years), or speeding (fines range €400–1,500 and include license suspension for three years).

Terrible as the figures may be, the French do seem to be making progress. Back in 1983, with far fewer cars on the roads, the annual death toll was 11,946. Even so, approach French highways with caution.

1995, 11,000 trucks trundled in daily; by 2000, there were 15,000. Authorities predict the figure will double by 2015.

Road Signs

Many French road signs are graphic icons. The type that prescribes a particular action uses a red circle with a white center. Applicable information is in black on the white center. The speed limit sign is a typical example, with black numerals on a white background, encircled by red. To designate "no left turn" or "no right turn," a similar sign is used, but with an arrow pointing in the forbidden direction and a diagonal red slash across it. Other such signs include a black figure of a person walking on the white center encircled by red; this indicates a crosswalk where you must yield to pedestrians.

Signs indicating possible dangerous situations are triangular in shape, but continue the motif of a red outline and white center, with a black symbol to indicate to problem. Such signs might warn of a curve (a black arrow), narrowing lanes (two lines), or railroad tracks; some will simply have a black exclamation point within the red triangle and another sign with words beneath, such as *"sortie d'usine"* (exit from a factory). A black *X* on white enclosed by a red triangle, indicates a crossroad.

But probably the most common triangular sign is turned with the apex pointing down and a rectangular black and white sign below the apex saying *cedez le passage'*—meaning "yield the right of way." These often appear where a stop sign would be used in the U.S., and at the entry to a roundabout. The triangular shape is also used for signs designating temporary danger, such as when work is being done on the street or road. These signs use the red triangle, but a yellow background with black symbols.

A third class of road signs express an obligation. These use a white circle around a blue disk overprinted with white symbols, such as a bicycle to indicate a bike path or a white arrow indicating a required direction. When white numbers appear on a blue circle, it is a minimum speed limit; you might encounter such a sign at the entrance to a highway tunnel, for instance, where a slow vehicle would be a danger. A red diagonal slash through one of these signs indicates the obligation is ended.

Blue squares with white symbols are informative. Such a sign depicting a bus indicates a bus stop; one with a large P indicates parking. A red rectangle atop a white vertical means a dead end; a white arrow on a blue background indicates a one-way street in the direction of the arrow. (A red circle with a horizontal white bar means "do not enter.")

RENTING, LEASING, OR BUYING A CAR

New cars cost more in France than they do in the United States—the difference amounts roughly to the French TVA, the 19.6 percent sales tax. For about €15,000 ($20,250), you get a small, basic vehicle. Another €3,500–4,500 ($4,725–6,075) will fetch you a larger, more powerful car. Spend €22,250 ($30,038), and you get a full-size sedan. Vans go for a premium, as do luxury models.

Diesel-engine cars, far more prevalent in Europe than in the States, are usually more expensive, although manufacturers often discount this difference in special promotions. Diesel fuel is about 10 percent cheaper than gasoline, however, so they may be more economical in the long run. Depending on many factors, the cost of buying and operating a car three years old or less for 10,000 kilometers a year will run approximately €305–915 ($412–1,235) per month. These costs will be less for older vehicles. When you purchase a vehicle, you'll pay a one-time tax and registration fee, but no more such fees as long as you own it.

If you plan to buy a car while in France, pick up the national weekly tabloid, *l'Argus,* for current prices on various makes of cars sold in France. Classified ads for used cars often refer to *prix Argus,* indicating the asking price mirrors what *Argus* states is the price for a similar vehicle.

However, used cars purchased from a franchised dealer may cost more than the *Argus* price. This is because most of them come with a three- to 12-month guarantee, depending on the car's age. My experience with such guarantees has been quite positive; the elevated price usually includes new parts and a thorough inspection of the vehicle. If there is a mechanical failure in a guaranteed vehicle, it is repaired at no cost to you—but you do have to put up with the inconvenience.

Part of your car maintenance expenses will be a required mechanical safety inspection once every two to four years. Additionally, any car at least four years old must undergo such an inspection within the six months prior to its sale. The seller is obligated to furnish proof of this to the buyer, but is not required to make the repairs. While the inspection is helpful in assessing steering and suspension, lights and brakes, and emission level, it does not account for other repairs that might be necessary.

Insurance should never be taken off a vehicle, because the owner

Don't Get Taken for a Ride

Used car dealers don't have the best reputation in the United States (something lower than a snake and more crooked than a pig's tail). This is not the case in France. Although there is always some possibility of chicanery (or, more likely, failure to notice a defect), you can go to a franchised dealer and expect to find used cars guaranteed to be in excellent mechanical condition.

The dealer's guarantee in France varies somewhat, depending on the age and condition of the car, but it is usually for three, six, or 12 months and will cover both parts and labor. Even a car five or six years old may merit a guarantee. Moreover, if the used car you buy is the same make that the dealer sells new, the guarantee will be good anywhere in France and probably in Europe. Some dealers extend this universal guarantee to any car they sell; others will limit it to repairs at their own garage, if it is a make other than their franchise.

In other words, if you buy a fairly new used Renault from a Renault dealer, you will get one-year guarantee for parts and labor good anywhere in Europe. Not includ-ed are parts that are expected to wear, such as tires or brake pads. The same goes for other makes as well. But you'll pay a premium for this peace of mind. Dealers routinely sell cars for €800–1,000 ($1,080–1,350) above the average selling price on the open market for a similar vehicle.

Buying from an individual is no different than in the U.S., but you will have one advantage: French vehicles more than four years old must undergo an independent inspection every two years and within no less than six months of being sold. This inspection does not guarantee mechanical perfection, but it does insure that brakes, steering, and other factors that might affect the safe operation of the vehicle—such as suspension—are in working order.

The difference is this: Buy a car from a dealer, and if the starter or alternator or the water pump fails within the time of the guarantee, it will be replaced without any cost to you beyond inconvenience. Buy from an individual, and you're on your own, although the savings may be worth the risk.

remains liable for any damages, even if the damage occurred after the vehicle had been stolen. For this reason, when individuals buy or sell a vehicle, they are careful to ensure that the termination of the seller's policy and the inception of the buyer's coincide.

Renting a car in France is no different from renting one in the United States. All you need are a valid driver's license and money, preferably a credit card. The rental agencies themselves will be familiar to you: Hertz, Avis, and Budget are the big ones in France, with offices in all the cities and airports. Avis has a special relationship with SNCF, the

French railroad, that permits you to pick up and return a car at the depot itself. This is a great convenience, given the congestion and one-way streets that often surround depots.

You should not overlook the possibility of a lease for stays of less than one year. France has a lease-purchase arrangement that avoids the 19.6 percent tax normally applied to car rentals. A couple will usually be able to use one partner for the first six months, and the other for the second half of the year. The license plates of such vehicles are identifiably red and silver. These vehicles, usually with *"faible kilometrage"* (low mileage) are often good deals when purchased from franchised agencies.

TAXIS

Taxi service in France is an expensive convenience. Fares vary by region, but in Paris, the basic rate is €0.62 ($.84) per kilometer. However, there is a minimum €2 ($2.70) pickup fee, and if the cab is called by phone, the meter begins running whenever the driver gets the call, not when the customer gets into the cab. There is a minimum rate of €5.10 ($6.89) for short trips.

The rate per kilometer increases outside of Paris to €1.06 ($1.43) in adjacent departments and €1.24 beyond ($1.67). A small tip, not more than 10 percent, is sufficient. In the countryside, where many older people do not have cars, taxis are not uncommon. They are used for transporting patients to hospitals or clinics for tests and examinations and are paid for by the health-care system.

Most train stations are served by taxis, with the number depending on the population of the city or town. However, taking a taxi into the countryside is necessarily an expensive proposition, because the driver has to make a round trip, and his chances of picking up a return fare are nil. A trip of about 24 kilometers (15 miles) from the Carcassonne depot to a rural village costs €35 ($47.25), for instance; for the chauffeur returning to the depot seeking another fare, it is a trip of 48 kilometeres (30 miles). Likewise, if you request a local village taxi to take you to the Carcassonne depot, the rate will be the same for the same reason.

By Boat

With the advent of the rail tunnel beneath the English Channel and discount airlines, ferries have diminished in importance as a means of travel from the UK directly to the Continent. Nonetheless, they continue to function, transporting people and vehicles headed to Normandy, Brittany, and points south. These days, ferries may provide services similar to a cruise ship.

A one-way fare in the spring from Portsmouth to Le Havre for a couple with a sedan costs about €150 ($202.50). A round trip between Plymouth and Caen costs about €475 ($641.25). During the summer and vacation periods, the fares increase.

Housing Considerations

Your home in France is your castle. Foreigners have the same rights to rent, buy, and own property as the French themselves. Nationality makes no difference in purchase or rental. Where and how you live is largely up to you—it all depends what you can afford and what you can find.

For many expatriates, the search itself is often the most trying part. Often people come to France with a preconceived idea of what they want—a little cottage in the country surrounded by a garden, a spacious city apartment with a view overlooking a park and a smart bistro down the block for morning coffee or before-dinner aperitifs. Just the sort of image you have seen in dozens of films.

But then you bump into reality. You find what you want, but can't afford it. Or price is no object, but nothing's for sale or rent in your desired location. You may indeed find your dream home or apartment in France—and even be able to afford it—but it's nevertheless wise to have realistic expectations about what's available and how much it will cost, just as you would back in the States.

Finding the Right Place

To begin with, you should familiarize yourself with the ways in which French housing differs from its American counterpart. Most notably, middle-class homes and apartments tend to be smaller, with fewer rooms and less square footage. Apartment kitchens are often postage-stamp-size; appliances are smaller as well. (A side-by-side refrigerator is called an *"americaine."*) New two-bedroom, one-bath homes are not uncommon in France, yet virtually none are being built in the States any more, where the three-bedroom, two-bath house is almost a minimum.

Your home in France is your castle.

There are other differences as well. Floors are more likely to be tile than wood or carpet; heating derives from hot water radiators, rather than forced air; and garages are less common—not extraordinary differences, but noticeable. You'd be wise to look at many possibilities, so you're able to distinguish normal differences from downright substandard housing. True, kitchens may be smaller, but not as small as *this* one. Yes, electrical outlets are not as numerous as they are in American housing, but a room without any is not up to par.

For help in finding the right location, as well as getting settled once you decide, visit the *mairie* (mayor's office) of your town. The staff can provide you with helpful information on public transportation, parking, garbage collection, and recreation facilities and opportunities. This information might help you decide how pleasant or convenient life there might be. The *mairie* is also where you go to register a child for school.

A great source of information about housing in France is the Agence Nationale pour l'Informations sur le Logement (ANIL). This agency provides information to the public on various aspects of housing, including financing, taxation, and legal matters such as owners' and tenants' rights. The local chapters are also clearinghouses for information about new properties for sale or rent.

Common Housing Terms

Any search for real estate will inevitably lead to the *petites annonces* (classified ads). A house or apartment may be said to have *carac.* (character), or to be *charm.* (charming), *coq.* (cute), *except.* (exceptional), or *rav.* (delightful). Here is a glossary to help you decode the jargon and abbreviations of this specialized text.

à louer: for rent or lease

asc. (ascenseur): elevator

à vendre or *AV:* for sale

bal. (balcon): balcony

boxe: parking place

caution: security deposit

cft. (confort): conveniences; such as a dishwasher, carpeting, etc.

ch. or *chb. (chambre):* bedroom; a *chambre de bonne* is a maid's room

chauf. cent. (chauffage centrale): central heating

com. (commission): agent's commission

cour.: courtyard

cuisine eq. (equipée): major appliances installed

dche. (douche): shower

et. el. (étage élevé): upper floor

garçonnière: bachelor's apartment; a small studio or room

grenier: attic; a room under the roof

imm. (immeuble): building; it may be an *imm. mod.* (modern), an *imm. anc.* (old), an *imm. nf.* (new) or an *imm. rec.* (recent)

interméd. (intermédiaire): agent

jar./jdn. (jardin): garden

kit.: kitchenette

lux.: luxurious

loyer: the rent

m2 (mètre carré): square meter, about 10.76 square feet

meublé: furnished

moq. (moquette): wall-to-wall carpeting

p. (pièce): rooms, not including bathroom

poss. (possibilité): possibility of

poutres apparentes: beamed ceilings

pr. cpl.: couple preferred

ref. nf. (refait neuf): newly remodeled

sl (sur): on

slle. (salle): large or formal room; *salle de réception* is a large living room; *salle à manger* is a formal dining room; *salle d'eau* is a room with water (sink, shower, etc.); *salle de bains* is a bathroom

ss. (sans): without

stdg. (standing): a classy, fashionable address; *gd. stdg.* or *tr. gd. stdg.* means deluxe

terr.: terrace

ttc (toutes charges comprises): all charges included; *chgs. (charges)* means there is a supplementary monthly fee in addition to rent *Ttc:* literally, *toutes taxes comprises;* this is widely understood to indicate a complete price

ventes: listings for sale

vide: empty, unfurnished

w.c.: water closet, meaning the toilet is in a room separate from the bath and sink

RENTING VERSUS BUYING

Several factors will influence your decision of whether to rent or to buy. An important one is location. Renting is far more common in metropolitan areas, where there are few houses but many apartments, than it is in rural areas and small towns. Another is cost. Not only are home prices high in metro areas, the typical 30-year American mortgage is not yet common in France. Seven to 15 years is the norm, requiring larger monthly payments—even people of ample means may be unable to afford to buy a house or a large apartment in Paris. Renting makes the most sense for those who wish to live amid the city's cosmopolitan splendor.

You may be able to afford your ideal home or apartment, only to discover nothing for sale that meets your requirements when you're ready to buy. In that case, renting makes the most sense. Once established comfortably in a neighborhood, you can wait for the sort of apartment or house you want to come on the market. During your wait, you will enjoy the benefit of becoming knowledgeable about the neighborhood's good and bad points without having made the commitment of a purchase.

In contrast, in rural areas and villages, you will find fewer rentals available. There is a far higher percentage of owner-occupied housing, and apartments are few. Buying a home makes more sense in these locations, because you will have a much greater chance of obtaining a suitable residence. In some thinly populated areas, building a new home may be the best solution. The price of new construction may be only slightly more than that of complete renovation, and in the end, you will have exactly what you want, rather than a compromise made by accepting what is available.

In or near a provincial city, you will probably have the greatest choice of both rentals and homes for sale. In most cases, prices will be more reasonable than in Paris, and you'll find a relatively large stock of both houses and apartments on the market. Especially for those considering retirement in France, these cities may be the ideal locations, and not only for their selection in housing. While proximity to or residence in a medium-sized city will mean higher prices for either purchase or rental, it also means easier access to cultural events and institutions, medical care, and air and rail transportation.

Remember, aside from Paris, Marseilles, Lyon, and Lille, France does not have large cities by U.S. standards. Major cities such as Nice, Bordeaux, and Toulouse have a population of less than one million in the metropolitan area. By choosing carefully, you can find small towns with good services within 20 kilometers (12.4 miles) of most cities. You will also likely find an international airport, TGV (high-speed train) service, and fully equipped hospitals in the metropolitan area.

Whatever housing option you decide to pursue, bear in mind that housing prices in much of France have risen sharply in the past five years. While New Yorkers and San Franciscans may find them reasonable, many others will not. The crux of the matter is that the housing market in France is now an international one. Buyers from Northern Europe, the UK and former colonies such as Australia, Canada and South Africa, now compete with the French for vacation and/or retirement homes, be they apartments on the Riviera, houses in a rural village, or country estates.

Add to this the increasing urbanization of France that concentrates employment in its cities—which protect their historic character, rather than bulldoze it in favor of new construction—and you have a very competitive situation. Demand increases, while supply remains static. For some French, the answer has been moving to the suburbs and commuting—a solution which many French, as well as foreign purchasers, shun. The result has been a marked increase in the value of the older housing stock, while the cost of construction for new houses continues to increase.

Between 1998 and 2004, apartment prices in Paris rose 72 percent; in the provinces, they rose 55 percent, with most of that in the last three to seven years. In 2003–2004, the increase in housing prices for the country as a whole was 14.7 percent. Will this rate of increase continue indefinitely? Some point to the late 1980s, when prices also shot up. But in 1991, when Paris prices averaged €4,200 ($5,670) per square meter, nearly as high as in 2005, prices crashed. In the recession of that period, they continued dropping until they hit their 1998 low of €2,500 ($3,375) per square meter. In the provinces during that period, the drop was not so great—from €1,686 per square meter to €1,462 ($2,276 to 1,977).

But the provincial rate increases in 2005, unlike those in Paris, outstripped their 1991 peak by nearly €600 ($810) per square meter; and many observers noted a pause in late 2004 in the rate of increase, especially at the high end of the market. In rural villages, as well as in cities, houses and apartments stayed on the market longer, with some not selling at all and some at reduced prices. Some analysts saw this as a possible peak, similar to that of 1991, with the market set to turn down in the face of a stagnating recovery.

Most analysts, however, now expect the market to continue slowly upward for some very good reasons. Demand continues to outstrip supply, with more young people forming families and more divorces increasing the demand. Rents have likewise gone up to the point where many tenants now consider ownership the only effective way to assure themselves of suitable housing in the future. Nor are they ignorant of the financial wisdom of ownership: With annual increases of 10 percent, property is one of the better investments available. To buy their own homes, they are taking out longer mortgages, commuting from longer distances, and tapping their families for help.

Foreign investment is also unquestionably part of this increasing demand. Throughout the South of France, both Northern Europeans and the British have bought tens of thousands of properties in the past decade, from wine domains to luxury apartments to village houses that are little more than a roof and four walls. While the French have been building new houses and apartments on the outskirts of towns, foreigners have repopulating the centers and countryside.

Buyers should also be aware of the seasonality of the housing market in France. Prices tend to increase the most during the second and third quarters, between March and October. In the rising market that began in 1998, prices did not actually decline from September to April—they just didn't increase as rapidly. If a property that interested you in August is still for sale in November, your chances of negotiating a lower price may be much better. On the other hand, property you like in May may well be sold by July.

Renting

Renting in France is different in some ways from renting in the United States. For one thing, the typical month-to-month or one-year agreement for an unfurnished apartment is not the norm. Instead, tenants typically sign a three-year lease for unfurnished property owned by individuals, who may also give short-term leases; or six years if the owner is a corporation. Furthermore, there are often charges you would not expect in the States. Foremost among these is the *taxe d'habitation* that the tenant, not the owner, must pay. There can also be a variety of maintenance charges. It makes no difference whether you rent an apartment or a house—the rules are the same.

Additionally, the tenant must have insurance in France. A landlord can demand proof of this insurance, and termination of the policy can be grounds for terminating the lease. This insurance protects the proprietor of the building from losses that might be caused by a tenant—fire, water damage, explosions, and so forth. These policies should also provide against damages to third parties, such as neighbors. Proof of this insurance should be presented annually to the landlord. Your finances will also be of concern to a landlord. You should be prepared to prove a monthly income of at least three times the rent.

Renting makes the most sense for those who wish to live amid the city's cosmopolitan splendor.

In France, unfurnished often means bare walls, ceilings, and floors. Light fixtures, kitchen cabinets, and appliances may all belong to a tenant. (Furnished rentals do include these amenities, of course. What's more, they do not require a written lease and may be occupied for shorter periods.) The lease also describes the parts of the premises for the exclusive use of the tenant and areas that are for communal use.

The laws governing rentals are actually quite complex. Landlords who rent four or fewer furnished apartments have different obligations from those who rent more than four; corporate landlords have some different obligations than individuals. Renting an apartment in a big building in a large city from an agency will certainly be a different experience than renting a house in a small village with the landlord living nearby. In any event, it is good to have an understanding of your responsibilities and those of the landlord's.

The rental of an apartment or house may require a large initial outlay of cash, although not so great as a purchase. If the rent is €900 per month, the real estate agent handling the rental receives a fee of 8 percent of the annual rent, and a two-month deposit is required, the total payment required to move in is €900 + €864 + €1,800 = €3,564 ($4,811), plus any extra charges that might be involved.

If there are to be increases in rent during the period of the lease, the landlord should specify them. Rent is usually based on last year's rent, plus any increase in the cost of construction index, although landlords may be able to justify greater increases following renovations. As in the

States, you'll typically pay rent once a month. If you pay more than three months in advance, a deposit should not be necessary, because landlords may not require deposits of more than two months' rent.

When you decide to leave, you should give notice at least three months in advance (many people vacate apartments before the three-year lease is up). Inform the various utilities and services of your departure date.

Electricité de France (EDF) will read your meter on your last day and forward the bill to your new address. You may also want to make an appointment to have the electricity turned on in your new residence. Follow the same procedure with the telephone company. The post office will forward mail for six months to another address, but will charge a one-time fee of €16.77 ($22.64)) to do so. Also let your insurance agent know that you're moving out, and change the policy to reflect your new address.

The landlord should go over the premises with you using the *états de lieux* (state of the premises) inventory form that was completed when you moved in. This is important in seeking the return of a deposit. If the landlord finds any damage that was done during your stay, he or she will withhold all or part of the deposit. Deposits must be paid to the tenant within two months after he or she moves out.

After you move, the prefecture must be informed of your new address; an electric or telephone bill will serve as proof. The same must be done for automobile registration. If you have moved to a different department, the annual tax on your car will change. Your health insurance must also be changed to your new address. and if your bank account has also changed, you should provide the new information.

Buying

Many people who have the means to move to France will sooner or later buy a residence. The security of owning your own home, whether a house or an apartment, is quite comforting to most of us. Moreover, for those who leave their native land to settle elsewhere, property ownership makes a definite statement: My home is here. And for those who look at property realistically, rather than as speculators intending to get rich off their purchase, French property has been a good investment.

Purchasing a home in France is similar to the same process in the States. You find a property for sale and make an offer. If the offer is accepted, you sign a *compromis de vente* (agreement of sale) and pay a deposit, usually not more than 10 percent of the purchase price. This deposit is a guarantee of good faith and will be forfeited if the buyer reneges on the deal. It is returned if the seller reneges. When the title is cleared, usually within a month or two, and the wishes of the buyer and seller have been met, the final papers are signed and the balance is paid.

It is now required that the seller of any house built before 1997 have it inspected for asbestos; houses built before 1949 must be inspected for

Rising Prices and the Falling Dollar

Americans looking for property in France these days must face two grim pieces of news. First of all, real estate prices have escalated throughout the country since 1998, and the rate accelerated even more after 2001. This is especially true in cities and nearby villages within easy commuting distance. (Yes, the French are becoming a nation of commuters!) In the six years from the beginning of 1998 until 2004, there was an increase of 70 percent nationally in housing prices. In Paris, its surrounding area, and other major cities, the annual increase was even greater. In selected neighborhoods, real estate agents saw the price of individual properties double more than once within that period.

The second is the falling dollar. Take, for example, a house for sale for €250,000 ($337,500) in the summer of 2003. At that price, you could have bought it for $225,000. By the end of 2004, the same €250,000 house would have cost $337,500. Neither the price nor the value of the property changed in France; what changed was the value of the dollar relative to the euro. Despite statements from Washington that the administration favors a strong dollar, the facts indicate otherwise.

How serious is this increase? Here's an illustration: In 2000, newer apartments near the Sorbonne in Paris's 5th *arrondissement* ranged €4,575–7,625 per square meter. In dollars, that amounted to $6,176–10,294, with larger units commanding higher prices. In 2004, you could expect to pay €6,300–9,000 per square meter for comparable units. That is, $8,500–12,150.

This wasn't just Paris that saw that kind of increase. In one chic Bordeaux neighborhood, buildings that sold twice between 1999 and 2003 doubled in price with each sale. In the heart of Lille, prices increased 20 percent in 2003; in old Marseille, the increase was 22 percent that year. While most cities and neighborhoods cannot match such increases, be prepared for "sticker shock," even if you looked at prices two years ago.

Those looking for bargains in French property these days are advised to search in rural areas well away from centers of employment, and/or for the fixer-upper where you can build up "sweat equity."

lead paint as well. In areas where termites are known, a termite inspection is also mandatory. These three inspections must be carried out by independent experts. However, the requirement of such inspections is relatively new, and there is little control over the qualifications of inspectors. Consumer organizations warn that there are many cases of real estate agents requiring kickbacks from the inspectors they employ and/or of employing those who give favorable reports.

There are two organizations that have tried to insure competency and professionalism among the experts. It is worthwhile checking if the expert employed in your case is certified by Qualicert or the Centre Technique du Bois et de l'Ameublement (CTBA). Both have websites.

Another requirement is that the surface area of the residence be measured. This can be done by anyone, including the seller, but errors greater than 5 percent are actionable, and the price can be reduced proportionately.

Keep in mind that even if you jump through all those hoops, there are still a few twists that can snag a deal. First of all, it is important to know that property sales—even those originating with a real estate agency—go through a *notaire* (notary). The French *notaire* does much more than an American notary public, although he or she does serve that function as well. While the preliminary agreement may be drawn up by a real estate broker, it is the *notaire* who draws up the *acte authentique de vente* (deed).

The *notaire* performs two important public functions: He guarantees the title—that is, verifies the seller has the right to dispose of it; and collects taxes due on the sale. For this, he receives a not insignificant fee fixed on a sliding scale that amounts to about €6,500 per €100,000 ($8,775 per $135,000) of the purchase price on a house more than five years old. On new homes, the fee drops dramatically, to about €2,000 per 100,000 ($2,700 of $135,000) of purchase price. If a real estate agent's fee—from four to 10 percent—is added, the price can mount, and you must take this into consideration.

The *notaire* can also perform a private function, serving as a knowledgeable third party involved in the negotiations, and can arbitrate between buyer and seller. Knowing the history of the property, the *notaire* may be in a position to reason with a seller who makes a questionable demand. Or, he may be able to make clear to the buyer the reasons for the seller's demands. Property sales are anything but unemotional affairs—particularly when the property may have been the seller's lifelong home, and the buyer is a foreigner—and a cool-headed arbiter may be the key to a successful purchase.

The other hurdle to clear before a piece of property can change hands is the commune's right of first refusal in any sale. The commune is the basic geographical unit of France, combining the urban planning and zoning powers of both city and county in the United States. Unlike American cities, in which jurisdiction stops at the city limits, the French commune's boundaries extend beyond the limits of the village and take in surrounding countryside; at the boundary begins the territory of another commune. As a result, the land surrounding the town remains under the commune's control. The discrepancy between strict city zoning laws and lax county rules that have permitted so much uncontrolled development surrounding American cities simply does not exist in France.

French law gives the commune an option on all the property within its boundaries. When a bona fide offer is made, the *notaire* presents the offer to the *mairie,* giving the town the two months to buy the property at that same price and use it for some public project.

In most cases, the commune does not exercise its right, and the deal proceeds as negotiated. Tenants also have a right to buy a property when it is put up for sale, even if the owner does not intend to sell it until after the lease is up. The rights of tenants to preempt a sale extend to farmland as well, where the situation becomes a more complicated legal affair.

Anyone who spends much time looking for property in France is certain to hear tales about paying part of the price under the table, with the buyer and seller declaring a lesser price to reduce taxes and notary fees. While some of these stories are factual, a foreigner should be especially wary of any such arrangement.

First of all, a low price may result in either the commune or a tenant exercising their right of preemption, so that you don't get the property after all. Second, you enter your new community known as someone willing to circumvent the law. Third, this practice is illegal and could backfire. Suppose the day after the property becomes yours, it is destroyed; is any insurance company going to reimburse you more than the declared purchase price? Exaggerated examples, perhaps, but worth consideration.

In France, as in the United States, there are private developers who buy land and build on it, selling the houses or apartments even before the work is complete. Agreement to buy such a residence may be done under a reservation contract, with payments spread out as the work is completed.

BUILDING A NEW HOME

An alternative to buying an existing house is to have one built, buying land separately and contracting for the work to be done, just as you would in the States. However, not all land may be built upon. Remember, a commune's limits extend to the border of the next commune, and development may not occur unrestrained, as sometimes happens in the U.S.

Determining whether a piece of land is buildable, or if a building might be converted to a residence, is easily done at the *mairie,* where you request a *certificat d'urbanisme* for the property. This will be provided without charge, and you need not be the property owner to obtain it. However, it is not a building permit; it simply tells you that a particular piece of land may be considered for a building permit.

Building plans will have to be approved by local authorities, and this means a French architect must draw them up. Some builders will have plans on hand or will have them drawn for a specific site for a flat fee. This is probably less expensive than hiring an architect yourself, who will charge a percentage of the total contract for his or her efforts.

However, there is an important consideration: The architect you hire is working for you; the architect the contractor hires is working for him. If you prefer to have that professional advice, plus the oversight of construction, that an architect provides, it's certainly wise to select your own. To have someone who knows the locale and climatic conditions, and can advise you of advantages and disadvantages of various materials and practices, is surely worthwhile.

On the other hand, a contract for a single-family home is a powerful document in France, with lots of protections for the client included. The contract with the builder should specify exactly the quality of the materials used in the construction. Since France has national standards for construction, these are well-known and easily determined. If you ask at least two builders for a bid, their materials can be compared, and each should be able to show examples of their previously constructed properties.

An architect may also take over many of the responsibilities a general contractor would handle in the United States. These include putting the various subcontracts out for bid, selecting craftspeople known to be skilled and reliable, and ensuring that the materials used are the ones specified and paid for.

The contract should also contain financial guarantees for completion of the work on time and at the agreed-upon price. If the contractor should fail to do so, the guarantor would be responsible for continuing the work. It should also contain a guarantee of perfect completion, whereby the contractor agrees to perform any necessary work for a year after delivering the house; a guarantee of good working order that ensures equipment added but not constructed by the contractor, such as plumbing fixtures and heaters, will work for at least two years; and a 10-year guarantee against defects related to the construction.

The contract for building a single-family home is strictly regulated by law in France, so its provisions are easily enforceable. For instance, it includes a schedule of payments to be made as work is completed. The contractor cannot demand payment except as set forth in the following schedule (percentages are cumulative):

The date the contract is signed—5 percent
The date the building permit is received—10 percent
The date construction begins—15 percent
The date the foundation is finished—25 percent
The date exterior walls are up—40 percent
The date the roof is in place—60 percent
The date interior walls and windows are installed—75 percent
The date plumbing, carpentry, and heating are finished—95 percent
The date the buyer accepts the house—100 percent

For those who decide to have a single-family home built, there is a special kind of insurance that should be purchased as part of the contract. Despite the guarantees within the contract, should there be a problem, the homeowner may face a lengthy and perhaps costly process to remedy the situation. This is especially true if a number of years have passed since construction; the builder may have gone out of business, for instance.

The solution is *l'assurance dommages-ouvrage* (insurance against faulty work). This insurance covers necessary repairs for the homeowner and puts the burden of pursuing recovery of damages on the insurance company. Courts have held that a home is worth substantially less if this insurance was not included in the construction. So, if you think

Finding a Fixer-Upper

Those looking for rural property at a low price to renovate themselves should also be prepared to do much of the searching themselves. Real estate agents work on commission in France, just as they do in the U.S., so it is not surprising that these agents prefer to spend time helping clients who expect to pay €150,000 ($202,500) or more, rather than those who seek a €40,000 ($54,000) (or less) bargain. Nor are agencies that interested in listing lower-priced properties—they don't stand to gain much when they are sold, and such properties do not project an image that will attract more affluent buyers. However, one or two such displayed in an agency's window may serve to attract prospects, who can then be sold a more expensive place.

Nonetheless, such properties exist. One place to start the search is with a *notaire*. A French *notaire* is a real estate broker, tax collector, legal expert, and notary public all rolled into one. Villages with a population of at least 1,000 will often have one, with his or her office marked by the gold shield over the door. Owners in the village or surrounding area with the kind of property to sell that you are looking for will often list it with the *notaire*.

Another place to go is the *mairie* (mayor's office), where property records for the commune are kept. If you have seen a place that appears to you to be a near ruin, indicating that the owner takes no interest in its upkeep and therefore might be interested in selling it, this is where you can find the name and address. Also, it is possible that someone in the *mairie* knows of such a property for sale, and can direct you to the owner. It is worth inquiring. Village officials are often interested in getting an abandoned property back on the tax rolls, as well as providing income to local merchants and artisans.

you might want to sell your house less than 10 years after construction, you'd be well-advised to consider this insurance, even if you have full confidence in the builder.

RENOVATING AN OLDER HOME

When it comes to deciding between renovation and new construction, relative overall costs play a small role, because there may be little difference between them. Much more important factors include the site, construction materials, and availability.

If you simply must have old stone walls, there is no alternative to renovation. When many of those old walls went up three or more centuries ago, there was no electricity and perhaps no running water. Such modern conveniences have to be added. If they have already

You will need to be persistent, but not insistent. That is, keep following leads but don't be obnoxious; no one is required to help you. If you find a helpful and sympathetic *notaire* who has nothing to offer initially, check back at reasonable intervals. If you were offered something that you did not like, explain why it was not suitable, thus refining your requirements. This indicates serious intent, but keep in mind that the type of property you are seeking may be rare. In some areas, for instance, isolated houses in the country are rare because historically, people lived in walled villages for protection. In many old villages, attached gardens are rare.

In other words, when you are told that there are no properties available that match your desires, it may not be a brush-off, but a statement of fact. When there are few such properties and a great demand, they often pass by word of mouth. Chat with local people, and not just about houses; try to get a sense of the community and how you might fit in. The more people who are aware of your potential as a neighbor as well as a buyer, the more likely someone is to mention a property they know. After all, they may be doing a friend or a relative a favor by helping them sell the property.

Once you do find a property, try to get a realistic idea of both the costs and problems of its restoration in the style you expect before making an offer, even if you plan to do most of the work yourself.

For example, wiring and plumbing are modern additions to many houses, and some people have no problem with exposed pipes or conduit. But if you cannot abide them, expect their concealment to increase the cost of renovation. Likewise, replacing many old elements with modern equivalents, such as concrete blocks for stone walls, sheetrock for plaster, or stone or old tile floors with modern surfaces, may not be aesthetically pleasing. Yet obtaining original materials may be prohibitively expensive.

been adequately installed, the cost will certainly be included in your purchase price.

The decision to renovate an old house is often intensely personal. It may result from a lifelong dream, a challenge, or even just a passing fancy. Any of these are sufficient reason to undertake such a project. Certainly, many foreigners who move to the French countryside rather than the cities come with this idea in mind. But before making the decision, you should consider several points:

• How much of the work will you do yourself? Renovation may involve any or all of the following crafts: masonry, electricity, plumbing, roofing, landscaping, and tiling. Aside from the skills involved and the unfamiliar materials, remember that construction work is hard physical labor. Are you up to it?

- Can you stand clutter? Any construction project is going to make a mess for a period of time. If you hire professionals to do it, it will probably take less time than if you do it yourself—meaning less time you have to live in a construction zone.
- Will you be satisfied with the results? An amateur may be able to cover a wall with plaster, but never achieve the perfectly flat surface that is desired. In much the same way, you can add electrical circuits or tile a floor, only to discover later that you did not do an adequate job due to your inexperience. Know your own abilities, or wait until you've gained the needed skill working on lesser jobs.
- Do you have the time to devote to such a project? Whether you do the work yourself or hire it done, renovating an entire house takes time, usually months. Installation of a new roof or even a skylight might be delayed for weeks due to rain, for instance.
- Is your spouse or partner in agreement? Even strong relationships can be stretched to near breaking by either a move to a new country or by a major home remodeling project. To undertake both at the same time when only one of you is enthusiastic about the project is bound to cause problems.

Many old houses in France may be little more than shells by today's construction standards. For instance, they may be wired for electricity, but it is totally inadequate for a home filled with appliances such a washer and dryer, dishwasher, heaters, etc. Plumbing may exist, but again be inadequate both in the size of the water pipes and the number of bathrooms. There may be a leaky roof or no insulation.

Putting all this right in an older house may be more expensive than starting from scratch in new construction. You can have a new house built in many rural villages on a site of your choice for less than €150,000 ($202,500). Obviously, the price goes up with the value of the land and the size and quality of the construction. But to live in a new house is not why many people want to move to France.

One approach is to find an older house that you consider livable, then renovate it while living there. This is certainly feasible. However, it should be noted that you can also have a house built, specifying in the contract that certain jobs will be done by the owner, rather than the builder, thus reducing the final cost. In any case, using your own labor may make a particular property affordable if time is not of the essence.

For those who choose to hire the work done, France is full of skilled artisans. One way to proceed is one step at a time. Craftspeople will give a written *devis* (estimate) for a job. It will break down materials and labor. Discuss the project with the craftsperson and ask his opinion of your plans. Many people arrive in France ignorant of local construction materials and techniques, and he may have other suggestions.

Start with a relatively small job, and see if you are satisfied before launching a large project. But remember that the better craftspeople may also be the busiest, so you may have to wait. (Contractors are the same the world over, and even the most carefully planned schedules do fall apart.) Also, a good electrician may be able to recommend a plumber or mason, or vice versa. Anyone who takes pride in his own work is not likely to tarnish his reputation by suggesting a person he knows will do a second-rate job.

The underlying rule is to hire licensed tradespeople. They stand behind their work, and it will be of a certain standard. Well, it's not a perfect world, and not all workmanship is equal. But by and large, the person who has to stand or fall on the quality of his or her work within a community will do a better job than someone supplementing a welfare check with odd jobs.

Furthermore, the licensed craftsperson has his or her own insurance and pays taxes, so you won't be liable for unpaid taxes or held financially responsible if they are injured on the job. It is the law that the employer—and that's what a homeowner who hires an unlicensed handyman becomes—must pay Social Security taxes for workers, and French authorities will not ignore this requirement if it is brought to their attention. And one of the licensed, tax-paying craftspeople in town may see that they hear about it.

Hiring a licensed craftsperson also provides a side benefit to you as a newcomer in a community. Good craftspeople are usually well-respected, and people value their opinions. Establish a good relationship with yours, and you will have made a worthwhile local acquaintance. In small villages, these people will be your neighbors; you probably also want them to be your friends.

If you opt to buy a house in unlivable condition, it may be a good idea to turn to an architect. For one thing, changes to the exterior will require drawings for approval. For another, the architect should be familiar with local craftspeople and know their strengths and weaknesses. Finally, the architect may have a bit more clout in getting workers to arrange their work schedules—since the architect represents not only the project at hand, but potential future jobs as well.

Perhaps the most important bit of housing advice for anyone buying property in France is simply: Don't get in over your head. No matter how carefully you select a property, the unexpected can occur, and you should have the reserves to deal with it. Your own health, the rate of exchange, or your family situation are only the most obvious problems that could affect your purchase.

Despite the rapid increase of property prices in recent years, it may not continue, just as the boom of the '80s peaked and values declined. You cannot be sure that a residence will be worth more tomorrow than it is today, or even that a buyer at today's price can be found tomorrow.

Household Expenses

UTILITIES

There is only a single provider of electricity in France, Electricité de France (commonly called EDF). There is a fixed monthly fee for service, depending on the amount of electricity it is estimated you will need, and then you will also have to pay for any electricity used. In recent years, EDF has closed many small offices and taken a more centralized approach to its services. For ordering service, they have a national number to call, or you can check the telephone directory for the number of your local agency. Normally, connections will be done weekdays, and you will need an appointment. They also have a website that offers information in both French and English. See the *Contacts* section of the *Resources* chapter for details.

Natural gas is not available everywhere in France, particularly in small villages. The single national supplier is Gaz de France. One of their websites offers information as to whether or not a particular town has gas service. In places without natural gas service, small bottles of butane are commonly available at grocery stores and other shops to serve as fuel for kitchen ranges.

Resources

Contacts

Consulates and Embassies

FRENCH CONSULATES IN THE UNITED STATES

There are 10 French consulates in the United States, including the one adjoining the embassy in Washington, D.C. Each consulate serves the surrounding geographical area. Apply for your visa application at the consulate nearest your residence. If applying in person, check hours of operation before you go; visa applications may be accepted only during certain hours. You can find links to consulates' individual websites at www.info-france-usa.org. Each consulate's site is different and also serves the French community in the U.S., giving an insight into life in a foreign country.

Atlanta
3475 Piedmont Rd. NE, Ste. 1840
Atlanta, GA 30305
tel.: 404/495-1660
fax: 404/495-1661

Boston
31 St. James Ave.
Park Square Building, Ste. 750
Boston, MA 02116
tel.: 617/542-7374
fax: 617/542-8054

Chicago
205 N. Michigan Ave., Ste. 3700
Chicago, IL 60601
tel.: 312/327-5200
fax: 312/327-5201

Houston
777 Post Oak Blvd., Ste. 600
Houston, TX
tel.: 713/572-2799
fax: 713/572-2911

Los Angeles
10990 Wilshire Blvd., Ste. 300
Los Angeles, CA 90024
tel.: 310/235-3200
fax: 310/312-0704

Miami
1395 Brickell Ave.
Espirito Santo Plaza, Ste. 1050
Miami, FL 33131
tel.: 305/403-4150
fax: 305/403-4151

New Orleans
1340 Poydras St., Ste. 1710
New Orleans, LA 70112
tel.: 504/523-5772
fax: 504/523-5725

New York
934 Fifth Ave.
New York, NY 10021
tel.: 212/606-3600
fax: 212 /606-3620

San Francisco
540 Bush St.
San Francisco, CA 94108
tel.: 415/397-4330
fax: 415/433-8357

Washington, D.C.
4101 Reservoir Rd. NW
Washington, D.C. 20007
tel.: 202/944-6195
fax: 202/944-6148

U.S. EMBASSY AND CONSULATES IN FRANCE

Following are the addresses and phone numbers for the various U.S. consulates in France. However, only Marseille and Strasbourg are full consulates; the others are called American Presence Posts and do not offer all services. American Presence Posts are only open by appointment and during limited hours. Check with the consulate in Paris for full details. These offices are closed on all French and U.S. holidays. The general website is www.amb-usa.fr.

Bordeaux
1 rue Fernand Phillipart
33025 Bordeaux

tel.: 05 56 48 63 80
fax: 05 56 51 61 97

Lille
107 rue Royale
59000 Lille
tel.: 03 28 04 25 00
fax: 03 20 74 88 23

Lyon
1 quai Jules Courmont
69002 Lyon
tel.: 04 78 38 36 88

Marseille
U.S. Consulate
Place Varian Fry
13006 Marseille
tel.: 04 91 54 92 00
fax: 04 91 55 09 47

Paris
U.S. Consulate
2 rue St. Florentin
75001 Paris
tel.: 01 43 12 47 08
fax: 01 49 27 92 65

U.S. Embassy
2 avenue Gabriel
75008 Paris
tel.: 01 43 12 22 22
fax: 01 42 66 97 83

Rennes
30 quai Duguay Trouin
35000 Rennes
tel.: 02 23 44 09 60
fax: 02 99 35 00 92

Strasbourg
U.S. Consulate
15 avenue d'Alsace
67082 Strasbourg
tel.: 03 88 35 31 04
fax: 03 88 24 06 95

Toulouse
25 allée Jean Jaurés
31000 Toulouse
tel.: 05 34 41 36 50
fax: 05 34 41 16 19

Planning Your Fact-Finding Trip

ACCOMMODATIONS
Paris and the Île-de-France
Au Manoir St-Germain-des-Prés
153 bd. St-Germain
tel.: 01 42 22 21 65
fax: 01 45 48 22 25
www.paris-hotels-charm.com

Bourgogne et Montana
3 r. Bourgogne
tel.: 01 45 51 20 22
fax: 01 45 56 11 98
www.bourgogne-montana.com

Général
5 r. Rampon
tel.: 01 47 00 41 57
fax: 01 47 00 21 56
www.legeneralhotel.com

Printania
19 r. Château d'Eau
tel.: 01 42 01 84 20
fax: 01 42 39 55 12
www.hotelprintania.fr

Val Girard
14 r. Pétel
tel.: 01 48 28 53 96
fax: 01 48 28 69 94
valgirar@club-internet.fr

Midi and Languedoc
Beaux Arts
1 pl. Pont-Neuf, Toulouse
tel.: 05 34 45 42 42
fax: 05 34 45 42 43
www.hoteldesbeauxarts.com

Grand Hôtel Français
12 r. Temple, Bordeaux
tel.: 05 56 48 10 35
fax: 05 56 81 76 18
www.grand-hotel-français.com

Nimotel
152 r. Claude Nicolas Ledoux,
   Nîmes
tel.: 04 66 38 13 84
fax: 04 66 38 14 06
www.nimotel.com

Princes de Catalogne
r. Palmiers, Collioure
tel.: 04 68 98 30 00
fax: 04 68 98 30 31
www.hotel-princescatalogne.fr

Ulysse
338 av. St-Maur, Montpellier
tel.: 04 67 02 02 30
fax: 04 67 02 16 50
www.hotelulysse.com

Provence and the Côte d'Azur
Boscolo Park Hôtel
6 av. Suède, Nice
tel.: 04 97 03 19 00
fax: 04 93 82 29 27
www.park.boscolo.com

Durante
16 av. Durante, Nice
tel.: 04 93 88 84 40
fax: 04 93 87 77 76
www.hotel-durante.com

Edmond Rostand
31 r. Dragon, Marseille
tel.: 04 91 37 74 95
fax: 04 91 57 19 04
www.hoteledmondrostand.com

Ibis Gare St-Charles
esplanade Gare St-Charles,
  Marseille
tel.: 04 91 95 62 09
fax: 04 91 50 68 42
www.accor-hotels.com

Manoir
8 r. Entrecasteaux, Aix-en-Provence
tel.: 04 42 26 27 20
fax: 04 42 27 17 97
www.hotelmanoir.com

Normandy
L'Absinthe
1 r. de la Ville, Honfleur
tel.: 02 31 89 23 23
fax: 02 31 89 53 60
www.absinthe.fr

Bristol
31 r. 11-Novembre, Caen
tel.: 02 31 84 59 76
fax: 02 31 52 29 28
hotelbristol@wanadoo.fr

Dieppe
pl. B. Tissot, Rouen
tel.: 02 35 71 96 00
fax: 02 35 89 65 21
hotel.dieppe@wanadoo.fr

Grand Cerf
21 r. St. Blaise, Aleçon
tel.: 02 33 26 00 51
fax: 02 33 26 63 07
legrandcerf-alencon@wanadoo.fr

Vieux Carré
34 r. Ganterie, Rouen
tel.: 02 35 71 67 70
fax: 02 35 71 19 17
vieux-carre@mcom.fr

Brittany
Anne de Bretagne
12 r. Tronjolly, Rennes
tel.: 02 99 31 49 49
fax: 02 99 30 53 48
hotelannedebretagne@wanadoo.fr

Cité
26 r. Ste-Barbe, St. Malo
tel.: 02 99 40 55 40
fax: 02 99 40 10 04
hoteldelacite@wanadoo.fr

Gradlon
30 r. Brest, Quimper
tel.:02 98 95 04 39
fax:02 98 95 61 25
hotel-gradlon@wanadoo.fr

Lecoq-Gadby
156 r. Antrain, Rennes
tel.: 02 99 38 05 55
fax: 02 99 38 53 40
lecoq-gadby@wanadoo.fr

Paix
32 r. Algésiras, Brest
tel.: 02 98 80 12 97
fax: 02 98 43 30 95
hoteldelapaixbrest@wanadoo.fr

Burgundy and the Rhône Valley

Bellevue
416 quai Lamartine, Mâcon
tel.: 03 85 21 04 04
fax: 03 85 21 04 02
bellevue.macon@wanadoo.fr

Collège
5 pl. St Paul, Lyon
tel.: 04 72 10 05 05
fax: 04 78 27 98 84
www.college-hotel.com

Grand Hôtel
18 cours République, Roanne
tel.: 04 77 71 48 82
fax: 04 77 70 42 40
granotel@wanadoo.fr

Hotel des Ducs
5 r. Lamonnoye, Dijon
tel.: 03 80 67 31 31
fax: 03 80 67 19 51
hoteldesducs@aol.com.

Phénix Hôtel
7 quai Bondy, Lyon
tel.: 04 78 28 24 24
fax: 04 78 28 62 86
phenix-hotel@wanadoo.fr

FOOD

Paris

Virtually any kind of food from anywhere in the world is available in Paris, from the humblest hamburger to the haute cuisine of three-star restaurants.

Ambassade d'Auvergne
22 r. Grenier St-Lazare
tel.: 01 42 72 31 22

Astier
44 r. J.-P. Timbaud
tel.: 01 43 57 16 35

Atelier Maître Albert
1 r. Maître Albert
tel.: 01 56 81 30 01

Saudade
34 r. Bourdonnais
tel.: 01 42 36 30 71

Sukhothaï
12 r. Père Guérin
tel.: 01 45 81 55 88

Midi and Languedoc

L'Arapède
rte. Port-Vendres, Collioure
tel.: 04 68 98 09 59

La Compagnie des Comptoirs
51 av. Nîmes, Montpellier
tel.: 04 99 58 39 29

L'Estaquade
quai Queyries, Bordeaux
tel.: 05 57 54 02 50
fax: 05 57 54 02 51
www.lestacade.com

Nimotel
152 r. Claude Nicolas Ledoux,
    Nîmes
tel.: 04 66 38 13 84

Rôtisserie des Carmes
38 r. Polinaires, Toulouse
tel.: 05 61 53 34 88

Provence and the Côte d'Azur

Seafood fresh from the Mediterranean is a specialty in this coastal region. Also look for North African dishes such as couscous, a lamb stew.

Boscolo Park Hôtel
6 av. Suède, Nice
tel.: 04 97 03 19 00

Brasserie Léopold
2 av. V. Hugo, Aix-en-Provence
tel.: 04 42 26 01 24

Chez Vincent
25 r. Glandeves, Marseille
tel.: 04 91 33 96 78

Edmond Rostand
31 r. Dragon, Marseille
tel.: 04 91 37 74 95

Mireille
19 bd. Raimbaldi, Nice
tel.: 04 93 85 27 23

Normandy

Fresh seafood from the Atlantic is featured all along the coast. Also, cheeses such as camembert and époisse come from here. Cider and calvados, the brandy distilled from it, are traditional beverages.

Bistrot du Chef en Gare
Buffet-Gare, Rouen
tel.: 02 35 71 41 15
Located in the depot, with railway memorabilia.

Le Chapeau Rouge
117 r. Bretagne, Alençon
tel.: 02 33 26 57 53

Grenouille
16 quai Quarantaine, Honfleur
tel.: 02 31 89 04 24
Frog legs are a specialty.

P'tit B
15 r. Vaugueux, Caen
tel.: 02 31 93 50 76

Quatre Saisons
pl. B. Tissot, Rouen
tel.: 02 35 71 96 00
Roast Rouen duck is the
    specialty here.

Brittany
Fresh seafood fills menus here.
Also, crêpes and galettes (flat pan-
cakes made with buckwheat flour
and filled with either sweet or sa-
vory ingredients) are traditionally
eaten with cups of apple cider.

Bistrot de Jean
6 r. de la Corne de Cerf, St. Malo
tel.: 02 99 40 98 68

Fleur de Sel
1 quai Neuf, Quimper
tel.: 02 98 55 04 71

Lecoq-Gadby
156 r. Antrain, Rennes
tel.: 02 99 38 05 55

Maison de l'Océan
2 quai Douane, Brest
tel.: 02 98 80 44 84

Petit Sabayon
16 r. des Trente, Rennes
tel.: 02 99 35 02 04

Burgundy and the Rhône Valley
Bistrot des Halles
10 rue Bannelier, Dijon
tel.: 03 80 49 94 15
Opposite the covered market.

Charolais
71 r. Rambuteau, Mâcon
tel.: 03 85 38 36 23

Mère Brazier
12 r. Royale, Lyon
tel.: 04 78 28 15 49

Paul Bocuse
au pont de Collonges Nord, Lyon
tel.: 04 72 42 90 90
The chef is in a class by himself.

Relais Fleuri
Allée Claude Barge, Roanne
tel.: 04 77 67 18 52

Making the Move

MOVING COMPANIES

The search for a firm to ship household goods to France might well begin with the Yellow Pages of any metropolitan area phone book. All the big national firms such as Allied, Bekins, and North American Van Lines generally have a local agent, if not a branch in most cities. Many reputable local moving and storage firms that do not themselves provide international shipping offer referrals to ones that do. In many cases, the local office will refer you to a central bureau for international moves. Following are some websites of international shippers:

Allied International
www.alliedintl.com

Bekins
www.bekins.com

Infinity Moving
tel.: 888/545-8400 (U.S. only)
www.infinitymoving.com

Moving Star
www.movingstar.us

All American Moving and Storage
www.moveus.net

North American Van Lines
www.navl.com

Stevens Worldwide
www.stevensworldwide.com

RELOCATION AGENCIES

European Relocation Association
www.eura-relocation.com

Mary Rix-Miller's Expat Assistance
8 rue Dr. Baudet
31170 Tournefeuille
tel.: 05 61 07 53 46
www.expatassistance.com

Syndicat National des Professionels de la Relocation et de la Mobilité
www.relocation-france.org

Language and Education

LANGUAGE AND EDUCATOR RESOURCES

Alliance Française
www.afusa.org

Association des Centres Universitaires d'Études Françaises pour Étrangers
(ADCUEFE CUEF)
Université Stendhal-Grenoble 3,
    BP 25
38040 Grenoble Cedex 9
tel.: 04 76 82 43 27
fax: 04 76 82 41 15
cuef@u-grenoble3.fr

Berlitz
www.berlitz.com
www.berlitz.fr

Eurolingua
www.eurolingua.com

Groupement Français
Langue Étrangère
Éspace Universitaire Albert-Camus
17-bis avenue du
    Professeur Grasset
34093 Montpellier Cedex 5
tel.: 04 67 91 70 00
fax: 04 67 91 70 01
ulys@fle.fr
www.fle.fr

Ministry of Education
www.education.fr

Mission Interuniversitaire de
Coordination des Échanges
Franco-Américains (MICAFA)
www.micefa.org

National Office for the Guarantee of Language Training and
Overseas Stays
(Office National de Garantie des
    Séjours et Stages Linguistiques)
8 rue César Franck
75015 Paris
tel.: 01 42 73 36 70
fax: 01 42 73 38 12
infos@loffice.org
www.loffice.org

SOUFFLE
Éspace Charlotte
83260 la Crau
tel.: 04 94 00 94 65
fax: 04 94 00 92 30
www.souffle.asso.fr
courrier@souffle.asso.fr

Student Traveler
www.studenttraveler.com

L'Université Inter-Âges
de Paris-Sorbonne
1 rue Victor-Cousin
75230 Paris Cedex 05
tel.: 01 40 46 26 19
formation.continue@paris4
    .sorbonne.fr
www.paris4.sorbonne.fr

L'Université de Tous les Saviors
(UTLS)
www.tous-les-savoirs.com

Universités Populaires

Union Française des Universités
Tous Âges(UFTA)
Headquarters: L'Evenière
Université de Rennes

1 avenue du Général-Leclerc
35042 Rennes Cedex
tel.: 02 99 63 66 76
www.assoc.wanadoo.fr/ufuta

Université Populaire du Rhin
Alsace
www.u-p.asso.fr

Health

RESOURCES FOR THE DISABLED

Maison de la France
www.franceguide.com
France's national tourist office
maintains a list on its website
of accommodations for the disabled, organized by region. It's
not comprehensive, but makes
a good starting point.

Mobility International USA
www.miusa.org

**Secrétariat d'État aux Personnes
Handicapées**
(Secretary of State for Handicapped Persons)
www.handicap.gouv.fr

SAFETY

Ministry of Health
www.sante.gouv.fr

The ministry's website maintains
a page called Renseignements
Practiques that lists telephone
numbers/hotlines for spe-
cial services, such as suicide
prevention (01 45 39 40 00),
AIDS ("SIDA" in French)
information (0800 840 800),
and rape (0800 05 95 95). The
0800 numbers are free.

Emergency Contacts

There is a single emergency number
to call from a cell phone: tel.: 112.

Fire Department
tel.: 18

Medical Emergencies
tel.: 15

Police
tel.: 17

Employment

JOBS AND INTERNSHIPS

American Chamber of Commerce in France
www.amchamfrance.org

Emailjob
www.emailjob.com

Emploi Center
www.emploicenter.com

Etudis
www.etudis.com

SELF-EMPLOYMENT

Ministry of Employment and Labor (Agence pour la Création d'Enterprises, or APCE)
www.apce.com

Finance

American Foreign Exchange
www.afex.com
International firm that specializes in currency trading.

Ministry of Finance
www.impots.gouv.fr
At this tax-focused website, you can make your annual Declaration of Revenue and pay online.

Communications

INTERNET SERVICE PROVIDERS

These are the major Fournisseurs d'Access Internet (FAIs) in France. Because of the volatility of the industry and ever-changing technology, you should visit each company's website to check offers and requirements. You will often find promotional CDs in computer stores that will give you initial access to the service.

AOL
www.aol.fr

Cegetel
www.cegetel.fr

Club Internet
www.club-internet.fr

Easyconnect
www.easyconnect.fr

Free
www.free.fr

Neuf Télécom
www.neuf.fr

Tele2
www.tele2.fr

Wanadoo (France Télécom)
www.wanadoo.fr

PHONE COMPANIES

France Telecom, now a public corporation, is no longer a government monopoly, but it still maintains all physical phone lines and is responsible for installation of telephones. However, other companies now offer service within France, competing with a confusing array of offers usually tailored to the particular needs of individual subscribers. Listed below are major providers of fixed telephone service.

Cegetel
tel.: 08 05 77 77 78
www.cegetel.fr

France Telecom
tel.: 1014
www.francetelecom.fr

One Tel
tel.: 3238
www.onetel.fr

Tele2
tel.: 08 05 04 44 44
www.tele2.fr

Teleconnect
tel.: 08 05 02 40 00
www.teleconnectfrance.com

Mobile Phone Service

The major providers of mobile phone service are listed below. Supermarkets also sell phones and service, and companies often have boutiques in shopping malls.

Bouygues
tel.: 08 25 32 73 26
www.bouyguestelecom.fr

Orange (France Telecom)
tel.: 08 25 00 57 00
www.orange.fr

SFR
tel.: 06 10 00 19 63
www.sfr.fr

SUPPORT SERVICES

Association of American Wives of Europeans
www.aawe.fr

Counselling in France
www.counsellinginfrance.com
This helpful link lists psychological counselors in various parts of the country.

SOS Help
tel.: 01 46 21 46 46
You can call this crisis hotline in France any afternoon or evening for friendly, English-speaking help, sympathy, and practical advice.

Housing Considerations

GENERAL INFORMATION

Agence Nationale pour
l'Informations sur le Logement
(ANIL)
www.anil.org

INSPECTOR CERTIFICATION

Centre Technique du Bois et de
l'Ameublement (CTBA)
www.termite.com.fr

Qualicert
www.sgsgroupe.fr

UTILITIES

Electricité de France (EDF)
tel.: 0 810 333 776
www.edf.fr

Gaz de France
www.gazdefrance-distribution.com

AGENCES IMMOBILIÈRES
(REAL ESTATE AGENCIES)

Bordeaux Region

Axel Immobilier
24 avenue Thiers
33100 Bordeaux
tel.: 05 56 86 18 18
www.axel-immobilier.fr

JB Immobilier
51, cours Tourny
33500 Libourne
www.jb-immo.com

Maisons du Canal
8 Le Bourg
33190 Hure
tel.: 05 56 71 25 51

Bourgogne Region

Immofamily.com
32 rue de Lyon
71000 Macon
tel.: 03 85 21 11 00
www.immofamily.com

Optim Immobilier
6 rue du Temple
21000 Dijon
tel.: 03 80 44 17 00
www.weboptim.com

Bretagne Region

Cabinet Martin
2 rue d'Isly
35000 Rennes
tel.: 02 99 67 22 44
www.cabinet-martin.fr

Lyon Region

A2C Immobilier
128 rue Bossuet
69006 Lyon
www.a2c-immo.com

Laforet Grand Lyon (20 agencies)
55 avenue Jean Jaures
69007 Lyon
tel.: 04 37 28 30 28
www.laforet-grandlyon.com

Marseille Region

Agence Haton (Century 21)
12 rue de la Buffa
06000 Nice
tel.: 04 93 88 34 94
www.rivieradeal.com

Agence I.P.A.
2 place des Prêcheurs
13100, Aix en Provence
tel.: 04 42 38 28 16
www.aixenprovence.com/
   immobilier

Eurimmo
23 boulevard Louis Salvator
13006 Marseille
tel.: 04 91 54 48 00
www.eurimmo-marseille.com

Sovagim (4 agencies)
24 boulevard Georges
   Clémenceau
83001 Draguignan Cedex
tel.: 04 98 10 28 80
www.sovagim.com

Montpellier Region

Imag'Immo Lattes (21 agencies)
Place d'Aragon
34970 Lattes
tel.: 04 67 20 15 19
www.imagimmo.com

Les Maisons du Soleil
55 rue Bize
34830 Clapiers
tel.: 04 67 59 44 99

Patrick Harlow Agency
Avenue Jean Mermoz
Immeuble L'Atalante
34000 Montpellier
tel.: 08 25 88 68 58
www.patrick-harlow.com

Normandy Region

Smart Immobilier
28 rue Armand Carrel
76000 Rouen
tel.: 02 32 76 31 52
www.smart.groupe-hinfray.com

Paris Region

Agence Ateliers Lofts & Associes
21 rue Greneta
75002 Paris
tel.: 01 53 00 99 00
www.ateliers-lofts.com

Agences Réunies (30 agencies)
Agence Etoile
3 boulevard Magenta
75010 Paris
tel.: 01 44 52 57 57
www.agences-reunies.com

Groupe ACM Immobilier
66 rue de Paris
78600 Maisons-Lafitte
tel.: 01 39 62 85 33
www.acm-immo.com

Hoche Immobilier
63, avenue de St. Cloud
78000 Versailles
tel.: 01 39 20 37 47
www.hocheimmo.com

Home Safari
9 rue Mollien
92100 Boulogne-Billancourt
tel.: 01 46 03 90 16
www.home-safari.com

Téoulé Immobilier
23 rue de la Paroisse
77300 Fontainebleau
tel.: 01 64 22 17 97
www.teouleimmobilier.fr

Toulouse Region
Levignac Immobilier
Avenue de la Save
31530 Levignac sur Save
tel.: 05 62 136 836

ORPI (25 offices)
37 allée Jean Jaures
31000 Toulouse
tel.: 05 61 99 21 21
www.orpi-toulouse.com

Shoe and Clothing Sizes

French shoe and clothing sizes are quite different from American ones, since they are derived from the metric system, rather than from U.S. feet and inches. Thus, men think of women with hourglass figures as 91-57-91, rather than 36-24-36.

In general, French men seem to have smaller feet than Americans; finding the equivalent of a size 12 or 13 shoe may be difficult. In women's shoes, equivalents are not exact.

Since so many articles of clothing are made outside of the countries where they will be sold, many of them now carry labels denoting size equivalents. Also, many stores in France display a chart showing corresponding sizes. In any case, it is always wise to try on any article of clothing prior to purchase, since there is often variation in size between manufacturers, regardless of the size marked on the label.

Women's Clothing

American	6	8	10	12	14	16	18
French	36	38	40	42	44	46	48

Men's Clothing

American	34	36	38	40	42	44	46
French	44	46	48	50	52	54	56

Shirt Collars

American	14	14.5	15	15.5	16	16.5	17
French	36	37	38	39	40	41	42

Women's Shoes

American	6	6.5	7	7.5	8	8.5	9
French	36	37	37	38	39	41	42

Men's Shoes

American	7	8	9	10	11	12	13
French	40	41	42	43/44	44/45	46	47

French Phrasebook

Bienvenue à Paris! Despite the unflattering stereotypes you may have heard about Parisians, you'll find that many are happy to help you negotiate their city, and most speak at least rudimentary English. That said, however, please note that the friendliness of the locals increases exponentially when you initiate conversations in French. Even if you've never studied a word, just try. It's a clear sign of respect, and it will be appreciated. Politesse is also a must: Begin every interaction with *"Bonjour, monsieur/madame,"* and disperse thank you's *(merci)* liberally. Note: *J* sounds are pronounced like the *g* in "massage."

Numbers

zero — *zéro*
one — *un*
two — *deux*
three — *trois*
four — *quatre*
five — *cinq*
six — *six*
seven — *sept*
eight — *huit*
nine — *neuf*
ten — *dix*
eleven — *onze*

twelve — *douze*
thirteen — *treize*
fourteen — *quatorze*
fifteen — *quinze*
sixteen — *seize*
seventeen — *dix-sept*
eighteen — *dix-huit*
nineteen — *dix-neuf*
twenty — *vignt*
one hundred — *cent*
one thousand — *mille*

Days of the Week

Monday — *Lundi*
Tuesday — *Mardi*
Wednesday — *Mercredi*
Thursday — *Jeudi*
Friday — *Vendredi*
Saturday — *Samedi*

Sunday — *Dimanche*
this week — *cette semaine*
this weekend — *ce weekend*
today — *aujourd'hui*
tomorrow — *demain*
yesterday — *hier*

Months

January — *Janvier*	October — *Octobre*
February — *Février*	November — *Novembre*
March — *Mars*	December — *Décembre*
April — *Avril*	this month — *ce mois*
May — *Mai*	this year — *cette année*
June — *Juin*	winter — *hiver*
July — *Juillet*	spring — *printemps*
August — *Août*	summer — *été*
September — *Septembre*	fall — *automne*

Time

What time is it? — *Quelle heure est-il?*
It is… — *Il est…*
eight o'clock — *huit heures*
half past ten — *dix heures et demi*
quarter to five — *cinq heures moins quart*
noon — *midi*

midnight — *minuit*
during the day — *pendant la journée*
in the morning — *le matin*
in the afternoon — *l'après-midi*
in the evening — *le soir*
at night — *la nuit*

Greetings and Basic Expressions

Good day. — *Bonjour*
Good evening. — *Bon soir*
Welcome. — *Bienvenue*
Excuse me. — *Excusez-moi*
Pardon. — *Pardon*
Sir — *Monsieur*
Madam — *Madame*
Miss — *Mademoiselle*
Do you speak English? — *Parlez-vous anglais?*
I don't speak French. — *Je ne parle pas français.*

How are you? (formal) — *Comment allez-vous?*
Very well, thank you. — *Très bien, merci.*
How's it going? (informal) — *Ça va?*
It's going fine. — *Ça va bien.*
My name is… — *Je m'appelle…*
What's your name? — *Quel est votre nom?*
Please. — *S'il vous plaît*
Thank you. — *Merci*
You're welcome. — *Je vous en prie*

No problem. — *De rien*   Yes. — *Oui*
I'm sorry. — *Desolé*   No. — *Non*
Goodbye. — *Au revoir*

Getting Around

How do I get to... ? — *Comment puis-je me rendre à... ?*
Where is... ? — *Où est... ?*
the subway — *le Métro*
the airport — *l'aéroport*
the train station — *la gare*
the train — *le train*
the bus stop — *l'arrêt de bus*
the bus — *l'autobus*
the exit — *la sortie*

the street — *la rue*
the garden — *le jardin*
a taxicab — *un taxi*
a hotel — *un hôtel*
a toilet — *une toilette*
a pharmacy — *une pharmacie*
a bank — *une banque*
a tourist office — *un bureau de tourisme*
a telephone — *un téléphone*

Food

I would like... — *Je voudrais...*
a table for two — *une table pour deux*
the menu — *la carte*
breakfast — *petit déjeuner*
lunch — *déjeuner*
dinner — *dîner*
the bill — *l'addition*
non-smoking — *non fumeur*
a drink — *une boisson*
a glass of... — *une verre de...*

water — *l'eau*
beer — *bière*
wine — *vin*
I am... — *Je suis...*
a vegetarian (male) — *végétarien*
a vegetarian (female) — *végétarienne*
diabetic — *diabétique*
allergic — *allergique*
kosher — *kascher*

Shopping

Do you have... ? — *Avez-vous... ?*
Where can I buy... ? — *Où puis-je acheter... ?*
May I try this? — *Peux-je l'essayer?*
How much is this? — *Combien?*

cash — *argent*
credit card — *carte de crédit*
Too... — *Trop...*
small — *petit*
large — *grand*
expensive — *cher*

Health

Help! — *Au secours!*
I am sick. — *Je suis malade.*
I am hurt. — *Je suis blessé.*
I need… — *J'ai besoin de…*
the hospital — *l'hôpital*

the doctor — *le médicin*
an ambulance — *une ambulance*
the police — *la police*
medicine — *médicament*

Glossary

acte authentique de vente: deed of sale

arrondissement: district; specifically, one of the administrative areas into which large French cities are divided

artisan: craftsperson

l'assurance dommages-ouvrage: insurance against faulty work; as in the construction of a house

autoroute: highway

le baccalauréat, or *le bac:* the degree granted after passing a national exam at the end of secondary school

bandes dessinées: comic books

les banlieues: the suburbs

le bon goût: good taste

le bon mot: literally, "the good word"; a clever remark

bouffer: rough equivalent of "pig out"

brandade: a purée of salt cod, olive oil, and milk

brasserie: a restaurant with a bar inside

bricolage: do-it-yourself construction

brocante: used household goods

canton: small territorial division in rural districts

un carnet: a money-saving 10-pack of tickets for the Paris Métro

carte de commerçant étranger: foreign merchant's visa

carte grise: the title slip for a car

carte integrale: a special ticket good for one year of rides in all eight zones comprising the Paris Métro and RER train lines

carte de séjour: residency permit

cassoulet: a casserole of beans, herbs, and meat

certificat d'urbanisme: a certificate of verification from the mayor's office that confirms a particular piece of land may be considered for a building permit

chambre d'hôtel: bed-and-breakfast

chambre des notaires: chamber of commerce

charcuterie: butcher's shop

charcutier: butcher

cohabitation: a government in which the French president and prime minister belong to different parties

college: middle school

commerçant: merchant

compromis de vente: an agreement of sale; as for the purchase of property

conjoint collaborateur: the spouse of the sole proprietor of an *enterprise individuelle* who also works in the business

convoi exceptionelle: a truck with an oversized load

devis: estimate (n)

dictée: dictation

domaines: Web designations or domains, such as .com, .org, .edu, and .fr

la douane: customs (at the airport)

échoppes: little, stone, one-story houses built for laborers during the 19th century; now both common and coveted in the Bordeaux region

école élémentaire: elementary school

école maternelle: daycare/preschool

entreprise individuelle: a business owned and run by a sole proprietor

étang: lagoon or pond

états de lieux: a "state of the premises" inventory form that must be completed with your landlord when you move into a rental residence

exploitations: business concerns

le fisc: the tax system

forfait: also known as a *micro-régime,* this special tax plan for small business avoids direct collection and payment of the value-added tax (TVA)

fournisseurs d'accès Internet: Internet service providers, or ISPs; the French acronym is FAI

galettes: crêpes made with buckwheat flour; an essential element in Breton cuisine

garrigue: brush composed of live oak, pine, Scotch broom, and thyme; it thrives in Mediterranean France

gendarmerie nationale: the national police force organized under the Ministry of Defense

gendarmes: police

gite: weekly vacation rental

haut debit: broadband

integration: assimilation

joie de vivre: joy of life

lattes: pieces of wood about .25-inch thick and two or three inches wide; used in the construction of French beds

lavoir: wash house

lettres recommandées: registered letters

"Liberté, égalité, fraternité": liberty, equality, brotherhood; a popular slogan employed socially and politically in modern France

lycée: high school

maison: house

marches: during Charlemagne's time, the lands on the frontier of a kingdom

mairie: mayor's office

maison de retraite: a community-operated assisted-living establishment and/or nursing home

maison secondaire: vacation house

marquis: military rulers under Charlemagne

"La Marseillaise": the French national anthem

mère: mother

le Métro: the Parisian subway system; the same term is used for subway systems in other major cities

moules: mussels

non: no

notaire: notary

nouveau roman: literally, "new novel"; a text written using a narrative technique that ignores many conventions of structure, plot, and character development

oui: yes

PACA: short for Provence-Alpes-Côte d'Azur, a region in the South of France

PACS: short for "pacte civil de solidarité," the French term for legally recognized domestic partnerships

pastel: a plant from the mustard family that yields a beautiful blue dye

patrimoine: national heritage

pays: country or region

père: father

périphérique: the beltway that surrounds Paris

petite annonce: classified ad

plafond de verre: glass ceiling

police nationale: a 145,000-person force that performs major crime investigations

pompier: firefighter

la poste: mail; when capitalized as La Poste, it refers to the French Postal Service

poste restante: general delivery

poulardier: poultry producer

préfecture: police headquarters

pré-inscription: letter of admission to a school or university

proche banlieues: nearby suburbs (in Paris)

puce: computer chip

régime de base: basic health-care coverage granted to all French citizens

sans-papiers: literally, "without papers"; people without proper visas

SIDA: the French acronym for AIDS

siret: a registration number signifying a legal business; businesses must apply for and receive one of these numbers to be considered legitimate in France

solidarité: literally, "solidarity"; a populist concept of obligation to one another for the good of all

stage: a period of professional development; akin to internships in the United States, with minimal pay (if any) but often excellent training

syndicat: syndicate; a union of workers

tabac: shop or bar-café where cigarettes and phone cards are sold

taxe d'habitation: the tax owed each January 1 by the person occupying a property

taxe foncière: property tax

telecopie: fax

thalassothérapie: spa treatments that include mineral baths, mud baths, seaweed packs, and plenty of curative water *travail au noir:* literally, "working black"; that is, as an illegal worker who does not pay taxes

tu: you (singular and informal)

tutoyer: to address someone as *tu;* that is, informally

universités populaires: Popular Universities

vieux: old

vin de pays: regional wine; generally sold only in the small area where it is produced

vous: you (plural and formal)

Index

U.S.~Metric Conversion

1 inch	=	2.54 centimeters (cm)
1 foot	=	.304 meters (m)
1 yard	=	0.914 meters
1 mile	=	1.6093 kilometers (km)
1 km	=	.6214 miles
1 fathom	=	1.8288 m
1 chain	=	20.1168 m
1 furlong	=	201.168 m
1 acre	=	.4047 hectares
1 sq km	=	100 hectares
1 sq mile	=	2.59 square km
1 ounce	=	28.35 grams
1 pound	=	.4536 kilograms
1 short ton	=	.90718 metric ton
1 short ton	=	2000 pounds
1 long ton	=	1.016 metric tons
1 long ton	=	2240 pounds
1 metric ton	=	1000 kilograms
1 quart	=	.94635 liters
1 US gallon	=	3.7854 liters
1 Imperial gallon	=	4.5459 liters
1 nautical mile	=	1.852 km

To compute Celsius temperatures, subtract 32 from Fahrenheit and divide by 1.8. To go the other way, multiply Celsius by 1.8 and add 32.

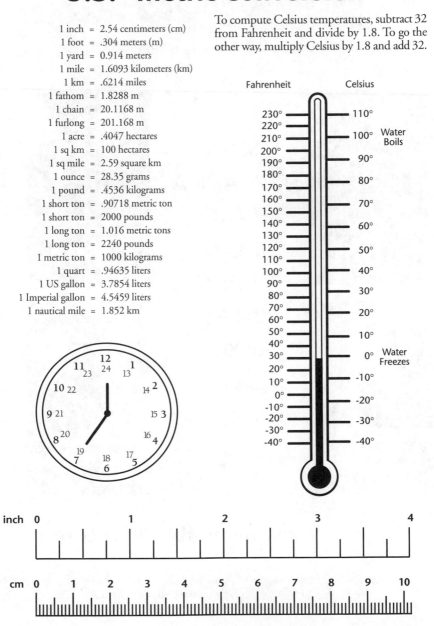

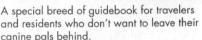

Living Abroad in France
Avalon Travel Publishing
1400 65th Street, Suite 250
Emeryville, CA 94608, USA
www.livingabroadin.com

Editor: Sabrina Young
Series Manager: Erin Raber
Design: Jacob Goolkasian,
 Amber Pirker
Copy Editor: Mia Lipman
Graphics Coordinators: Justin Marler,
 Tabitha Lahr
Production Coordinator:
 Darren Alessi
Map Editor: Kevin Anglin
Cartographers: Kat Kalamaras, Amy Tan
Cartographic Manager: Mike Morgenfeld
Indexer: Laura Welcome

ISBN-10: 1-56691-920-7
ISBN-13: 978-1-56691-920-3
ISSN: 1555-5526

Printing History
1st edition—October 2005
5 4 3 2 1

Text © 2005 by Terry Link.
Maps © 2005 by Avalon Travel
Publishing, Inc.
All rights reserved.

Avalon Travel Publishing
an Imprint of
Avalon Publishing Group, Inc.

Some photos and illustrations are used
by permission and are the property of
the original copyright owners.

Front cover photo: © John Elk III

Printed in the USA by Worzalla

Keeping Current

Although we strive to produce the most up-to-date guidebook that we possibly can, change is unavoidable. Between the time this book goes to print and the time you read it, the cost of goods and services may have increased, and a handful of the businesses noted in these pages will undoubtedly move, alter their prices, or close their doors forever. Exchange rates fluctuate—sometimes dramatically—on a daily basis. Federal and local legal requirements and restrictions are also subject to change, so be sure to check with the appropriate authorities before making the move. If you see anything in this book that needs updating, clarification, or correction, please drop us a line. Send your comments via email to atpfeedback@avalonpub.com, or write to the address above.